Serenade of Suffering

Serenade of Suffering

A Portrait of Middle East Terrorism 1968–1993

RICHARD J. CHASDI

LEXINGTON BOOKS
Lanham • Boulder • New York • Oxford

LEXINGTON BOOKS

Published in the United States of America
by Lexington Books
4720 Boston Way, Lanham, Maryland 20706

12 Hid's Copse Road
Cumnor Hill, Oxford OX2 9JJ, England

British Library Cataloguing in Publication Information Available

Library of Congress Cataloging-in-Publication Data

Chasdi, Richard J., 1958–
    Serenade of suffering : a portrait of Middle East terrorism,
1968–1993 / Richard J. Chasdi.
        p.   cm.
    Includes bibliographic references (p.   ) and index.
    ISBN 0–7391–0057–2 (alk. paper)
    1. Terrorism—Middle East.   I. Title.
HV6433.M5C53   1999
303.6'25'0956—dc21   98–52753
                                                                  CIP

Printed in the United States of America

♾™ The paper used in this publication meets the minimum requirements of American
National Standard for Information Sciences—Permanence of Paper for Printed Library
Materials, ANSI/NISO Z39.48–1992.

For Sharon M. Applebaum and Neal A. Tolchin

Contents

Figures

Tables

Foreword

It must be understood how little systematic events-based analysis exists in the study of terrorism and how much of our "knowledge" of the process of terrorism is based on media presentations of a relatively few major events. We have been so inundated with images of terrorism in the Middle East over the past quarter century that we cannot but conclude that we know all about the origins and patterns of terrorism and that it is simply time for governments with a will to put an end to the perpetrators. Our daily dose of terrorist news coverage often would have us believe that there is little more to understanding terrorist behavior than a knowledge of chance and opportunity.

That is why the careful events-based research that is at the heart of this book is of such merit. Richard Chasdi provides the opportunity to look beyond the headlines to explore the actual patterns of terrorist events and their connection to the development of political movements which employ terrorist strategies and their organizational growth and disintegration. Chasdi views the terrorist organizations as multidimensional, not to approve of their actions or to score points in a political debate, but rather to try and better understand the process by which terrorism is chosen, whom terrorists target, and what can be done to prepare for such actions.

He explores, chronicles, and tests the explanatory variables for target selection that widely recognized writers in the field deem important. Further, he examines the underlying reasons for why there may be terrorist group patterns or variations among specific types of groups according to region.

Eight Middle East terrorist groups are studied. They are differentiated according to ideology, the presence or absence of a charismatic leader, and recruitment patterns. Chasdi identifies how they differ with respect to the targeting behavior.

The analysis reveals discernible and at times dramatic patterns of terrorist group targeting behavior when Middle East terrorist groups are broken down according to three defining characteristics: ideology, goals, and recruitment patterns.

Chasdi provides meaningful insight into the formative processes of terrorist groups, their splintering, and their decline. In short, he sheds considerable light on why terrorist groups form the way they do and why they evolve in particular ways and how this evolution impacts terrorist behaviors.

The data indicate special attention ought to be devoted to potential government targets with respect to Jewish fundamentalist and Arab nationalist-irredentist groups with charismatic leaders and Marxist-Leninist nationalist-irredentist groups without them.

Thus, it is clear that policymakers and scholars both should profit from this research that reveals regular patterns in the target selection process of Middle East terrorist groups. At a functional level, this research should strengthen the capability of government officials to assess and respond to the threat or use of unconventional warfare. At a more theoretical level, this work provides new insight into the study of terrorism which can be replicated for other regions.

Chasdi hopes that the basic structure of his work can assist others in their work and contribute to a cumulative integration of scholarly work. If others invest the careful effort in data collection and analysis for which Dr. Chasdi has shown the way, this will occur.

PROFESSOR MICHAEL STOHL
Department of Political Science
Purdue University
West Lafayette, Indiana
December 18, 1998

Acknowledgments

First and foremost, I am indebted to my mentor and friend, Professor Michael Stohl of Purdue University, for his invaluable assistance and steadfast support. I am also indebted to Professors Louis Rene Beres, Lyn Kathlene, James McCann, Robert Melson, Keith L. Shimko, Michael Weinstein, and Frank Lee Wilson, all of Purdue University. I am also very grateful to Professor Frederic S. Pearson, Director of the Center for Peace and Conflict Studies at Wayne State University, whose invaluable assistance helped me transform a Ph.D. dissertation into a varnished monograph. Dr. Pearson has been a colleague and teacher to me and has provided me with innumerable opportunities for growth in both professional and personal ways. Many thanks are also due to Penelope A. Morris for layout, typesetting, and copy editing assistance and unflagging commitment to the project. I am very grateful to Professor Ian S. Lustick, Department Chair, Richard L. Simon Term Professor in the Social Sciences, Department of Political Science, University of Pennsylvania, for his kind assistance providing me with access to his personal files on Jewish fundamentalist terrorist groups and Jewish fundamentalism in Israel. I would also like to thank Dina Rodrigues, Franc Gianino, and Gary Gaub for proofreading, artwork, and data collection in Philadelphia, respectively. On a personal level, many thanks to Sharon, who stands by me always, Neal, Dick, Herb, Kenneth, my mother, Reed and Freida, and my beloved Tiffany Anne, for their unconditional assistance and support.

Chapter One

Introduction

In many ways, terrorism represents the last unexplored frontier for studies about political violence. Such luminaries as Clausewitz, Jomini, Mahan, and Douhet have written extensively about conventional warfare, making substantive contributions with respect to unraveling its various strands and identifying its underlying structure. Similarly, the dynamics of ethnic conflict in various parts of the world have been explored with intellectual rigor.[1] In contrast, comparatively little has been written about terrorism that focuses primary attention on the causal factors that generate and sustain terrorism. To be specific, we know precious little about the behavior of terrorist organizations, and their sources and origins.

The purpose of this study is twofold. First, it will investigate the empirical behavior of different types of Middle East terrorist groups that have carried out terrorist assaults from 1968 to 1993. Hence, it will isolate and identify particular types of targeting behavior and provide a description of terrorist event "attributes" according to terrorist group-type. Clearly, that is important for a better understanding of what Middle East terrorism is all about and addresses one facet of what counter-terrorism planners need to know to craft more effective counter-terrorism measures.

The second objective of the work is to provide meaningful insight into the formative processes of terrorist groups, their splintering, and their decline. In other words, why do terrorist groups form the way they do, and why do they evolve? This issue is especially crucial in the post Cold War world, where terrorism, already an expression of national sentiments by sub-national actors and some nation-states, may, with its opaque set of interconnections, be increasingly used by certain nations to carry out assaults in an international political system militarily dominated by the United States.[2]

The Threat of Terrorism

The threat of terrorism is not necessarily confined to smaller organizations that may be acting on their own. Nowadays, terrorism is also used as a "proxy tool" by some nations to express grievances, anger, or political demands and aspirations. As far back as 1991, Noel Koch, the former Director of Special Planning for the U.S. Department of Defense, testified that Saddam Hussein, viewed by many Palestinians as a hero for surviving the Persian Gulf War, remains capable of committing or supporting many acts of terrorism against the United States. Koch reports that, "in fact Saddam Hussein is as much of a menace as he ever was, he's probably more powerful as a result of this war and the way it ended as he ever was, [and] he's a hero to Arab nationalists for having survived this adventure...."[3]

Nowadays, terrorism abounds as a means to influence the political process ordinarily reserved for leaders of nation states, evolving nation-states (e.g., Yasser Arafat's Palestinian National Authority in Gaza and parts of the West Bank, the Taliban movement in Afghanistan), and "supra-national organizations" such as the United Nations and the European Community. For example, terrorism has happened in Northern Ireland in reaction to the new peace framework agreement hammered out between Catholic and Protestant leaders there, and the leaders of England and Ireland, under the aegis of former U.S. Senator George Mitchell.

The threat of terrorism in the United States is a significant one. In addition to the Oklahoma City bombing, the bombing of New York's World Trade Center and terrorist plans to destroy major commuter tunnels in New York City highlight the scope of the challenge.[4] In Saudi Arabia, the presence of U.S. forces, viewed as provocateurs by Islamic militants, may have generated and sustained terrorist assaults against a U.S. supported military reserve training camp in 1995 and the Khobar facility bombings in 1996. Indeed, as this book goes to press, world-wide attention is almost singularly focused on the nearly simultaneous bombings of the U.S. embassies in Nairobi, Kenya and Dar-as-Salaam, Tanzania and U.S. retaliatory responses against supposed terrorist bases and facilities in Afghanistan and Sudan.[5]

Challenges and Opportunities

One of the challenges and opportunities of such work revolves around the central question of what *is* terrorism. One generally recognizable problem that contributes to the underlying imprecision of terrorism studies is that terrorism remains ill-defined. That is the case largely because political considerations intrude into the realm of less partisan efforts to conceptualize what exactly constitutes terrorism. Different definitions of terrorism abound, many with different levels of emphasis, be they political or even legal in nature. For example, legal definitions may differ for purposes of war or for purposes of prosecution.[6] Illustrative of that is how the FBI excludes assaults on abortion clinics in its appraisal of U.S. domestic terrorism events.[7]

Largely as a result of those political considerations, a comprehensive, meticulous, and widely shared definition of terrorism is not available.[8] One leading authority on terrorism claims that U.S. government agencies have by themselves used over one hundred different definitions over a forty-five year period. Schmid "listed 109 different definitions of terrorism provided between 1936-1981 and there have been more since; the U.S. government alone has provided more than half a dozen, which are by no means identical."[9] Laqueur tells us a definition of terrorism that is inclusive of its many shapes and ideological premises is not available.[10] This lack of consensus on so fundamental an issue makes it relatively easy to forgo rigorous attempts to define terrorism and fall back on shopworn approaches that focus almost exclusively on "terrorist thinking" and the physical devastation that terrorist attacks cause.

Seen from this angle, there are implications for counter-terrorism policy. For one thing, without a uniform definition of terrorism, each nation, strenuously competing with other nations in a world characterized by decentralized legal and political systems, will be more likely to tailor its counter-terrorism policy with geopolitical considerations in mind. In this Westphalian world, where states must prepare for the prospect of war and, to use Hobbes's metaphor, stand poised like soldiers with their swords drawn, state leaders perceive this process to be in their best self-interest.[11] That, in turn, increases the likelihood that international law will be compromised or ignored outright.

Another source of confusion is that writers begin their analyses at very different starting points. For example, some authors are content to devote almost singular attention to a particular region and write what essentially amounts to a descriptive case study.[12] Others begin with broader and more abstract approaches that emphasize theoretical considerations over qualitative detail.[13] Still others place a longitudinal emphasis on their work that chronicles the historical progression of terrorism.[14]

To make matters worse, the bulk of what has been written about terrorism is almost entirely vacuous from the vantage of empirical investigation. Many of those works are characterized by simple narratives about the principal actors and terrorist acts they commit and are peppered with empty rhetoric that all too often distills down to invectives that advocate remedial use of unbridled force.[15]

Equally troublesome is the all too frequently encountered and, I think, largely incorrect assumption that terrorists are psychotic individuals who somehow have the chance to be able to act out their pathologies on a stage of world-wide proportions.[16] In fact, many leaders of subnational organizations who later became national leaders have taken "terrorist" actions that in their own minds presuppose and derive from the idea of "pre-emptive defense." To be sure, they are still afforded the assumption of rational decision-making. For example, Menachem Begin, Yitzhak Shamir, and Nelson Mandela have all engaged in terrorist activity as leaders of the Irgun, The Stern Gang (Lehi), and the "MK," the military arm of the African National Congress, respectively.[17]

Distinguishing Types of Terrorism

Terrorism can be categorized according to whether the perpetrators of terrorist assaults are state or non-state actors. That is important because who the perpetrators of terrorist acts are has implications for counter-terrorism strategies that are consistent with international law. For example, terrorists who are non-state actors pose special problems with respect to prosecution because the International Court of Justice can invoke sanctions only against states and not groups of individuals. In other words, in the absence of an international penal court, state terrorism and states that support terrorists are liable for punishment by the International Court of Justice, but terrorist groups acting without state support are able to escape the brunt of punishment.[18]

The conceptual fuzziness of "terrorism" is highlighted when particular terrorist group classification schemes are under consideration. To be sure, a more in-depth analysis of existing classification schemes and typologies is offered in Chapter Two, but for now, consider the following: Mickolus tells us that "transnational terrorism" is terrorist activity "carried out by basically autonomous non-state actors, whether or not they enjoy some degree of support from sympathetic states."[19] For example, many terrorist organizations in the Middle East that are frequently written about, such as Hamas and the Palestine Liberation Front (PLF), are non-state actors that undertake "transnational terrorism." We are also told that "international terrorism" refers to terrorist acts "carried out by individuals or groups controlled by a sovereign state."[20] The author suggests a terrorist group in this situation is a state agent, and as such, has access to that state's resources and its territory, which can be used as a staging ground for attacks and a "safehaven" for sanctuary.

So, what's wrong? At a substantive level, while Mickolus's terrorist group delineations may serve well for purely descriptive accounts of various terrorist groups and events, it gives us precious little in the way of analytical utility. It is evident that Mickolus's "international terrorism" category is not mutually exclusive and is therefore unable to capture qualitative distinctions between different types of international terrorism. For example, *Mossad* operations conducted outside Israel can be viewed as both international and state terrorism. Clearly, those types of state operations by *Mossad,* or *CIA,* or *MI5* for that matter, are different from other types of international terrorism under consideration here.

In a similar vein, how is Mickolus's scheme operational? For example, where is the threshold that distinguishes between those international terrorists "controlled by a sovereign power" and "transnational terrorist" groups that are not? How is that threshold measured and hence made operational? Issues similar to these must be addressed in order to conceptualize a functional typology as opposed to a taxonomy for pedagogical purposes.

Compounding the matter even more, it is commonplace to note that terrorism is also broken down into spheres of domestic and state terrorism.[21] Yet "domestic terrorism" is a relatively broad term that describes terrorism conducted by perpetrators indigenous to the state where a terrorist assault is carried out. It is important to recognize that the term "domestic terrorism" really remains open-ended and vague because domestic, transnational, and state terrorism are not mutually exclusive classifications.

For example, Hamas "Izzadine al Quassam" terrorist assaults can be viewed as both transnational terrorism, because of Hamas's relative autonomy with respect to states (and evolving states) in the region, and as domestic terrorism, since the majority of its activists come from the West Bank and Gaza. Similarly, Israeli "counter-terrorist" operations conducted against suspected terrorists and their families in the West Bank and Gaza can be viewed as examples of state terrorism and domestic terrorism simultaneously. At the heart of the matter, a classification scheme fit for analytical utility must be able to separate groups so that one type of terrorist group cannot fall into more than one category.

What distinguishes state terrorism from other forms of terrorism is that acts of terrorism are conducted by government agencies of a nation-state in pursuit of political objectives. For example, the pro-Soviet Afghan government secret police the Khad (Khedamat Amiat Daulati or state security service) reportedly killed at least 11,000 political prisoners during the first twenty months of its existence. At the same time, state security apparatus of several nations including Britain and Israel have carried out state terrorism operations directed against political opponents.[22] Clearly, the study of state terrorism is important, but an analysis of causal factors at work in the context of nation-state processes, such as bureaucratic decisionmaking, is beyond the scope of this work.[23] At the same time, in Chapter Two, we will discuss "the state" in terms of why conformance of counter-terrorism measures with international law is really a "net gain" for counter-terrorism analysts and the leaders of nation-states who rely on their judgment.

The Case for a "Functional Typology"

In the broader sense, the purpose of this study is to inject a high dosage of scientific rigor and uniformity into the field of terrorism studies through the construction of a "functional" typology of Middle East terrorist group-types. In essence, its very nature helps to highlight new and probing questions about how and why terrorist groups form, splinter, and decline. In other words, the typology also serves as a touchstone to probe the fundamental issues of how unknown terrorist groups coalesce, and take responsibility for their terrorist assaults, as happened with the "Real IRA" and the World Islamic Front for Jihad Against Jews and Crusaders groups involved in 1998 bombings.[24] While the focus and application of this typology is on Middle East terrorism in the hope that it may somehow alleviate human suffering in that part of the world, its basic structure and the theoretical premises that derive from it are applicable to the study of terrorism world-wide.

In the narrower sense, this typology is constructed so it can account for the dissolution of terrorist group-types and the formation of new ones, in contrast to those typologies that classify terrorist groups according to location of incident or the type of terrorist activity undertaken. The idea of crafting a typology to classify terrorist group-types is certainly neither new nor original. What makes this terrorist group-type typology unusual is that it is "functional" in the sense that it can be used to reveal what types of targets particular group-types favor. That knowledge is useful to counter-terrorism planners for predictions about where particular terrorist groups may strike and how to strengthen potential targets.

The first step in the creation of such a typology is to conceptualize a suitable definition of terrorism that has a reasonable chance of acquiring wide-scale recognition. This study uses international law as the basis of that definition in part because it has legitimacy and widespread acceptance. At the heart of the matter, international law makes it possible for scholars and policymakers alike to distinguish clearly between legitimate insurgent activity and acts of terrorism.[25]

The structural shape of the typology is based on three defining characteristics that distinguish between group-types. Those defining characteristics are ideology, goals, and recruitment patterns. This typology, which draws from Starr and Most's work on third world conflicts, can be represented as a three-dimensional cube with the characteristics ideology, goals, and recruitment, each posited along one axis.[26] An underlying theme of the typology is the considerable conceptual distance between ideology and goals, or ideology and behavior, the latter being tactical alternatives, as in the case of Islamic fundamentalist terrorist groups, the emergent reality of a single Islamic state, a confederation of Islamic states, the destruction of Israel, or the destruction of contemporary Sunni regimes.[27]

"Lower Order" and "Higher Order" Terrorism— Some Reflections

The foregoing leads to the fundamental issue of why distinguish between "lower order" terrorism, namely terrorism that makes use of conventional weapons, and "higher order" terrorism that involves the use of chemical, biological, or nuclear weapons. Are the underlying explanatory models or frameworks under consideration the same or different when "lower" or "higher order" strategies are under consideration? Do terrorists employ a cookie-cutter approach in terms of strategy?

The answer, in my judgment, is that when decisions about the use of conventional or non-conventional weapons are made, the models differ. One way of thinking about these classifications involves a complex set of interconnections between terrorism event "purpose," locale, and the continuously evolving international political environment.

For one thing, the "purpose" of terrorism may vary with respect both to aims and to how terrorist leaders view the most effective means to achieve their aims. Some terrorists may perceive themselves to be "defenders of the community," engaged in "pre-emptive assaults." Hence, in some cases, the goal is to get persons to relocate elsewhere, as opposed to a more strategic plan to wrest power away from a movement and have "the movement give up." It seems plausible in this context that conventional terrorism is more

Figure 1   A 3-Dimensional Typology Cube of Middle East Terrorist Group-Types

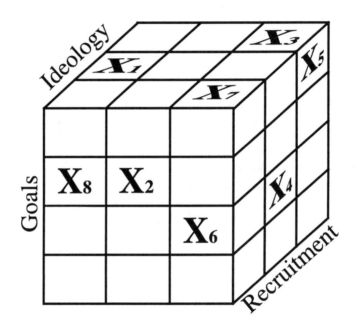

X$_1$ = Theocentric
X$_2$ = Theocentric charismatic
X$_3$ = Ethnocentric
X$_4$ = Ethnocentric charismatic
X$_5$ = Ideo-ethnocentric
X$_6$ = Ideo-ethnocentric charismatic
X$_7$ = Jewish theocentric
X$_8$ = Jewish theocentric charismatic

Source: Chasdi, Richard J. 1995.
"The Dynamics of Middle East Terrorism 1968-1993:
A Functional Typology of Terrorist Group-Types."
Ph.D., dissertation, Purdue University.

effective in terms of political message sending, namely the need for structural political change. In addition, terrorism, if used with restraint, thereby in effect falls short of a "violence threshold" that would evoke a massive counter-terrorism campaign that would more than offset any political gains hoped for or made.

On the other hand, if realistic political accommodation or structural political change are not underlying themes of the group under consideration, "higher order" terrorism may demonstrate the essentially "nihilistic or anarchistic" nature of a terrorist group. Consider the terrorist assault by the Japanese cultist group Aum Shinrikyo, which discharged sarin nerve gas into the Tokyo subway system in 1995, apparently after several "test runs" of germ acquisition, germ cultivation, and germ warfare terrorist assaults were made at several geographical sites.[28]

In their discussion about the looming catastrophe of "higher order" terrorism, Falkenrath, Newman, and Thayer tell us that over and beyond the exceptional behavior of Aum Shinrikyo, there is no proof positive that other "sub-national" terrorist organizations have ever carried out terrorist assaults with chemical, biological, or nuclear weapons.[29] At the same time, the authors issue a caveat when they assert, "Of course, this explanation for mass-casualty aversion applies mainly to terrorist organizations that adopt rational strategies to achieve political aims, not to the full gamut of potentially violent state actors. Apolitical or religious terrorists may not be bound by this logic...."[30]

In a similar vein, locale plays a major role with respect to whether "lower order" or "higher order" weapons are used. Clearly, the geographical configuration of the locale under consideration is important. For example, it makes precious little sense for either a Protestant or Catholic terrorist group in Belfast to release toxins into the environment. Faced with that enormous calamity, many "constituent group" members on both sides would die, and the terrorist assault would provoke a massive counter-terrorist campaign.

The continuously evolving international political landscape may also be an explanatory variable in terms of choice between "lower" and "higher" order weapons. At a functional level, nuclear proliferation continues in the post Cold War world with "higher order" materials available on "black-markets" and former Soviet state employees' "scientific knowledge for sale," yet the ability to miniaturize weapons to be usable by terrorists is still evidently rare. While it is conjecture at this stage, it seems plausible that as events in the international political system unfold, terrorist groups may feel "pushed off" the stage, thereby in effect paving the way for greater interest in "higher order" terrorist assaults.

Terrorist Group Leaders and Followers

Another way of thinking about terrorist organizations is to distinguish between groups led by a "charismatic leader" and those that are not. At the most fundamental level, this classification scheme draws from what we see around us, and may help explain splintering of one group to form others, as with Dr. George Habash's Popular Front for the Liberation of Palestine (PFLP), Naif Hawatamah's Democratic Front for the Liberation of Palestine (DFLP), Sabri al-Banna's Abu Nidal Organization (ANO), Wadi Haddad's Popular Front for the Liberation of Palestine-Special Operations Group (PFLP-SOG), Rabbi Meir Kahane's Jewish Defense League (JDL), and Kach.[31] An underlying justification for this approach is that even beyond the sphere of the terrorist world, we notice that persons from many cultural settings and geographical sites seem to have a certain predilection for charismatic authority in general that makes them more prone to the allure of charismatic leaders who are not terrorists, such as Jim Jones in Guyana and David Koresh's "Branch Davidians" in Waco, Texas. Bearing in mind that this phenomenon transcends national and cultural boundaries, it is probably no exaggeration to say that control for culture and region suggests other psychological make-up factors at work.

At a more theoretical level, one way to think about how terrorist groups coalesce with respect to leaders and followers, and why, is to apply Reiss and Roth's schema that describes "social" and "individual" explanatory variables for violence and their interconnections within and across different "levels of analysis."[32] Why is that important? For one thing, not everyone burdened with the strains and tensions of life becomes, willy nilly, a terrorist. Reiss and Roth's ideas that in some ways presuppose and derive from Gurr's "theory of relative deprivation" are intriguing.[33] The underlying theme of this work is "the interplay" of a host of "social level" (i.e., "macrosocial"; "microsocial") and "individual level" (i.e., "psychosocial"; "biological") factors with what the authors describe as "predisposing," "situational," and "activating" factors.

It is important to note that precious little is understood with respect to precise mixtures of factors that generate and, in some cases, sustain violent outcomes. The authors tell us that "a major problem in understanding violence is to describe the probability distributions of predisposing factors, situational elements, and triggering events at the biological, psychosocial, microsocial and macrosocial levels."[34] We should use the foregoing model as a pedagogical tool that has the capacity to provide insights and formulations, the validity of which need to be tested empirically in the future.

To illustrate some of the issues under consideration, we can use the

Jewish Defense League (JDL) as a case study. The JDL was established in Brooklyn, New York in 1968 by Meir Kahane, generally recognizable as a reactionary American rabbi.[35] Its mission was twofold: to train Jews in the arts of self-defense against would be assailants and engage in protest against those states and their agents considered to be enemies of the State of Israel. At a functional level, Sprinzak tells us that the JDL was broken down into two components. The first of those, the *"chaya"* (animals), were the activists who carried out terrorist assaults against targets considered antithetical to Jewish interests, organizations, or persons in the political fray. The second component was the so-called *"scholars"* group.[36] Presumably, the "scholars" group engaged itself, among other things, with aspects of fund raising and administrative work.[37]

Perhaps the single most intriguing question here is why the Jewish Defense League came about in the first place. Hoffman suggests the answer is a relatively straightforward matter. For Hoffman, "The religiously orthodox residents ... had long been prey to muggers, vandals and the various other malevolent denizens of America's urban areas. The majority of these crimes were perpetrated by young Blacks and Puerto Ricans who lived in the ghettos surrounding the beleaguered Jewish neighborhoods."[38]

For Friedman, Kahane seems to have evoked a remarkable degree of self-importance and other similar feelings at an early age as a "Betar" youngster in New York. For example, Friedman relates how one of Kahane's peers recalls that, "at one meeting, Kahane stood at the lectern in his brown-shirted uniform, contemptuous, angry, power hungry, strutting. ... He started to rant about turning Israel into a theocracy, and that only he could save the Jewish people. I got the feeling I was at a fascist rally."[39] The foregoing description that Friedman provides of Kahane's psychological disposition offers another tantalizing clue to the story, but his emphasis still seems makeshift, never complete.

Reiss and Roth's schema, when applied, seems especially new and probing, since it introduces flexibility into an analysis of the Jewish Defense League. We know that not everyone who, to use Hoffman's words, has "been prey to muggers, vandals and ... other malevolent denizens...." will become standard-bearers for what Hoffman describes as "a vigilante gang" and later, "a political pressure group."[40] In explaining what makes for the genesis of terror, we must first explain what factors contribute to a condition where group identity is threatened.

Here, Gurr and Harff's analysis is a useful vehicle because it delineates seven factors that outline a way of thinking about group reactions. The Gurr and Harff framework involves "concepts" and "indicators" that revolve around the themes of: "economic and political discrimination"; "group iden-

TABLE 1 Reiss and Roth's Risk Factors Matrix

Matrix for Organizing Risk Factors for Violent Behavior

Units of Observation and Explanation	Proximity to Violent Events and Their Consequences		
	Predisposing	Situational	Activating
Social			
Macrosocial	Concentration of poverty Opportunity structures Decline of social capital Oppositional cultures Sex-role socialization	Physical structure Routine activities Access: Weapons, emergency	Catalytic social event medical services
Microsocial	Community organizations Illegal markets Gangs Family disorganization Preexisting structures	Proximity of responsible monitors Participants' social relationships Bystanders' activities Temporary communication impairments Weapons: carrying, displaying	Participants' communication exchange
Individual			
Psychosocial	Temperament Learned social responses Perceptions of rewards/ penalties for violence Violent deviant sexual preferences Cognitive ability Social, communication skills Self-identification in social hierarchy	Accumulated emotion Alcohol/drug consumption Sexual arousal Premeditation	Impulse Opportunity recognition
Biological	Neurobiologic[a] "traits" Genetically mediated traits Chronic use of psychoactive substances or exposure to neurotoxins	Transient neurobiologic "states" Acute effects of psychoactive substances	Sensory signal-processing errors Interictal events

[a]Includes neuroanatomical, neurophysiological, neurochemical, and neuroendocrine. "Traits" describes capacity as determined by status at birth, trauma, and aging processes such as puberty. "States" describes temporary conditions associated with emotions external stressors, etc. Authors Reiss, Albert J. Jr., and Jeffrey A. Roth, 1993 *Understanding and Preventing Violence.* National Academy Press (NAP). Reprinted with the kind permission of NAP.

tity"; "ethnic political leadership and group cohesion"; the "political environment" namely the type of "political institutions" in place; "use of violence by governments"; means of "external support"; and "international economic status."[41]

As with the Reiss and Roth analysis, Gurr and Harff's analysis does not provide precise measures of factors or trace the arc of interconnections between them. What both can do, however, is provide a framework of thinking about the problem that recognizes distinctions between factors and acknowledges interconnections, sometimes direct, sometimes indirect, that resonate between them.

What seems significant here is that processes are at work that transform conflict, oftentimes really pedestrian in nature, into full blown violent political undertakings. Picture a situation where two Jewish persons are chased by some stone-throwing kids yelling anti-Semitic epithets. To be sure, this is loathsome, but that or some variation of that happens to many people. As I am fond of telling my students, not everyone who experiences a "road rage" event views it as a set of challenges and opportunities to fight. Likewise, not everyone burdened with the strains and tensions of life becomes, willy nilly, a terrorist. At the heart of the matter, there is the enormous ideological and substantive difference between experiencing a stone-throwing incident, albeit distasteful, and attempts by some to put into practice the Kahane maxim of "every Jew his .22."[42]

While it is beyond the scope of this study to flesh out a more complete JDL "matrix," it is possible to mull over some issues that an approach like this would include. Accordingly, to use Reiss and Roth's "matrix" terminology, at a "macrosocial-predisposing level" one might find empirical evidence of "oppositional cultures," such as what one might see in the orthodox Jewish section of Crown Heights in Brooklyn. In a similar vein, at the "microsocial-predisposing level" one might focus on "community organizations," namely that myriad set of Jewish religious-social institutions that anchor much of Jewish life in this and similar locales. In turn, with respect to more at the "microsocial-situational level" of analysis one might focus on "family disorganization" (e.g., family dysfunction, which may or may not presuppose and derive from assimilation issues) in specific families or persons.

In terms of Reiss and Roth's "individual" level of analysis, it is probably no exaggeration to say that Kahane followers, and indeed Kahane himself, may have had processes at work that were somehow different from many of us. At a "psychosocial" level, Kahane and Kahane-types may have had "temperament" or "communication skills" (e.g., rage management) problems. In terms of the "biological" level the authors, by extrapolation, articulate that chemical or genetic make-up may have been contributory factors in terms of cognitive processing and expression, and ultimately terrorist assaults. To be sure, particular readings of history, in this case Holocaust history, also may be involved here. What seems significant here is that in some form or fashion, those factors could converge in ways within and between "levels of analysis" to increase the likelihood of terrorism happening.

In short, what Reiss and Roth delineate is a multivariate analysis to explain violent assaults when conditions are ripe, both at personal and social levels. Kahane's psychological disposition, along with his followers, coupled with the manifestations of socio-economic conditions associated with poor, disenfranchised members of society (what Hoffman describes as "young Blacks and Puerto Ricans") really coincide, in the case of JDL, to create a cauldron of potentially explosive behavior ready to boil over. The usefulness of Reiss and Roth's analysis, when applied to the case of Meir Kahane in the locale of Brooklyn, New York, and subsequently Israel, is important because it provides insight into the formative processes of terrorist groups in particular settings. This study will offer more in depth analysis of the Jewish Defense League and its offshoot group, Kach, in Chapter Four.

All in all, results from analysis of the behavior of different types of terrorist groups that derive from the typology mentioned previously, coupled with the formulation and application of theory about "prevailing ideology," and terrorist group sources and origins, will accomplish several objectives. First, the study will present a clear picture of what types of targets different types of terrorist groups prefer and the characteristics of terrorist attacks according to group-type. Second, theoretical discussion about the Middle East, in a broader sense, will be articulated within a framework that delves into the fundamental matter of why terrorist assault attributes may vary by terrorist group-type. Lastly, even though a qualitative analysis of all terrorist groups under consideration is beyond the scope of this work, our theoretical discussion will provide insight into, and flesh out descriptions of, how some groups rise and fall. Hopefully, the findings will serve as a foundation for further research and for more effective counter-terrorism stratagems.

Notes

Albert J. Reiss and Jeffrey A. Roth's "Risk Factors Matrix" reprinted with the kind permission of National Academy Press from their work, *Understanding and Preventing Violence.*

1. Earle 1994. Examples of well written studies about ethnic conflict abound. For a comprehensive analysis of ethnic conflict, see Horowitz 1985. For a broad overview of its various forms, see von der Mehden 1973.

2. Nye 1993, 191-192. Karber and Mengel tell us of a set of interconnections between "political context," as they put it, and terrorist group "change" and the "splinter" process, thereby in effect clearly capturing, in the narrow sense, part of the picture of the splintering process as it pertains to government reactions (Karber and Mengel 1983, 24-25). The qualitative analysis offered here will flesh out that underlying premise and other premises about terrorist group sources and origins through an application of the Reiss and Roth "risk factor matrix" to Middle East terrorism.

3. Senate Governmental Affairs Committee, 15 July 1991; "Terrorism after the Gulf War"; broadcast on C-SPAN 2 July 20, 1991; C-SPAN Video #91-07-16-02-2. Illustrative of Saddam Hussein's capacity to support terrorist assaults against U.S. targets and/or interests are recent reports that link him to the bombing of the U.S. Embassies in Kenya and Tanzania. For example, Myers et al. tell us, "The United States believes that senior Iraqi scientists were helping to produce elements of the nerve agent VX at the factory in the Sudan that American cruise missiles destroyed. . . . Concern was heightened because of links of Osama bin Ladin, the suspect in the bombing, and the Sudan government." Myers et al. 1998, A1, A6.

4. Fishkoff 1993, 1; Chasdi 1994, 62.

5. McKinley Jr. 1998a, A-1, A-8; McKinley Jr. 1998b, A-1, A11.

6. One of the underlying problems for terrorism analysts that presupposes and derives from the existence of several definitions of terrorism and a Westphalian legal and political world is that terrorism definitions differ with respect to the operational settings in which they are used (Louis Rene Beres, discussion 1993, Purdue University). For example, prosecutors have an enormous capacity for "politically correct" definitions of terrorism used to deny routinely POW status afforded by the Geneva Conventions and Protocols. In the broadest sense, Blakesley tells us that the political offense exception is afforded to terrorists when in fact, the political offense exception should not be afforded to them at all, but only to members of a lawful insurgency or participants in civil war or revolution. See Blakesley 1992, 75-76; Chasdi 1994, 80. Faced with that situation, one would hope that for prosecution purposes, there would be a standard more generally accepted, as well as more acceptable outside the juridical framework (Louis Rene Beres, discussion, December 1993, Purdue University). The following conventions describe protections afforded to POW's: UN 1950a, Weston, Falk, and D'Amato 1990, 147-154; UN 1950b, Weston, Falk, and D'Amato 1990, 155-159; UN 1950c, Weston Falk, and D'Amato 1990, 160-169; UN 1950d, Weston, Falk, and D'Amato 1990, 170-180; UN 1978a, Weston, Falk, and D'Amato 1990, 230-246; UN 1978b, Weston, Falk, and D'Amato 1990, 247-252.

7. Dr. Frederic S. Pearson, Wayne State University, attended an FBI briefing of World Affairs Councils, Washington, DC, November 1997.

8. Walter Laqueur and Grant Wardlaw suggest that important point in their discussions about terrorism. See Laqueur 1987, 380-381; Wardlaw 1986, 283-284; Chasdi 1994, 63. Brian Jenkins (1981, 171) also alludes to that point.

9. Laqueur 1987, 380-381; Schlagheck 1988, 1.

10. Ibid.

11. Hobbes's "posture of war" as found in Holsti 1985, 25. Holsti extends the Hobbesian metaphor to cover international politics during the Cold War.

12. For example, Harris (1989) and O'Day (1989, 1994) devote considerable attention to "The Troubles" in Northern Ireland. Alternately, Harkabi (1974) focuses attention on terrorism that presupposes and derives from the Arab-Israeli conflict.

13. Several statistical studies about terrorism are characterized by that emphasis. For example, see Osmond 1979, Oots 1984, Hewitt 1988, Flemming 1992, Miller 1986, and Weinberg and Eubank 1988.

14. Rapoport is one author who embraces that perspective. See Rapoport 1984, 1987.

15. For example, consider Livingstone's appraisal of the problem. "Many observers," he contends, "believe that World War III has begun.... Although it is strategic warfare on the cheap, its stakes are no less significant or meaningful to the United States and other nations of the West than a direct clash between the two superpowers.... Moreover, the day may not be far away when foreign terrorists strike at the very heart of civilization in the United States, and the nation must not be found unprepared" (Livingstone 1986, 2-3, 9-10).

16. Parry (1976) and McKnight (1974) are two writers who embrace that approach. For Parry, the opportunity to plan and carry out terrorist acts also has an economic dimension. He claims that "all the long way from Robespierre to Arafat there is one significant constant: The prevailing origin of terror's leadership is in the middle class, particularly the upper middle class—numerically a small proportion of it, but a proportion strong socio-economically and eccentric psychologically" (Parry 1976, 525).

17. Fischbach 1994; AbuKhalil 1994. We are told by Juckes (1995, 102-103) that the first of a series of "MK" (Umkonto we Sizwe- "Spear of the Nation") assaults took place on December 16, 1961 at various locales in South Africa. *The New York Times* reports that "Among the places hit were a suburban post-office, several African-affairs offices and an electric power station. The sites were mainly around Johannesburg and Port Elizabeth" (*New York Times* 1961, 3).

18. Chasdi 1994, 70; United Nations 1945c, Weston, Falk, and D'Amato 1990, 33-38. Several attempts to create an international penal court have been proposed over the years. M. Cherif Bassiouni chronicles these in his work. See

Bassiouni 1986, 77 n73. Bassiouni tells us, "The 1948 text of the Human Rights Conventions drafted by the Human Rights Commission of the United Nations included a proposal for an International Court of Human Rights open to individuals as well as states." Paris Peace Conference, Confer. Doc {Gen} I.B. 13, at 444-45 {1946}; see also Goldberg, "The Need for a World Court on Human" 11 How. L.J. 621 {1965}; see generally del "Russo, supra note 54 at 757." Other plans included an International Court of Habeas, an altered form of the Permanent Court of International Justice, and an International Criminal Court. Bassiouni 1986, 77 and citations 75, 76, 74; Falvey 1986, 343-344, 357-358.

19. Flemming 1992, 4.

20. Ibid.

21. This section of the study draws on Flemming's discussion about different types of terrorism. See Flemming 1992, 4, 5.

22. John F. Burns, "Afghans Disclose Deaths of 11,000," *New York Times,* 9 November 1989, A-15. Burns reports it is estimated by Muhajadin rebels that the Khad has killed some 80,000 persons. "Accounts that have been circulated for years in Kabul, the Afghan capital, have spoken of prisoners of war who were thrown into pits and buried alive, and others who had their hands and feet bound and were run over by tanks. Other accounts have told of prisoners being lined up to be used as targets by army recruits." "Clemency Declined by Britain For Six Convicted Irishmen" *New York Times,* 30 January 1988, sec A. The British government has long refused to treat IRA activists as privileged combatants subject to the laws of war. Instead, they are treated as criminals, to delegitimize Irish nationalism. IRA activists who violate *jus in bello* (justice in war) criteria are not tried as war criminals. Here it is reported that "Home Secretary Douglas Hurd refused to exercise the royal prerogative of mercy, which empowers the Government to free convicts despite court rulings." For more on *jus in bello* criteria, see Chapter Two.

23. For an especially probing and insightful discussion of bureaucratic decision making dynamics, see Art 1974.

24. Clarity 1998, A1, A7; Benac 1998, 3.

25. Bassiouni 1978; Bassiouni 1986; Beres 1987; Beres 1988a; Beres 1988b; Beres 1990; Blakesley 1992; Blakesley and Lagodney 1991; Brierly 1963; Detter De Lupis 1987; Murphy 1978; Falvey 1986; Fried 1985; Gal-Or 1985.

26. Harkavy and Neuman 1985, 32-52; Chasdi 1997, 70.

27. Chasdi 1997, 107 n5.

28. Broad, William J. 1998, A-1, A-10.

29. Falkenrath, Newman, and Thayer 1998, 44-52.

30. Ibid., 51.

31. Long 1990, 18-19, 211; Taheri 1987, 89; Parsons 1964, 361; Chasdi 1997, 73, 107.

32. Reiss and Roth 1993. My thinking was also influenced by Nye's risk factor analysis about the likelihood of war happening (Nye 1993).

33. Rubenstein 1989, 308; Graham 1989, 334-338; Gurr and Harff 1994, 82-95.

34. Reiss and Roth 1993, 299.

35. Hoffman 1984, 10-15; United States Department of Justice 1985, hereafter USDOJ, 295-316; Lustick 1988, 67; USDOJ 1986, 20; Gurr 1988, 570-571; Homer 1983, 169; USDOJ 1983, 17; Goodman 1971, 32, 33, 115-116, 118-119, 121-122.

36. Sprinzak 1993, 234.

37. Friedman 1990. One sphere of activity with a powerful allure is the set of interconnections that Friedman tells us existed between Kahane, Geula Cohen, the standard-bearer of the ultranationalist religious Tehiya party, and former Prime Minister Yitzhak Shamir. Friedman asserts "the secret relationship between Cohen, Shamir, and Kahane was forged one blustery cold morning in December 1969" (Friedman 1988, 420). To be sure, such an opaque arrangement reported by Friedman to have been consummated without Prime Minister Golda Meir's knowledge remains murky and equally troublesome and requires further investigation and confirmation.

38. Hoffman 1984, 11. Although Hoffman hints at some socio-economic factors, his analysis really begs the question, since it is not especially probing with respect to the complex set of factors and their interconnections that seem to be at work. Regrettably, Hoffman's argument about the origins and sources of JDL is a tautology because an explanation of "Jewish violence" that points to violence is a redundancy.

39. Friedman 1990, 39-40.

40. Hoffman 1984, 11.

41. Gurr and Harff 1994, 82-95.

42. Mergui and Simonnot 1987, 16.

Chapter Two

Definitions, Politics and Terrorism, Typologies

In terms of terrorism studies, there is a need for greater understanding of this relatively neglected, but increasingly important area of international politics. In the case of the Reagan and Bush administrations, conventional reflexive reactions to terrorism emanating from Libya and Lebanon happened. In turn, President Clinton's use of "cruise missile diplomacy" against Saddam Hussein of Iraq in June of 1993 and Osama bin Laden in August of 1998 still demonstrates how inadequate conventional military tactics are against a type of warfare where land, sea, and airpower are largely inconsequential.[1]

Although the United States has a host of decision-makers who can appraise the relative military strengths and subsequent threats that conventional nation states pose, there seems to be an equally impressive scarcity of counter-terrorism analysts in government who are knowledgeable about the set of factors that generate and sustain terrorist movements and distinguish terrorism from more conventional military threats.[2]

There is a need to generate theory about terrorism to gain a better understanding of its subtleties and nuances. As previous research has suggested, ideological and religious fanatics are not deterred by policy calling for prompt "retaliation" and "retribution." For example, Stohl suggests that a policy like the Reagan administration's approach of "pre-emptive retaliation" against Hezbollah in Lebanon can be deleterious to U.S. interests at two levels. First, tactical mistakes with respect to military operations can be made to create an image of incompetence. Second, in its perceived role of provocateur in the Middle East, the U.S. loses more of its moral standing in the eyes of many in the world community.[3]

Stohl tells us, "'Preemptive retaliation' was turned on the Hizbollah and its leaders. The United States involved itself with Lebanese intelligence operatives through a CIA operation to train and support counter-terrorist units for strikes.... On March 8, 1985, members of one of those units, reportedly acting without CIA authorization, hired others in Lebanon to detonate a car bomb outside the Beirut home of militant Shiite leader Shaykh Fadlullah.... Beyond the questionable morality of the action, by aligning itself with parties of dubious merit the Administration appeared, once again incapable of competent action."[4] Clearly, Stohl's analysis reverberates in terms of thinking about the rage evoked among many Sudanese after President Clinton's cruise missile assault against a pharmaceutical plant in Sudan and reports that surfaced of a cruise missile striking a Pakistani site by mistake.[5]

Those "rough and ready" policy prescriptions, while increasingly popular among the public and politicians because of their rather simplistic reliance on the threat or use of force, are particularly ill-suited for responding to a "people's war of ideology" and other political and social campaigns throughout the world spawned by secular and religious nationalist fervor. Problems abound with that approach at two levels. First, from the vantage of efficiency, those robust sounding anti-terrorism policies are vacuous. After all, as Crozier puts it, "terrorism is a weapon of the weak."[6] Laqueur and Alexander tell us that terrorism, with its many ideological shapes and structural forms, continues to thrive in an effective and sustained way.[7] Second, counter-terrorism policies that embrace the underlying themes of retaliation and retribution have the potential to cause serious domestic problems.

Several authorities on international law have discussed the insidious effects of counter-terrorism policy driven by geopolitical considerations and how ignoring international law in favor of short term political gain increases the chance of illegal activity taking place at home. The French reaction to terrorism in Algeria, for example, is perhaps the most glaring case of that happening. In response to the Algerian National Front (FLN), the French created an ultra-nationalist right wing organization in the Organisation de l'Armee Secrete, or Secret Army Organization (OAS), that repeatedly made attempts to assassinate President Charles de Gaulle in the early 1960's because of his staunch support for an independent Algeria.[8]

What much of this distills down to is the need to isolate and identify more clearly what constitutes terrorism. If a more precise and generally recognizable definition could be constructed and accepted more widely, not only would counter-terrorism strategists be able to coordinate efforts more effectively, but American policymakers themselves would be able to make stronger and more consistent arguments about what constitutes terrorism as opposed to "just war" that would, in essence, lead to a better image of Americans in many parts of the world.

What is Terrorism? In Search of a Suitable Definition

International law provides useful insight into the development of a framework for thinking about an operational definition of terrorism. First and foremost, it provides a way to look at terrorism with increased precision that makes it possible to draw critical distinctions between terrorism and justifiable insurgency. The juridical touchstones of counter-terrorism policy are the standards of *jus ad bello* (justice of war),[9] *jus in bello* (justice in war),[10] and the post-Nuremberg conception of the human rights regime.[11]

In the case of *jus ad bellum* (justice of war), Beres tells us that the use of force is permissible under international law in four instances: in self-defense when an attack is imminent, in post-attack situations, for humanitarian intervention reasons either to protect a population at risk or a nation's own citizens from egregious violations of the human rights regime, and to fulfill collective security agreements.

With respect to *jus in bello* (justice in war), we are told that the legitimacy of an insurgency under international law is evaluated by three standards that must be met. First, the degree of force used by an insurgency must be consistent with the minimum amount of force necessary to acquire the political objective and proportionate to the amount of force that is wielded against the insurgency by opponents. Second, it is incumbent upon an insurgency to make a compelling case that the use of force is necessary. Faced with the looming catastrophe of warfare, the insurgency must make the case persuasively that all peaceful options have been pursued in an exhaustive manner without success. Third, it is essential for an insurgency to distinguish between military forces and non-combatants during its operations with the singular purpose of protecting non-combatants from harm.[12]

What seems critical here, however, is that definitions of terrorism that devote scant attention to what distinguishes terrorism from justifiable insurgency are all too often used as operational definitions by government agencies responsible for counter-terrorism activities, thereby in effect contributing to the political game-playing that is all too frequently a hallmark of counter-terrorism efforts. While definitions of terrorism that focus more attention on the physical characteristics, effects, or sources of terrorism may be useful for other works, this study needs a conceptual definition of terrorism for the larger world of action that makes the distinctions between justifiable insurgency and terrorism more focused and precise.[13]

The U.S. Department of State definition of terrorism highlights dramatically the problem of open-endedness that lends itself to political game-playing. From the U.S. Department of State viewpoint, terrorism is "the threat or use of violence for political purposes by individuals or groups, whether acting for, or in opposition to, established governmental authority, when such actions are intended to influence a target group wider than the immediate victim or victims."[14]

This definition of terrorism, however, seems afflicted with various difficulties. Imagine a set of circumstances, for example, in which an authoritarian regime violates peremptory *jus cogens* laws by committing egregious human rights violations that approach Nuremberg category crimes. Under international law, specifically article 51 of the Vienna Convention, if states decide to enact legislation at variance with natural or other peremptory law, insurgencies may be lawful and exhibit law enforcing behavior if the rules of proportionality, discrimination, and military necessity are adhered to by the insurgents.[15] Clearly, under the foregoing circumstances, citizen intervention against the government could be law enforcing rather than law violating behavior, because such activism fulfills agreements of human rights law.[16]

Unquestionably, perhaps the single most dominant principle underlying international law is the inviolability of states and the protection of sovereignty. That principle is codified by statutes in the Declaration on the Inadmissibility of Intervention in Domestic Affairs of States and the Protection of Their Independence and Sovereignty.[17] At the same time, it is permissible under international law for foreign powers to intervene in the domestic affairs of a state in very limited circumstances. That principle is supported by codified international law, namely article 49 of the Convention for the Amelioration of the Condition of the Wounded and Sick in Armed Forces in the Field, which concerns "grave breaches" of conduct, and the Agreement For the Prosecution and Punishment of the Major War Criminals of the European Axis Powers and Charter of the International Military Tribunal, which among other things, describes Nuremberg category crimes.[18] In addition, this principle of foreign power intervention under very selective circumstances is upheld by Emmerich de Vattel, a highly qualified publicist and as such a recognized source of international law.[19]

A second inconsistency with respect to the U.S. Department of State definition of terrorism is that it fails to acknowledge that it is permissible for foreign powers to intervene in the domestic affairs of sovereign states which enact municipal law that is in violation of *jus cogens* laws. That is important because if terrorism is practiced by a state, a definition like the foregoing does not highlight the responsibility other nations may have to try to stop state terrorism from happening.

Plainly, the Department of State ignores important sources underlying international law and readily accepts a makeshift but never really complete definition of terrorism.[20] What makes that U.S. Department of State definition makeshift relative to Vattel's definition, for example, is that the U.S. Department of State definition was designed to accommodate geopolitical considerations. Vattel's definition, however broad in scope, was not, and as such is certainly less dubious.

With respect to the development of a conceptual definition of terrorism, what does appear to be critical is that the term "terrorism" can be manipulated more easily than "insurgency" by decision-makers driven by geopolitical considerations to perpetuate an international political system in which politics comes before law. "Governments," Blakesley tells us, "including our own ... prey on the public perception of anarchy in the international arena. They use the public perception of that anarchy and fear of terrorism to promote their own policies of international vigilante justice."[21]

If the emotionally laden term terrorism can serve the interest of counter-terrorism in ways that lead to a condition where the counter-terrorists become the terrorists, the core of any conceptual definition of terrorism should be free from terms that exert a powerful pull on visceral emotions. Hence Professor Louis Rene Beres' way of viewing terrorism may be most useful. For Beres, "insurgent violence without just cause (*jus ad bellum*) and/or insurgent violence which falls outside of justice in war (*jus in bello*) is terrorism."[22]

Having said that, however, a conceptual definition of terrorism in purely jurisprudential terms somehow seems insufficient. Some writers have pointed out that a purely jurisprudential definition of terrorism seems to ignore the quality of terror itself as an especially important component of the phenomenon.[23] The task at hand is to encapsulate that component in the definition so that it does not distort or detract from the essentially jurisprudential character of the conceptualization. One way to do this, I think, is to look at the processes associated with the terrorist act.

A fruitful approach to that problem is to examine the imagery elicited by the act itself which serves as building blocks of that condition of profound

anxiety and dread commonly construed as terror.[24] What seems critical
here is that there is a duality to the effect of the imagery elicited by the
terror act: while the act itself engenders images of the terrorists' strength
and virility, the target population is affected by aspects of the act which
elicit images that emasculate or denigrate it. That "esthetic component" of
terrorism is most clearly seen in dramatic acts of terrorism such as the
Munich massacre of Israeli athletes and the hijacking of the *Achille
Lauro*.[25] Hence the conceptual definition of terrorism that this study
embraces is:

> the threat, practice or promotion of force for political objectives by or-
> ganizations or a person(s) whose actions are designed to influence the
> political attitudes or policy dispositions of a third party, provided that the
> threat, practice or promotion of force is directed against (1) non-com-
> batants; (2) military personnel in non-combatant or peacekeeping roles;
> (3) combatants, if the aforementioned violates juridical principles of pro-
> portionality, military necessity, and discrimination; or (4) regimes which
> have not committed egregious violations of the human rights regime that
> approach Nuremberg category crimes. Moreover, the act itself elicits a
> set of images that serve to denigrate the target population while
> strengthening the individual or group simultaneously.[26]

The Symbiotic Relationship Between Politics and Terrorism

In the broadest sense, this study will explore the origins and evolution
of terrorist groups and delve into different types of terrorist group behavior.
Both of these objectives are undertaken with an eye toward recognizing the
effect of political context and shifts in that setting on growth, maturity, and
decline of groups, and variations in the targeting practices of those groups.
From the vantage of exploring terrorist group behavior, the study needs to
relate political events happening in the region to terrorism, thereby in effect
giving a dynamic quality to the work.

One way of thinking about the interplay between politics and terrorism
is to explore whether or not terrorist groups act differently when political
events occur, such as the outbreak of war, movement in the "peace process"
between Israel, Arab confrontation states and the Palestinians, elections in
Israel or Egypt, assassinations, or structural changes in Israeli settlement
policies in the West Bank. With respect to each of these political event
types, and some others, it will be possible to review the data and determine
if any relationship between these events and terrorist assaults are revealed.
In other words, can this study determine if terrorist assaults are in most

cases linked to political events, or whether they are "independent events"?

Let us explore this idea of the relationship between political events and terrorism by placing some of Mickolus's data in the context of two models of conflict. In the broader sense, Azar, Jureidini, and McLaurin describe the role that violence plays in protracted communal conflict and suggest the analogy of a servo-mechanism to capture how political forces at work prevent political events from being too disruptive or too accommodating. In the narrower sense, Brecher and James construct a way of thinking about violence that hinges in part on whether or not participants view some sort of resolution to the political fray. What follows next are examples of Middle East terrorism that highlight some of the political event categories previously mentioned, and give substance to the aforementioned models of conflict.

Azar, Jureidini, and McLaurin tell us that intractable conflict is a process that regulates itself, acting as a type of servo-mechanism designed to keep political events in the region from being too belligerent or too coopera- tive.[27] This suggests a relationship exists between "cooperative" events and terrorism. For example, when an acute crisis such as the outbreak of war occurs, terrorist acts may decrease because of the fear that an increase in terrorism might make the crisis uncontrollable. At the same time, the authors report, "when the lower critical threshold is crossed, the crisis is due to an unusually cooperative event (such as, in the Middle East, President Anwar el-Sadat's visit to Jerusalem). Such an event would demand an answer that would constitute a threat to the national consensus as defined in the protracted conflict...."[28] In other words, the authors suggest that "cooperative" events beget disruptive events like terrorism.

Mickolus's data set seems to substantiate the notion that terrorist activity will be minimal during the outbreak of war. For example, he suggests that from June 6, 1967 to June 12, 1967, only one act of transnational terrorism could be linked to the Six Day War.[29] During that same period, only two acts of transnational terrorism were reported to have taken place by the *Jerusalem Post*. The "Assifa" organization claimed to have attacked two northern Israeli settlements on June 6, and an unknown group of terrorists attacked a portion of the Beersheba-Gaza railway line on June 8, 1967.[30]

Mickolus reports that between October 6, 1973, which marks the start of the Yom Kippur War, and December 1, 1973, there were only four transnational terrorist acts carried out by Palestinian terrorist groups worldwide.[31] Likewise, from June 6, 1982, which marks the start of Israel's invasion of Lebanon, to August 1, 1982, there were only four acts of international terrorism that seem to be linked to Israel's military action in Lebanon.[32]

Data which draws on Mickolus's work and the *New York Times* also seem to substantiate Azar, Jureidini, and McLaurin's idea that unusually cooperative events will elicit counter-weight events.[33] For example, when Sadat announced his intention to travel to Jerusalem to meet with Prime Minister Begin, terrorist acts directly linked to that trip were extremely prevalent throughout the Middle East. Consider the following terrorism events that took place during three days following Sadat's announcement.

Mickolus tells us that in Damascus, two bombs were detonated inside the Egyptian embassy by an unknown group on November 17, 1977, following President Sadat's visit there with Syrian President Hafaz-el-Assad.[34] On November 18, a bomb destroyed the offices of Egypt's national airline Egypt-Air in Beirut, and one of the Egyptian embassy's walls there was demolished by a rocket attack.[35] In Athens, a group of armed Palestinian protesters opened fire on the Egyptian embassy with pistols on November 18.[36] Mickolus reports that the Egyptian embassy in Pakistan was attacked by six students, reportedly Palestinians, who tried to set the embassy on fire.[37] In Tripoli, the Egyptian embassy was also attacked by arsonists demonstrating against Sadat's trip to Israel.[38]

Several years before Sadat's landmark journey to Israel various attempts at peace negotiations also elicited terrorist activity. For example, the Popular Front for the Liberation of Palestine General Command (PFLP-GC) attacked the northern Israeli settlement town of Kiryat Shmona and killed eighteen persons with the purpose of derailing Arab-Israeli peace accords on April 11, 1974.[39] On May 15, 1974, the Popular Democratic Front for the Liberation of Palestine (PDFLP) attacked an Israeli apartment building and a close-by school in the Israeli border town of Maalot to prevent peace negotiations between Israel and Jordan.[40] On March 5, 1975, al-Fatah activists attacked the Savoy Hotel on the waterfront in Tel-Aviv to disrupt the Israeli-Egyptian peace talks headed by Secretary of State Henry Kissinger.[41] Similarly, the Popular Front for the Liberation of Palestine (PFLP) attacked the Egyptian embassy in Madrid to protest the signing of the Egyptian-Israeli disengagement pact on September 15, 1975.[42]

At the same time, it should be mentioned here that the Jewish fundamentalist terrorist group Terror Against Terror (TNT) was planning its most spectacular mission as a direct result of the Camp David Accords. At the time of its demise, the Gush Emunim underground (TNT) was planning to bomb the Dome of the Rock on the Temple Mount in Jerusalem.[43]

Drawing on action-reaction models of group conflict, Brecher and James report that what is happening in the Middle East today is reflective of the predominant role violence plays in intractable communal conflict. The authors tell us that, "as long as adversaries see no end to their conflict, and as long as their struggle over incompatible threatened values persists.... That tendency ... induces a resort to violence ... and responsive violence by the adversary(ies)."[44]

Brecher and James's model of crisis management in the Middle East may explain what seems to be a strong relationship between assassination of terrorist leaders and retaliatory activity. The period following the Munich massacre of Israeli athletes in 1972 is especially revealing since Prime Minister Golda Meir's reaction to this act was immediate. She made it strikingly clear that Israeli security forces would systematically kill those terrorists associated with that event. Consider the four examples of that relationship which occurred during the seven month period between December 1972 and July 1973.

Mickolus reports that on December 8, al-Fatah and PLO official Mahmoud Hamshari was slain by a bomb blast in Paris by Mossad's "Wrath of God" assassination team.[45] On January 25, 1973, Abu Khair, an al-Fatah leader, was slain by a "Wrath of God" unit in Cyprus.[46] On January 26, 1973, Black September Organization (BSO) activists killed a Shin Bet officer in Paris in retaliation for Mossad's counter-terrorism operations.[47] In direct retaliation for Abu Khair's death, an Israeli business executive was assassinated by Black September activists on March 12, 1973.[48]

In April 1973, an Italian El Al worker was shot to death in retaliation for Black September leader Abdul Zuaiter's assassination by "Wrath of God" operatives on October 16, 1972.[49] On June 28, 1973 Mohammed Boudia, a Black September activist, was slain in Paris, again reportedly by "Wrath of God" bombers.[50] Three days later, an Israeli air force ace was shot to death in Washington, D.C. to avenge Mohammed Boudia's death by a group calling itself "Voice of Palestine."[51]

One of the hallmarks of intractable communal conflict in general and lengthy terrorist campaigns in particular is that watershed political and military events have a profound and lasting effect not only at the immediate time and place they happen, but in the future and at shifting geographic and political sites.[52] Azar, Jureidini, and McLaurin make the important point that "protracted conflict has, as we have seen, forcefully captured and held important segments of national identity." If "moves that signal a potential termination to the conflict engender powerful identity crises in a personal and subcultural as well as national scale," then what happened in the past, especially if it is part of a commonly shared and tortured historical legacy, is equally important for cementing social solidarity and self identity.[53]

Azar, Jureidini, and McLaurin's idea suggests that anniversaries of landmark political events ought to be marked by terrorist incidents.[54] That theoretical proposition seems to be supported by the data. With respect to the commemoration of landmark events, several examples between 1975-

1978 are reported by Mickolus.

For example, Mickolus reports that al-Fatah placed a bomb on an Israeli bus on November 19, 1978, commemorating the first anniversary of Anwar el-Sadat's trip to Israel.[55] Similarly, a bomb was placed on a Jerusalem street on April 13, 1977 to mark the tenth anniversary of Israel's conquest of East Jerusalem during the Six Day War of 1967.[56] Likewise, al-Fatah detonated a bomb near a cafe in Jerusalem on November 13, 1975 to celebrate the anniversary of Yasser Arafat's landmark speech before the U.N. General Assembly.[57]

Brecher and James's model may also explain the seemingly strong relationship between shellings, air strikes, and retaliatory terrorist acts. For example, in response to Israeli shelling of southern Lebanon, a PDFLP bomb was detonated close to an Arab school in the Christian part of East Jerusalem on November 15, 1977, and a second bomb detonated in a Jewish suburb three hours afterwards.[58]

In retaliation for Israeli bombing in southern Lebanon, a Palestinian group placed a bomb in the Bank Leumi le Israeli in Paris on November 27, 1977.[59] On May 20, 1978, the Black June Organization, conceivably in conjunction with the PFLP, assaulted El Al passengers at Orly Airport in Paris to retaliate directly for Israeli air strikes against Tyre where some two hundred Palestinian combatants were reportedly killed.[60]

An analysis of the relationship between political events and the outbreak of terrorism will be discussed in more detail in Chapter Four, Chapter Five, and Chapter Six. Chapter Four will discuss the sources and origins of several Middle East terrorist groups and make a set of interconnections to shifting political context. Chapter Five will discuss the methodology and constructs to be used for a quantitative analysis and offer the analysis of behavior patterns for several types of groups and the terrorist assaults they commit.

Typologies

"Aim Approach" Typologies

The aim of this chapter portion is to showcase three types of terrorist group typologies and provide discussion that underscores their strengths and shortcomings. The framework for discussion involves descriptions and critiques of "aim" approach typologies, "instrumental" approach typologies, and "psychological" approach typologies.[61] Examples of more prominent typologies that are illustrative of the strengths and shortcomings intrinsic to these "approaches" are offered to give the reader a sense of what is available with respect to typologies in the field of terrorism studies. Additional examples of terrorist group typologies similar in thematic emphasis are provided in the endnotes to flesh out a more complete picture.

"Aim typologies" are terrorist group typologies that focus primary attention on the aim or ideological function of the terrorist group, which presupposes and derives from motivational factors such as political goals that generate and sustain action. Such typologies oftentimes emphasize the importance of particular terrorist group attributes like degree of political commitment or political ideology. That is what Merari calls the "purpose" approach: it seeks to define the "purpose" of the terrorist group under consideration.[62]

Wilkinson distinguishes between four major types of terrorism: "ethnic minority, nationalist or autonomist"; "ideological sects or secret societies" that aspire to shape "revolutionary" economic and political change in the world; "exile or emigre groups" which embrace "irredentist, separatist or revolutionary aspirations ..."; "transnational gangs" who use violence "in the name of some vague 'world revolutionary goal'."[63]

Taken at first blush, it is clear that Wilkinson's categories are not mutually exclusive. For instance, Wilkinson's categories "ideological sects" and "transnational gangs" have substantial overlap. The Irish Republican Army (IRA), for example, can be categorized as a "transnational gang" because IRA activists attack targets in England as well as Ulster, and a "nationalist or ethnic minority" group.[64] Precisely for that reason, the ability of Wilkinson's typology to generate meaningful hypotheses to test about different terrorist group-types is practically nil.[65]

Johnson crafts a concise typology that consists of six terrorist group types: "minority nationalist," "Marxist revolutionary," "anarchist," the "syndicalism of immaturity," "neo-fascist (and extreme right-wing)," and "ideological mercenaries." For Johnson, terrorist groups like al-Fatah, the Basque ETA, the IRA, and the Front de Liberation du Quebec (FLQ) are "minority nationalist groups." Meanwhile, any Maoist, Guevarist, or Trotskyist terrorist group falls under the "Marxist revolutionary" group heading.

Terrorist groups such as the Iberian Liberation Movement (MIL) are classified as "anarchist groups," while groups like the Symbionese Liberation Army (SLA), the Baader-Meinhof gang, and the Weathermen comprise the "syndicalism of immaturity." Furthermore, terrorist groups like the Italian Ordine Nuovo and Avanguardia Nazionale are considered "neo-fascist and extreme right wing groups." Finally, the category "ideological mercenaries" is comprised of groups like Black September and the Japanese Red Army.[66] While substantive problems of category overlap are also present in Russell, Banker, and Miller's typology, this work stands out in part because of the rather odd and imprecise use of hyperbole to delineate between types of terrorist groups. To be persuaded that hyperbole is apparently an acceptable part of serious efforts to understand the dynamics of terrorism, we need only to consider the entirely vacuous description of nihilist terrorist groups. "They are," for the authors, "bent on destruction along the lines of the once heard call by black militants in the United States: 'Burn, baby, burn!'"[67]

Shultz differentiates between three different types of political terrorism. Shultz tells us that "revolutionary terrorism" is the threat and/or use of force with the aim of making structural revolutionary change within the existing political order.[68] "Sub-revolutionary violence" involves a lesser degree of change and upheaval; it is the threat and/or use of force to shape structural change in "... structural-functional aspects of the particular political system."[69] Lastly, "establishment terrorism" is the threat or use of force by an existing regime that can be directed against either internal and/or external opponents.[70]

Interestingly enough, Shultz focuses attention on a set of key variables he feels are relevant to the three kinds of political terrorism he articulates. Those variables are, "... sensitive to cross category comparison, while maintaining a degree of parsimony."[71] The variables Shultz cites are: causes, environment, goals, strategy, means, organizations, and participation.[72] Shultz's typology is one of the few examples of work on terrorism that actually posits key explanatory variables within the framework of the typology. At a substantive level, that is a meaningful contribution. Nonetheless, while Shultz's work enumerates those explanatory variables succinctly, it fails to realize the real potential that it has because there is no attempt to examine or elaborate on the relationship between them.

Merari presents a meticulous and well formulated typology that breaks down terrorist activity primarily along the lines of the group that is targeted and its headquarters of operation.[73] Accordingly, he seems to combine elements of "aim" and "instrumental" approaches. While he acknowledges that short term "situational" conditions can temporarily divert terrorist leaders from the pursuit of long range goals within the political landscape and hence from the original targets, Merari distinguishes between four basic types of terrorism.[74]

For Merari, "domestic based xenofighters" are terrorists who target foreign inhabitants, associations, or governments but wage war from a domestic site. "Foreign-based xenofighters," by contrast, are terrorists who wage war against foreign inhabitants, associations, or governments from sites overseas. "Domestic based homofighters" comprise groups that target indigenous government and/or competing organizations from local sites. "Foreign based homofighters," by contrast, are terrorists who target indigenous government and/or competing associations from sites overseas.[75]

Merari closely ties together the terrorist activities that he classifies and the explanatory variable goals. For each organization type, Merari lists a series of "operational goals" that are commonly pursued.[16] Merari extrapolates three generalizations about types of terrorist activity from his classification scheme.

First, "xenofighter terrorist groups" are inclined to mount operations that are more indiscriminate with respect to who is targeted than "homofighter terrorist groups." Illustrative of Merari's point, in my judgment, is the enormous devastation of the Nairobi, Kenya terrorist assault, where a "foreign based xenofighter group" (i.e., Osama bin Laden activists) destroyed the U.S. embassy there and killed some two hundred fifty persons in August 1998. Second, "foreign based terrorist groups" are inclined to carry out acts of international terrorism. Third, "foreign based terrorist groups" rely on generally recognized support and sympathy from foreign nations that sponsor them.[76]

While Merari's analysis gives a scintillating suggestion of the direction this work might have taken, Merari does not elaborate much on what he calls "the specific limitations" of terrorist groups and what causes them. Such a discussion would be a useful addition to a conceptualization that strongly alludes to the role that many variables play in terms of how they constrain terrorist group behavior.

Fattah's work is another example of an "aim typology" that has "instrumental" trappings. The typology focuses on the type of target selected but is based on "the type and aims of the terrorist group...."[77] For Fattah, targets are divided into four categories: "immediate and secondary," "appropriate and inappropriate," "accessible and inaccessible," and "personalized and generalized." "Immediate and secondary targets" are labels that Fattah uses to describe the primary victim(s) of a terrorist incident and other groups of people and persons of authority who are affected indirectly.

"Appropriate and inappropriate" targets are linked to whether or not "mass destruction terrorism," like rebellion, or "selective terrorism," such as political assassination, is taking place. Fattah explains that "... an appropriate target is one whose destruction or victimization would help best the cause of the terrorists and would assist them in achieving their goals."[78] What seems significant here is that Fattah does not fail to capture the possibility of change in terms of terrorist assault targets that may presuppose and derive from change in terrorist group "life-cycle" and political context.

At a tactical level, Fattah suggests a connection between goals and types of terrorist acts. At the most basic level, "accessible and inaccessible targets" is a category that refers to the vulnerability of a target. Delving deeper, the author suggests that target types such as government and business facilities may elicit different acts of terrorism: more symbolic acts like sabotage in the case of the former, and more coercive acts like kidnapping in the case of the latter.[79] That idea is extended into the realm of "personalized" and "generalized" targets. To be more specific, campaigns against the ruling elite seem to evoke attacks against "personalized" targets like government officials, while the aim of debilitating government is associated with terrorist attacks against "generalized" targets like bus stops and schools.[80]

The underlying strength of Fattah's typology is the emphasis that is placed on the connection between the type of target selected and political goals pursued by terrorist leaders. By extrapolation, the author suggests the process is sometimes more static, sometimes more fluid, as appraised by terrorist group leaders. While Fattah discusses political context and magnitude of the struggle, his typology, like both the Shultz and Merari typologies, would benefit from some more probing discussion about explanatory variables and the interconnections that resonate between them.

Seen from a slightly different angle, Crenshaw-Hutchinson constructs a terrorism assault typology in contrast to a terrorist group or terrorist group-type typology. The author develops a terrorist event typology that takes into account the multi-purpose objectives of a terrorist assault. We are told Crenshaw-Hutchinson's typology presupposes and derives from Thomas P. Thornton's schema and delineates a set of "proximate objectives" and "tactical considerations" inclusive of "targets," "responses," and "levels of discrimination" intrinsic to a terrorist assault. The "proximate objectives" that the author suggests are "short run" include: "morale building," "advertising," "disorientation," "elimination," and "provocation."[81] The author also suggests these are goals designed to affect aspects of inter-group interaction, as well as other targets, that can be seen as immediate, secondary, and tertiary in nature.

Crenshaw-Hutchinson describes elements of "response" at three target levels that can be viewed as immediate ("victim and identification group"), secondary ("mass"), and tertiary ("sympathizers") that in this case can be described as "positive targets." For the "victim and identification group," the response includes "despair and immobility" and "fear." In turn, we are told that "mass" targets experience "curiosity" and "anxiety." Lastly, "sympathizers" experience "enthusiasm" and other generally recognizable feelings. The author goes on to elaborate on "levels of discrimination" in terms of intensity, for example, that contributes to the desired response.[82]

What seems significant here is the real contribution Crenshaw-Hutchinson makes with respect to showcasing different levels of effect, both external and internal to the group, that terrorist assaults elicit. In other words, Crenshaw-Hutchinson's work on terrorism in Algeria after the Second World War really presupposes and derives from the continuously evolving nature of group "purpose," and thereby in effect group evolution within a political context. Interestingly enough, we are told that some prominent "terrorists" became part of the establishment after Algerian independence.[83] Clearly, Crenshaw-Hutchinson's special focus on the dynamics of terrorism in continuously evolving political landscapes, along with her reflections on the internal dynamics of terrorist groups under consideration, resonates deeply with many underlying themes of this work.

In terms of an appraisal of these "aim typologies," an underlying concern with many of them revolves around the central issue of theoretical utility. First, one problem all too frequently encountered is that the categories delineated are not mutually exclusive. With problems of category overlap, it is really not possible to operationalize a typology. In a similar vein, some typologies treated in the endnotes are overly articulated, such as the Mickolus and Bell efforts, while others, like Ronchey's, could be developed even more. Second, many of the typologies do not predicate themselves on distinctions made between terrorism and justifiable insurgency which, in my judgment, needs to be addressed in some fashion.

One issue area that stands out concerns the static nature of many of these works. While the Merari and Fattah typologies seem closer to the mark, all too many of these works seem overly rigid. Falling back on the Jewish Defense League example we used earlier, we know that a terrorist group's "aim" can change. Indeed, it is commonplace to note that the "aim" of the Jewish Defense League changed from purely self-defense motivations to more political ones that manifested themselves in the special, predominant JDL focus against Soviet targets that was a hallmark of JDL terrorist assaults in later years.[84]

At the heart of the matter, it seems that precious little among "aim type" terrorism typologies has been done to posit key explanatory variables for terrorism as an intrinsic function of the typology itself. Even more scarce, it seems, is work that attempts to isolate and identify interconnections between explanatory variables. The fundamental issue really becomes one of whether or not a typology is dynamic, namely whether or not it can take into account the sources and origins of terrorist groups, their growth, and even decline.

"Instrumental Approach" Typologies

A few writers embrace an "instrumental approach" in terms of the construction of terrorism typologies. That approach focuses more attention on the type of terrorist activity undertaken, rather than on what generates and sustains terrorism. Falk distinguishes between terrorism carried out by government "functionaries" and non-government "revolutionaries."[85] For Falk, "functionaries" embody a "statist logic" that revolves around the central idea that "total war" is a perfectly suitable way to acquire political gain. Indeed, Falk tells us that, "inflicting pain becomes in a very real sense what the war is all about."[86]

Alternately, terrorism, as practiced by "revolutionaries," embodies what Falk calls an "emancipation logic" that compels terrorists to "register its impact through shock effects or through expressive dramaturgy that relies on the media to transmit intimidating messages."[87] Falk makes the important point that terrorism elicited by "functionaries" and "revolutionaries" mirrors each other because they correspond in terms of the roles played by perpetrators, the target, and the audience, even though the underlying political reasons differ.[88]

What seems significant here is the Falk typology fails to capture terrorism practiced for less lofty reasons than revolution or maintenance of the status quo. Terrorism that does not embrace full-blown revolution, but rather practical political concerns instead, can be used to protest against political, social, or economic conditions.

For example, certain animal rights organizations in Canada target animal laboratories, meat-packing, or grocery establishments.[89] Indeed, one fundamental question really is, how do we really know what constitutes "revolutionary" terrorism anyway? For example, were the "Black Panthers" in the United States "revolutionary," to use Falk's term, or were they more an expression of the outrage against the political accommodation and change denied to African-Americans by White America?

Waugh distinguishes between "spillover terrorism," "integrated terrorism," and "external terrorism."[90] For Waugh, the primary feature of "spillover terrorism" is that the use of force by "foreign nationals" is focused against people from foreign lands and/or their possessions rather than against the reacting government.[91]

What distinguishes "integrated internal terrorism" from "spillover terrorism" is that the nationality of the victims and the terrorists are unalike, with either the victims or the terrorists coming from the "host state."[92] Lastly, "external terrorism" is characterized by the terrorist act taking place over and beyond the province of the target state.[93] Within that framework, Waugh also creates two sub-categories for location based on whether the terrorist act is internal or external to the province of the target state.[94]

The central idea behind Waugh's typology revolves around the appraisal of the terrorist group by the reacting government. We are told that "the typology is predicated on the perspectives of the responding governments with the acts categorized according to the jurisdictional relationships to the acts, the victims and the terrorists."[95] But we already know that definitions of terrorism and interpretations of terrorism events by reacting governments are all too frequently tarnished by geopolitical considerations. For example, what about distinctions between "rebellion and justifiable protest" that may be manipulated by the ruling elite?

One underlying concern here is how little attention is paid to the dynamics that account for terrorist group cohesion and development, such as shifts in political context and "predisposing factors" among particular individuals that serve to give shape to terrorist group self-identification. After all, it is the terrorist group leaders who actually shape the group's identity and direction in the larger world of action.

It follows that Waugh's conceptualization would benefit from a discussion about what elements help to create those outwardly visible features. After all, two groups with enormous ideological or motivational distance between them can target similar locales, assault "foreign nationals," or practice what Waugh calls "external terrorism." At the heart of the matter is why terrorist groups behave as they do and how the dynamics of the terrorist groups themselves influence particular terrorism outcomes.

For Pluchinsky, "indigenous terrorism" constitutes the lowest rung in his terrorist typology. "Indigenous terrorism" is distinguished by terrorist activity that is bounded by the geographical boundaries of a nation.[96] "Supra-indigenous terrorism," which comprises the next upward rung in the typology, is broader in scope but is constrained by regional boundaries.[97] "International terrorism," distinguished by terrorist assaults that almost always take place beyond the province of the target nation, forms the next ascending rung.[98] Lastly, "state directed terrorist activity," considered by Pluchinsky to be the "highest level" of terrorist activity, is focused against "external elements" of opposition that are found outside the jurisdictional province of the state which perpetrates that activity.[99]

But how does the foregoing scheme square with an underlying theme of this work, namely that terrorist group behavior and instrumentalities can change depending on a host of internal factors, and political context shifts, at both domestic and international systems levels? An underlying issue here is why create an ordinal terrorism group-type matrix, ranging from "lower to higher" level terrorism in the first place. Does a ranking like Pluchinsky's really capture meaningful differences between types of groups? For example, consider if Gurr's notion of "relative deprivation" can account for why certain terrorist groups remain "indigenous" or not.[100] In a similar vein, what factors contribute to the wider scope of "supra-indigenous terrorism"? If economic and political "deprivation" is addressed or ignored outright, is it not plausible to think of change in terrorist group behavior happening apace?

In the broader sense, underlying change in terrorist group behavior can happen for more pedestrian reasons. For example, if counter-terrorist measures are significantly enhanced, as was the case with Israeli airport security after a series of attacks on El Al aircraft during the late 1960's, a terrorist group that formerly engaged in "supra-indigenous terrorism" such as the PFLP might be compelled to strike abroad at the interests of the target state, thereby in effect changing it into an "international" terrorist organization.[101]

One fundamental issue of concern with "instrumental typologies" revolves around their inability to capture how the behavior and instrumentalities of terrorist groups can change. The enormous capacity for change in terrorism event lethality, or even a switch from "lower" to "higher" order terrorism, seems dependent on an array of internal and external factors. For example the "purpose" of a group can change, thereby in effect altering terrorist assault targeting or lethality. In the international sphere, political context does change, and that can help to transform terrorist organizations into fledgling governments, such as the case with the Palestine Liberation Organization (PLO), or it can conceivably enhance the scope, intensity, or frequency of terrorist assaults if terrorist groups feel outpaced by political events.

Furthermore, in the domestic sphere, demands and aspirations for political and economic change, and what those evoke from government, can transform the structural shape of the terrorist struggle, thereby in effect paving the way for "group splitting" or even the elimination of a terrorist organization's *cause celebre*. For example, we know that with the establishment of the State of Israel, the *raison d'être* of Menachem Begin's Irgun passed into eclipse. Perhaps that process was captured most symbolically by Prime Minister David Ben-Gurion's sinking of the Lehi munitions ship *Altalena*, which was blown to pieces off the shoreline of Natanya, to underscore Prime Minister Ben-Gurion's dominance of the Israeli political and military landscape.[102]

All of the aforementioned work on typologies really leads to the fundamental issue of whether or not this review of "instrumental approach" terrorist group typologies serves as a bellwether for more probing efforts to come. I think an answer of "yes" is the ineluctable conclusion. Perhaps the single most dominant lesson, in my judgment, is that terrorism typologies must be able to take the inevitability of change into account, with a capacity for analysis at different levels that includes, but may not be limited to: international and domestic political contexts and the dynamics of terrorist group "life cycles" that revolve around the central issues of terrorist group self-identification and cohesion, growth, evolution, and decline.

"Psychological Approach" Typologies

Typologies about terrorism that base classification schemes on the psychological and/or personal make-up of the perpetrators seem to be divided into two camps. On the one hand, there are typologies of terrorism that attempt to make more substantive analyses about the effect of personality on terrorist event outcomes. On the other hand, several typologies that embrace the "psychological approach" rely merely on narrative or emotive descriptions about what happened and who the terrorists are, rather than on what psychological factors interact with one another to produce terrorist behavior in certain people.

Goldaber creates a typology that devotes increased attention to the different personality types that generate three distinct types of terrorists. For Goldaber, "hostage-takers," and by extrapolation terrorists in general, are grouped according to three motivational "bases": "psychological," "criminal," or "political." In turn, each of those categories is broken down further according to personality types or characteristics.

In the case of "hostage-takers" motivated by psychological factors, three personality types are denoted: the "suicidal personality," the "vengeance seeker," and the "disturbed individual." In contrast, hostage-takers driven by criminal factors are classified as "cornered perpetrators," "aggrieved inmates," or "felonious extortionists." Lastly, persons motivated by political factors are grouped as "social protesters," "ideological zealots," or "terrorist extremists."[103]

While Goldaber's work reflects workman-like effort, his personality types seem overly rigid, and as such, do not seem to introduce a flexibility into the system that may more accurately reflect the murky complexities of explanatory factors at work. For example, it seems plausible, nay probable, that a "suicidal personality" is a "vengeance seeker" in some capacity, and also a "disturbed individual." While Goldaber's analysis is thought provoking, the reader, in my judgment, literally cries out for more in the way of flexibility, elaboration, and precision that would amount to work more probing and fresh.

Post crafts a substantive typology that draws on the psychological dynamics of the family. For Post, terrorist groups are divided into two kinds: "anarchic-ideologues" and "nationalist-secessionists." We are told that "anarchic-ideologues" are persons who have internalized basic conflict and anger against the family, particularly the father, thereby in effect transferring rage upon society. Groups like Italy's Red Brigade and the Federal Republic of Germany's Rote Armee Fraktion (Red Army Faction) fall under that category.[104]

Alternately, Post suggests "nationalist-secessionist" terrorists are persons who are in sync with their family's view of the world and therefore embrace the struggle for political independence. The author explains that "in the case of the individual who takes up the cause of the politicized ethnic or national minority—such as the Basque separatists—the split derives from the split within society and is a split in the sense of political identity."[105] Hence, terrorist groups like Basque Fatherland and Liberty (Euzkadi ta Askatasuna or ETA), the PIRA, and Palestinian nationalist groups like al-Fatah, belong in this category.[106]

While Post's typology is a tantalizing snapshot of the direction the work might have taken, the typology does not seem to delve deeply enough into the matter at hand. At the heart of the matter, we know that very few persons, even those with a tortured historical legacy, actually become terrorist activists, whether they, as Post suggests, internalize conflict or embrace a political cause. The observation that very few people become terrorists suggests a confluence of factors at work that coincide to create or increase the likelihood of terrorism happening.[107]

At a more basic level, Kaplan describes the psychological factors that cause specific types of terrorism. Although Kaplan's work is not a formal typology per se, it is treated as one because what amounts to nationalist and anarchist-nihilist terrorism is distinguished. For Kaplan, terrorist assaults within the context of national liberation struggles are in reality struggles to increase self-esteem by collectivities. Terrorists "... may have suffered a severe blow to their self-esteem—from a crushing military defeat for example. Or they may have become aware of the lack of something they never had, a firm basis of self-respect."[108]

In a narrower sense, the relationship between an urge for violence and an incomplete personality can result in terrorism of an anarchistic-nihilistic nature. Kaplan asserts, "terrorism can not only shore up a weakened ego; it can also shatter its walls altogether, freeing the self from what has come to be felt as a prison."[109] As an example, the author reports that Lee

Harvey Oswald, the alleged killer of President Kennedy, proclaimed that, "Happiness is taking part in the struggle where there is no borderline between one's own personal world and the world in general."[110]

The one obvious question is why not extend the analysis of "the weakened ego" in some form to encompass terrorists who operate within the context of national liberation struggles. After all, there seems to be enormous functional and substantive distance between terrorist activists on the one hand and constituent groups on the other. One can even conceive of a "spectrum" among constituent group members ranging from "hard-liners" to "hanger-ons" at the fringes. While Post and Kaplan provide some very useful tools to think about the problem, we need, in my judgment, to delve more deeply into the sources and origins of terrorism with special focus on various "levels of analysis" and contact points between them.

Rather than seeking to craft a typology that classifies groups and highlights differences between them, some writers who embrace the "psychological approach" seem to pay scant attention to isolating and identifying regular patterns of terrorist group behavior. For example, McKnight compiles a virtual repository of anecdotal accounts about terrorism. The underlying goal of this work is "to explain and reveal the mind of the terrorist, to show how a man may commit acts of blatant terror for political and ideological motives; how in fact he can face his own friends and family—perhaps sit down to share a meal with children—after planting a bomb in a crowded shopping street."[111] The book is divided into several sections, with chapter headings such as "Mid-East Madness," "Blood-soaked Isle," and "Ireland Death Dance," each describing terrorist activity happening in various parts of the world. Clearly, that type of vacuous description of terrorism, peppered liberally with well worn clichés, is not especially useful for this study.

In a similar vein, Parry's work suggests that terrorism can be broken down into categories that include "nihilist/anarchist" terrorism, "nationalist or irredentist" terrorism, "state terrorism," and "right-wing" terrorism.[112] The book is divided into several sections that run the gamut from the "nihilist/anarchist" type terrorism carried out by groups like the Symbionese Liberation Army (SLA), to the "nationalist/irredentist" terrorism of groups like the PLO, to the "state terrorism" perpetrated by the Jacobins, the Third Reich, and Mao Zedong, to the reactionary terrorism carried out by the Croats against the Serbs before the Second World War.[113]

While the foregoing description seems to suggest an "aim" typology, Parry uses the same style of analysis that McKnight uses, with similar results. For example, we are told that, "despite their lofty protestations, many political terrorists are acting out the disturbances of their minds and souls rather than out of political reasons. For their insane violence, blame their families, blame society if you will. But the true cause is deeper, in a configuration of fear and hatred, in their innermost drive to do violence."[114]

Parry's work is perhaps the foremost example of work on terrorism that pulls at the heartstrings of emotion rather than engaging in sufficiently rigorous analysis of what generates and sustains a highly complex phenomenon. Although Parry conveys the depth of misery and suffering that takes place as a result of terrorist actions, that information is not especially relevant for this study.

With respect to those writers on terrorism who undertake more serious inquiry, the basic problem with the "psychological approach" is that terrorist behavior is not shaped simply by the psychological predispositions of the terrorists. Clearly, other explanatory factors are critical in terms of how terrorist groups behave and why.

In terms of the "second camp" of writers, the basic problem with the "psychological approach" is that the time honored but well worn assessment of terrorists as "crazies" is a gross oversimplification and incorrect in most cases. Even though it may by generally correct to claim that some terrorists exhibit what Parry calls "abnormal tendencies," it is critical to acknowledge that many others do not.[115] Indeed, a considerable amount of the literature on terrorism underscores the notion that the rationality assumption in decisionmaking is as valid for terrorist tacticians as it is for the political leadership of nation-states.[116]

All of the aforementioned leads to the fundamental question of what can be learned from the literature on terrorist group or terrorism event typologies. In the narrower sense, it seems clear that when scholars are constructing typologies, most would benefit from paying closer attention to theoretical considerations, such as the development of categories that are mutually exclusive and, hence, able to capture distinguishing characteristics across terrorist group-types. To be specific, categories should take into account an array of distinguishing characteristics such as ideology, goals, and recruitment patterns.

In the broadest sense, it seems clear that many writers who focus attention on typologies of terrorism need to devote more consideration to rigorous analysis of explanatory variables and contemplate ways to identify the degree of influence those variables have on terrorist group behavior. All too frequently, the literature on terrorism typologies presents a rather fragmented picture that barely touches on the intricacies and distinctions that characterize this type of political violence.

For one thing, we know that only a small fraction of persons burdened with the strains and tensions of political struggles ever become terrorist activists. In fact, a much larger number of persons comprise "constituency groups" which are themselves comprised of persons with an array of opinions about acceptable and unacceptable terrorist practices.[117] In turn, this observation indicates particular factors at work in particular persons, which may "coincide" with factors in a social framework of what Gurr and Harff would call "economic and political deprivation" to produce terrorism.

Finally, what bodes ill for terrorism research in general is the still apparently acceptable practice among too many writers on terrorism of relying heavily on narratives that use gratuitous emotion to explain this dynamic and complex phenomenon. More attention and precision by researchers needs to be devoted to meaningful analysis of the sources and origins of terrorist groups and the root causes of variations in terrorist group behavior, rather than on polemics.

Conclusions

Policymakers and scholars ought to profit from research that reveals regular patterns in the target selection process of Middle East terrorist groups. At a functional level, this research should strengthen the capability of government officials to assess and respond to the threat or use of unconventional warfare. At a more theoretical level, this work should provide new insight into the study of terrorism, still a relatively neglected area of political violence studies.

Unquestionably, a fundamental obstacle that hampers more effective policymaking and research is the absence of a more precise and widely accepted definition of terrorism. Terrorism, in its many ideological shapes and structural forms, remains a difficult aspect of political violence to define. Different definitions of terrorism abound, some with political or legal emphasis, making it more difficult to focus on the ticklish question of what constitutes a terrorist act.[118]

The term terrorism is in itself problematic. That term is so emotionally laden that it can be manipulated by policymakers who will likely tailor counter-terrorism policy with geopolitical considerations in mind. In the narrower sense, a definition of terrorism that is operational is critical for this study for three reasons. At the most obvious level, an "operational definition" serves as a cornerstone for the development of a functional terrorist group-type typology. For another thing, an operational definition is crafted at the outset so that the pitfalls that surround a subjective interpretation of the data may be avoided, thereby adding to the overall quality of the work.

In the broadest sense, it is essential to conceptualize a definition of terrorism that distinguishes between terrorism and justifiable insurgency where in the case of the latter the principles of proportionality, military necessity, and discrimination are followed by groups that use violence in the political fray. Consequently, policymakers in the larger world of action would have a more uniform understanding of the distinctions between these two concepts, thereby in effect providing an opportunity to make foreign policy more consistent with international law. The conceptual definition of terrorism developed here draws on preexisting definitions but uses international law to provide valuable insight to accomplish that task. It is probably no exaggeration to say that a definition of terrorism that can make a distinction between terrorism and justifiable insurgency, and at the same time capture the sense of horror of the act, stands a real chance of acquiring wide scale acceptance and recognition.

An operational definition of terrorism that draws on international law makes it possible to craft counter-terrorism policy in accordance with international law. To be sure, that is important at two levels. First, as both Stohl and Beres suggest, ignoring international law in favor of retaliatory counter-terrorist activity that is generated and sustained largely by myopic geopolitical considerations increases tensions between potential adversaries and the potential of full-blown military conflict. Second, the political experience of established counter-terrorist organizations that have operated over and beyond the realm of international law demonstrates that ignoring international law in the realm of international politics increases the chance of illegal political activity taking place at home.[119]

Lastly, this work also emphasizes the importance of linkage between political events happening in the Middle East and terrorism. Indeed, it is an incumbent responsibility to make that linkage, thereby in effect giving a dynamic quality to the work. The work covers two frameworks for thinking about intractable conflict and implications for terrorist assaults happening in that context. A cursory review of the data indicates that some type of relationship may exist between political events related to the Middle East and terrorist assaults. As this research unfolds, those relationships, as well as others, will be explored and described in detail.

Notes

Material on terrorism and international law reprinted with the kind permission of *Shofar: A Jewish Journal of Interdisciplinary Studies*.
    1. Schmitt 1993, A1, A6; Friedman 1993, A1, A6.

2. For definition purposes, terrorist movements and guerrilla movements are not necessarily the same. Ian Smart distinguishes between guerrillas, whose primary focus is to eradicate the political and military forces of an enemy, and terrorists, who use force or the threat of force primarily to create abject fear while pursuing political objectives. For example, Mao Zedong was a guerrilla or an insurgent but not a terrorist. See Smart 1987, 4.

3. Stohl 1987, 168. Louis Rene Beres tells us that "negative physical sanctions unless they are devastating enough to ensure destruction of the group itself, are bound to be ineffective. Such sanctions might even have the effect of a stimulus" (Beres 1991, 140). See Wilkinson 1984, 298; DiLaura 1987, 32; Falk 1983, 23-24.

4. Ibid.

5. McKinley Jr. 1998a, A1, A8; McKinley Jr. 1998b, A1, A11; Myers et al. 1988, A1, A6.

6. Crozier 1960, 158.

7. Laqueur and Alexander 1987, 380-381.

8. Blakesley 1992, 56; Beres 1987, 1-19, 47-68; Bell 1975, 18; Chasdi 1994, 60; *Jerusalem Post* 1961; *Jerusalem Post* 1962a, 1; *Jerusalem Post* 1988a, 6; Carr 1958, 4; *Jerusalem Post* 1990b, 2; Carr 1962b.

9. Counter-terrorism policy ought to be designed to ensure the integrity of human rights which are *jus cogens* rights under international law. As mentioned previously, the use of force is permissible under international law in four instances: in self-defense when an attack is imminent, in post attack situations, for humanitarian intervention reasons either to protect a population at risk or a nation's own citizens from egregious violations of the human rights regime, and to fulfill collective security agreements. To the extent that counter-terrorism policy that employs force fulfills at least one out of those four criterion, it meets *jus ad bellum* criteria. The concept of "just cause" is extrapolated from a series of international conventions and a variety of non-convention sources which describe democratic norms to be upheld. International conventions ensure individuals have rights but the underlying problem that remains is that international law cannot enforce those rights. It is the conjunction of democratic norms clearly upheld by international law and the inability of international law to enforce law that allows for the use of force in certain circumstances. See Beres 1990, 132; Louis Rene Beres, interview, December 1993, Purdue University; United Nations 1945a, hereafter UN, Weston, Falk, and D'Amato 1990, 138-139; Intoccia 1985, 131-135; Wardlaw 1988, 235; Chasdi 1994, 60.

10. See Beres 1990, 133; Beres 1988a, 293; Intoccia 1985, 136-137; Joyner 1988, 37; Wardlaw 1988, 235. This part of the study draws from those discussions. Attention is focused on three elements that each state should consider to determine if an insurgency uses 'just means': proportionality, military necessity, and discrimination. The principle of proportionality is upheld

by article 35 of the 1978 Protocol of the Geneva Conventions (UN 1978a, Weston, Falk, and D'Amato 1990, 230-246). It is important to emphasize that this concern embodied in treaty law predates the Geneva Convention by several decades. For example, see United States Department of State 1910, hereafter USDOS; Weston, Falk, and D'Amato 1990, 129-135; Fried 1985, 107-108. Lastly, Professor Beres, an authority on international law, makes the important point that the notion of proportionality pertains also to the nature of force exerted vis á vis the given objective and not necessarily to the prior use of force by the enemy. Another measure of "just means" is the concept of military necessity. Faced with the looming catastrophe of warfare, the insurgency must make the case persuasively that all peaceful options have been pursued in an exhaustive manner without success (Grotius [1604] 1964, 97). The principle of discrimination is upheld in article 51 section 4 of the 1978 Protocol of the Geneva Conventions. See UN 1978a, Weston, Falk, and D'Amato 1990, 230-246. Summing up, Professor Beres tells us that every insurgency should really be evaluated twice: once for *jus ad bello* (justice of war) and *jus in bello* (justice in war). See Beres 1988a, 293; Beres 1990, 133; Chasdi 1994, 60, 72-73.

In accordance with article 38 of the Statute of the International Court of Justice, the writings of highly qualified publicists as well as international conventions (treaties) are sources of the concept of justice in war. Samuel von Pufendorf upholds that concept: "For He who has declared himself our enemy, inasmuch as this involves the express threat to bring the worse of evils upon us, by that very act, so far as in him lies, gives us a free hand against himself, without restriction. Humanity, however, commands that so far as the clash of arms permits, we do not inflict more mischief upon the enemy than defense, or the vindication of our right, and security for the future, require" (Pufendorf [1682] 1964, 139).

Emmerich de Vattel upholds the principle of the inviolability of non-combatants. "Women, children, feeble old men, and the sick are to be counted among the enemy (§ 70, 72), and a belligerent has rights over them, inasmuch as they belong to the Nation which he is at war, and because as between Nations, rights and claims affect the body of society, and with it all its members (Book II, § 81, 82, 344). But these are who offer no resistance, and consequently the belligerent has no right to maltreat or otherwise offer violence to them, much less put them to death (§ 140)" (Vattell [1758] 1964, 282).

Alberico Gentili also upholds the principle of the inviolability of non-combatants during war. In his discussion on the conduct of war relative to women Gentili states, "Further, to violate the honor of women will always be held to be unjust. For although it is not contrary to nature to despoil one whom it is honorable to kill, and although where the law of slavery obtains it is permitted according to the laws of war to sell the enemy together with his wives and children, yet it is not lawful for any captive to be visited with insult." As for children, "For since that time of life is not accustomed to do harm and cannot do so, it ought not be injured." As for the elderly who show no resistance, "What I have said of children I should also wish to apply to those of advanced years; for both those periods of life are feeble and their privileges are often similar" (Gentili [1612] 1964, 252, 260).

The concept of war is codified in several international conventions. See Declaration of St. Petersburg (1868) which states "that the only legitimate object which states should endeavor to accomplish during war is to weaken the military forces of the enemy; that for this purpose it is sufficient to disable the greatest number of men" as cited in Fenwick 1924, 438 n4, 463-464. See USDOS 1910; Weston, Falk, and D'Amato 1990, 129-135; UN 1950a, Weston, Falk, and D'Amato 1990, 147-154; UN 1950b, Weston, Falk, and D'Amato 1990, 155-159; UN 1950c, Weston, Falk, and D'Amato 1990, 160-169; UN 1950d, Weston, Falk, and D'Amato 1990, 170-180; UN 1978a, Weston, Falk, and D'Amato 1990, 230-246; UN 1978b, Weston, Falk, and D'Amato 1990, 247-252.

The concept of justice in war is incorporated in municipal law, specifically in codes of military justice. According to John H.E. Fried, those principles are incorporated in the U.S. Army Field Manual and the U.S. Air Force Treatise. See Department of the Army 1956, 12, hereafter DOA; Department of the Air Force 1976, 6-5, hereafter DOAF as cited in Fried 1985, 98 citations 4, 5.

11. See UN 1945a, Weston, Falk, and D'Amato 1990, 138-139. What constitutes an egregious violation of the human rights regime is drawn from several sources of codified international law. For example, see UN 1950a, Weston, Falk, and D'Amato 1990, 147-154; UN 1951a, Weston, Falk, and D'Amato 1990, 297-301.

The human rights regime is codified in several international conventions. See articles 55 and article 56 of UN 1945a, Weston, Falk, and D'Amato 1990, 138-139; Organization of American States 1948, hereafter OAS; Weston, Falk, and D'Amato 1990, 293-296; UN 1951, Weston, Falk, and D'Amato 1990, 297-301; UN 1948, Weston, Falk, and D'Amato 1990, 298-301; UN 1953, Weston, Falk, and D'Amato 1990, 302-309; UN 1954a, Weston, Falk, and D'Amato 1990, 310-313; UN 1954b, Weston, Falk, and D'Amato 1990, 314; UN 1954c, Weston, Falk, and D'Amato 1990, 315; UN 1960a, Weston, Falk, and D'Amato 1990, 316-321; UN 1955, Weston, Falk, and D'Amato 1990, 322-334; UN 1959a, Weston, Falk, and D'Amato 1990, 335-340; UN 1959b, Weston, Falk, and D'Amato 1990, 341-342; UN 1960b, Weston, Falk, and D'Amato 1990, 343-344; UN 1965a, Weston, Falk, and D'Amato 1990, 345-356; UN 1963, Weston, Falk, and D'Amato 1990, 357-362; European Treaty Statute 1968, hereafter Europ. T.S.; Weston, Falk, and D'Amato 1990, 363; UN 1969, Weston, Falk, and D'Amato 1990, 364-368; UN 1966, Weston, Falk, and D'Amato 1990, 369-370; UN 1976a, Weston, Falk, and D'Amato 1990, 371-375; UN 1976b, Weston, Falk, and D'Amato 1990, 376-385; UN 1976c,

Weston, Falk, and D'Amato 1990, 386-387; UN 1967b, Weston, Falk, and D'Amato 1990, 388-390; UN 1967a, Weston, Falk, and D'Amato 1990, 391; UN 1967c, Weston, Falk, and D'Amato 1990, 392-393; UN 1968, Weston, Falk, and D'Amato 1990, 394-397; Organization of American States 1978, hereafter OAS; Weston, Falk, and D'Amato 1990, 398-412; UN 1970, Weston, Falk, and D'Amato 1990, 413-414; UN 1971, Weston, Falk, and D'Amato 1990, 415-418; UN 1973, Weston, Falk, and D'Amato 1990, 419-422; UN 1976d, Weston, Falk, and D'Amato 1990, 423-425; UN 1977, Weston, Falk, and D'Amato 1990, 426-428; UN 1974, Weston, Falk, and D'Amato 1990, 429-432; USDOS 1974a; Weston, Falk, and D'Amato 1990, 433-434; Europ. T.S. 1978; Weston, Falk, and D'Amato 1990, 435-437; UN 1978c, Weston, Falk, and D'Amato 1990, 438; UN 1983, Weston, Falk, and D'Amato 1990, 439-442; UN 1981a, Weston, Falk, and D'Amato 1990, 443-447; Organization of African Unity 1986, hereafter OAU; Weston, Falk, and D'Amato 1990, 448-458; UN 1981b, Weston, Falk, and D'Amato 1990, 459-461; UN 1984, Weston, Falk, and D'Amato 1990, 462; UN 1987, Weston, Falk, and D'Amato 1990, 463-471; Organization of American States 1987, hereafter OAS; Weston, Falk, and D'Amato 1990, 472-475; UN 1985a, Weston, Falk, and D'Amato 1990, 476-478; UN 1985b, Weston, Falk, and D'Amato 1990, 479; UN 1986a, Weston, Falk, and D'Amato 1990, 480-484; UN 1986b, Weston, Falk, and D'Amato 1990, 485-488; International Labor Conference 1989, hereafter ILC; Weston, Falk, and D'Amato 1990, 489-497; UN 1990, Weston, Falk, and D'Amato 1990, 498-512.

12. Chasdi 1994, 60.

13. Chasdi 1994, 63. At the same time, scholarly endeavors to define terrorism would also benefit from the conceptual definition of terrorism fashioned here. For example, George H. Quester suggests that we adopt a typology where "all military activity is categorized by what is defended and by what is attacked." Under that taxonomy, "when we dispense with this attempt to defend, to hold a line, we ... are in a guerilla mode of operations.... What we normally mean by terrorism is then probably a guerilla campaign conducted in the countervalue (targeting non-military targets) mode of attack." For Quester, "terrorism is thus an approach that seeks to impose pain in an area where those perpetrating such pain cannot yet hope to establish a military monopoly or a system of law and order of their own" (Quester 1987, 227-228).

Be that as it may, there are glaring omissions in Professor Quester's definition of terrorism which reduce its effectiveness. Not the least of those is that a terrorist group could violate *jus in bello* laws, by unleashing weapons of mass destruction against military targets of any government including those innocent of committing Nuremberg category crimes and expect to avoid the brunt of punishment ordinarily reserved for terrorists (UN 1945a; Weston, Falk, and D'Amato 1990, 138-139). For example, if an organization like the Weathermen of the 1960's decided to destroy Department of Defense personnel with chemical or biological weaponry, that act, under Quester's definition of terrorism, could be construed as something other than terrorism.

An assault like the Weathermen example provided above would unquestionably violate international law. The Hague Convention Respecting the Laws and Customs of War on Land (1907) stipulates that armed forces which "employ arms, projectiles, or materials of a nature to cause unnecessary suffering" are prohibited (USDOS 1910; Weston, Falk, and D'Amato 1990, 129-135 as cited and discussed in Fried 1985, 99-100). Protocol I (1978) which augments the Geneva Conventions stipulates in article 35 section 2: "It is prohibited to employ weapons, projectiles and material and methods of warfare of a nature to cause superfluous injury or unnecessary suffering" (UN 1978a; Weston, Falk, and D'Amato 1990, 230-246). See Fried 1985, 100, for a discussion of the Protocol's antecedent, the Hague Convention, article 23 [e]; USDOS 1910; Weston, Falk, and D'Amato 1990, 133.

As if that critical omission were not enough, Professor Quester does not at any point address several important legal criteria, not the least of which is whether the armed struggle under consideration is sustained or spasmodic in nature. That is important because those who are privileged combatants are subject to the laws of war. Carrying out sustained operations within the context of an organized resistance qualifies combatants for POW status as opposed to those who carry out acts outside of that framework (Louis Rene Beres, interview, December 1993, Purdue University). Protocol II of the Geneva Conventions stipulates in article 1 that "this Protocol ... shall apply to all armed conflicts which are not covered by article 1 of the Protocol Additional to the Geneva Conventions of 12 August 1949, and relating to the Protection of Victims of International Armed Conflicts (Protocol I) and which take place in the territory of a High Contracting Party between its armed forces and dissident armed forces or other organized armed groups which, under responsible command, exercise such control over a part of its territory as to enable them to carry out sustained and concerted military operations and to implement this Protocol" (UN 1978b; Weston, Falk, and D'Amato 1990, 247-252).

It is conceivable that non-sustained military operations, for better or for worse, may meet the criteria of *jus in bello* (justice in war). In the narrower sense, the phrase "sustained and concerted action" was designed to preclude what might be considered criminal activity in the domestic jurisdiction of a state (Louis Rene Beres, interview, December 1993, Purdue University). Yet article 7 of the Resolution on the Definition of Aggression upholds "the right of self-determination, freedom and independence as derived from the [UN] charter of peoples forcibly deprived of that right...." (UN 1974b, Weston, Falk, and D'Amato 1990, 224-226). In the case of Hitler, for example, where there was always a larger or smaller resistance against him, the killing of Hitler or the attempt to do so would have fallen purposely and completely within the realm of an ongoing resistance even though the act itself is a "one shot" type of act. Accordingly, the assassination or attempted assassination of Hitler would meet *jus in bello* criteria (Louis Rene Beres, interview, January 1994, Purdue University; Blakesley 1992, 35-37; Chasdi 1994, 81, 63; UN 1974b; Weston, Falk, and D'Amato 1990, 224-226; Beres 1991, 130; UN 1945b; Weston, Falk, and D'Amato 1990, 16-32).

Returning to the Weathermen example, a member of that group or the Symbionese Liberation Army (SLA), for example, could not claim to be protected under international law because those groups did not carry out sustained and concerted military operations. In addition, neither group would have met the criterion of "just cause" because the United States did not commit egregious human rights violations approaching Nuremberg category crimes (see endnote 9 in Chapter Two; Chasdi 1994, 63).

14. See USDOS 1983; Stohl 1987, 168 n2; Norton 1988, 4. It is interesting to note that according to this U.S. Department of State definition of terrorism, the French and American Revolutions must be considered examples of terrorism. There is no provision in this definition of terrorism that concerns the concept of "just cause." Even causes that the United States supports for its own geopolitical interests, such as the Reagan supported Contras or the Kennedy supported Bay of Pigs invasion, are examples of terrorism under this definition of terrorism used by the United States government (Beres 1988a, 299 n14).

15. Chasdi 1994, 63-64; United Nations 1980a. Danileko suggests that *jus cogens* norms really presuppose and derive from the school of naturalism, which in comparison to the school of positivism asserts that, first and foremost, states are bound to uphold peremptory law. For Danileko, "It is well known that the doctrine of international *jus cogens* was developed under a strong influence of natural law concepts. In contrast to positivists, who advocate complete, or almost complete, freedom of contract, naturalists always taught that states cannot be held absolutely free in establishing their contractual relations" (Danileko 1992, 214). The sources of the rule of proportionality as a criterion for the concept of "just means" are chronicled in the Old Testament. For example, in Exodus, 21: 22-25, it is written that in the case of wrongful misconduct against a woman, "you shall give life for life, eye for eye, tooth for tooth, hand for hand, foot for foot, burn for burn, wound for wound, stripe for stripe." In Deuteronomy 19: 19-21, it is written that in the case of a witness submitting false testimony, "your eye shall not pity; it shall be life for life, eye for eye, tooth for tooth, hand for hand, foot for foot." In Leviticus 24: 17-21, it is written, "when a man causes a disfigurement in his neighbor, as he has done it, it shall be done to him, fracture for fracture, eye for eye, tooth for tooth; as he has disfigured a man he shall be disfigured." See Holy Bible Revised Standard Edition 1952, 78, 206, 130; Beres 1988b, 335.

The long standing idea of proportionality can be traced to the time honored principle that a state that has been subjected to another state's use of force, in the absence of efforts by that state to redress the grievance, is entitled to undertake reprisals proportionate in nature (Air Services Agreement Arbitration 1963, hereafter ASAA; Detter De Lupis 1987, 75; Naulilaa Arbitration 1928, hereafter NA; Intoccia 1985, 138-139).

In the case of discrimination, Ingrid Detter De Lupis, drawing on Keen's *The Laws of War in the Later Middle Ages* (1965, 190-191, 196), asserts that civilians, including women and children, had little or no defense against assaults before Grotius' time, "although there were isolated regulations such as that of Henry V of England in 1515, or the Holy Roman Empire of 1442, and 1570, whereby women, children, priests, monks and nuns were immune from attack" (Detter De Lupis 1987, 242, 242 n76). Under contemporary international law, the prohibition against indiscriminate attacks directed at non-combatants is codified in the Geneva Conventions of 1949 and Protocol I (Article 52 - General protection of civilian objects) and Protocol II (Article 13 - Protection of the civilian population; Article 14 - Protection of objects indispensable to the survival of the civilian population) (UN 1950a; Weston, Falk, and D'Amato 1990, 147-154; UN 1950b; Weston, Falk, and D'Amato 1990, 155-159; UN 1950c; Weston, Falk, and D'Amato 1990, 160-169; UN 1950d; Weston, Falk, and D'Amato 1990, 170-180; UN 1978a; Weston, Falk, and D'Amato 1990, 230-246; UN 1978b; Weston, Falk, and D'Amato 1990, 247-252).

According to Ingrid Detter De Lupis, the concept of military necessity is vague at best, but essentially has been used to justify activity to shorten a military conflict or operation. For Detter De Lupis, there will continue to be the balancing of humanitarian principles on the one hand with military necessity requirements on the other. See Detter De Lupis 1987, 334; Beres 1990, 132-133.

16. Chasdi 1994, 63-64. An interesting counter-argument against citizen intervention can be drawn from the Declaration of Independence, itself a document of international law because it embodies natural law. We are told, "Prudence, indeed will dictate that Governments long established should not be changed for light and transient causes; ..." (Louis Rene Beres, interview, January 1994, Purdue University).

17. Chasdi 1994, 64; see UN 1965b, Weston, Falk, and D'Amato 1990, 195-196. Specifically, it states: 1. No state has the right to intervene, directly or indirectly, for any reason whatever, in the internal or external affairs of any other state. Consequently, armed intervention and all other forms of interference or attempted threats against the personality of the State or against its political, economic and cultural elements are condemned.

18. UN 1950a; Weston, Falk, and D'Amato 1990, 147-154; UN 1945a; Weston, Falk, and D'Amato 1990, 138-139; Chasdi 1994, 64.

19. UN 1945c, article 38(d); Weston, Falk, and D'Amato 1990, 33-38. Vattel tells us: "But if a prince, by violating the fundamental laws gives his subjects a lawful cause for resisting him; if, by his insupportable tyranny he brings on a national revolt against him, any foreign power may rightfully give assistance to an oppressed people who ask for aid" (Vattel [1758] 1964, 131).

20. Louis Rene Beres, an expert on international law, argues that this is the case because U.S. foreign policy has traditionally been formulated with Cold War geopolitical considerations in mind. As such, the U.S. continued to support anti-communist regimes which continued to commit egregious violations of the human rights regime such as South Africa and Iran. At the same time, the U.S. has reflexively implemented aggressive foreign policy against regimes which embraced Marxist-Leninist political ideology such as the Ortega regime in Nicaragua. See Beres 1987, xi, 2, 4, 24, 54, 150; Chasdi 1994, 65.

21. Blakesley 1992, 52; Chasdi 1994, 65.

22. Chasdi 1994, 65; Chasdi 1995, Chapter I, Chapter II; Beres 1990, 133; Beres 1987, 106.

23. Robert McKim of the University of Illinois made this important point when he reviewed an early draft of my work, "Terrorism: Stratagems for Remediation from An International Law Point of View," presented at *International Studies Association\Midwest 1991 Annual Meeting,* Urbana-Champaign, IL, October 1991. Other writers who emphasize the quality of terror intrinsic to the act include Lasswell (1978, 258); Kupperman and Friedlander (1979, 54); DiLaura (1987, 29); Simpson (1982, 32); Hocking (1986, 297, 306); O'Brien (1985, 34).

24. Chasdi 1994, 65. While writers such as Lewis Coser and Gordon Allport discuss the role of the image of "outer enemy" and "outgroup" with respect to cohering a group within the context of group conflict, the terrorist act elicits imagery which is two directional in effect. While the imagery associated with the act serves to cohere the terrorist perpetrating the act, it also serves to denigrate the target population. For example, the circumstances involving the deaths of Leon Klinghoffer and Dora Bloch not only created images that empowered the terrorists, they also elicited images of incapacitated Jews who were killed because they were Jewish. That imagery affected Jews profoundly worldwide and helped make the names Dora Bloch and Leon Klinghoffer unforgettable. See Coser 1956, 110; Allport 1954, 244-145; Chasdi 1994, 65-66; Webster's 1977, 1204.

25. Chasdi 1994, 65. The "esthetic component" conceptualization is a concomitant to Lasswell's notion that terrorists engage in "… the symbolic enhancement of instruments or procedures of destruction (of which violence is the most extreme)" (Lasswell 1978, 258-259, 261). To be specific, Lasswell is concerned with the "devices of symbolic enhancement.… The ordinary revolver that you use to bump off someone, or the dagger—how do you symbolically

enhance this little piece of destructive technology? If you strangle a victim, how do you put the individual act of strangling into such an evocative form that has the fear-instigating quality that generates general apprehension and leads to broad political consequences?" (Lasswell 1978, 259). This conceptualization also follows Crozier's assertion that the net effect of terrorism is to reduce the resources of one target and increase those of a different one (Lasswell 1978, 262). We are told terrorism "may be used against the enemy or against members of one's own side" (Crozier 1960, 159-160).

26. Chasdi 1997, 74-75; Chasdi 1994, 66; Pearson and Rochester 1998, 448.

27. Azar, Jureidini, and McLaurin 1978, 43, 51-53.

28. Ibid., 53.

29. Mickolus 1980, 75.

30. *Jerusalem Post* 1967, 2.

31. Mickolus 1980, 413-419.

32. Mickolus, Sandler, and Murdock 1989a, 289-304.

33. Azar, Jureidini, and McLaurin 1978, 43, 51-53.

34. Mickolus 1980, 754.

35. Gage 1977; Howe 1977; *Jerusalem Post* 1977a, 2; *Jerusalem Post* 1977b, 1, 2; Mickolus 1980, 745-755.

36. Mickolus 1980, 755; Gage 1977; *New York Times* 1977; *Jerusalem Post* 1977a; *Jerusalem Post* 1977b, 1, 2.

37. Mickolus 1980, 755.

38. Mickolus 1980, 755; Howe 1977; *Jerusalem Post* 1977b, 1, 2.

39. Mickolus 1980, 446-447.

40. Mickolus 1980, 453-454.

41. Mickolus 1980, 512-513.

42. Mickolus 1980, 544-545.

43. Sprinzak 1988, 198, 200, 206, 209; Long 1990.

44. Brecher and James 1987, 10.

45. Mickolus 1980, 364.

46. Mickolus 1980, 371-372.

47. Mickolus 1980, 372.

48. Mickolus 1980, 380.

49. Mickolus 1980, 387.

50. Mickolus 1980, 395.

51. Mickolus 1980, 396.

52. Dutter 1987, 153; Holton 1977, 98-99.

53. Azar, Jureidini, and McLaurin 1978, 57.

54. Azar, Jureidini, and McLaurin (1978, 50, 57) suggest that idea in their discussion.

55. Mickolus 1980, 815.

56. Mickolus 1980, 694.

57. Mickolus 1980, 563.
58. Brecher and James 1987, 10; Mickolus 1980, 753.
59. Mickolus 1980, 756.
60. Mickolus 1980, 789.
61. This conceptualization is based on an analysis Merari makes about existing terrorist typologies. Merari distinguishes between typologies based on "group ideology," "group purpose or *raison d'être*," and "psychological motives." See Merari 1978, 331-346.
62. Merari 1978, 331-346.
63. Wilkinson 1979, 104.
64. Ibid. Flemming, Schmid, and Stohl use four categories to sort out terrorist typologies: group typologies, motivation typologies, modus operandi typologies, and origin typologies (Flemming, Schmid, and Stohl 1988, 153-195). In fact, Merari (1978, 333) makes the same point about the Irish Republican Army (IRA) in a critique of his work.
65. Iviansky's categorization scheme suffers from the same problem. Iviansky denotes three forms of "individual terror": "anarchist terrorism," "terrorist warfare" in conjunction with political and social crusades (social revolution), and terrorist warfare in pursuit of "national liberation" (Iviansky 1977, 51, 53, 55). For Iviansky, "anarchist terrorism" is characterized by "lone wolf" attacks by individuals who do not have a niche in the existing political and economic framework. In contrast, "terrorist warfare" conducted in the name of structural political and economic change is less of a "thunderous cry" and more of a political statement. Lastly, "terrorist warfare" carried out for national independence seeks to inflict punishment on institutions that symbolize foreign domination. To be specific, its purpose is "... to sow disorder and undermine the prestige of the alien power, so indicating the movement's determination to carry the struggle to a successful conclusion" (Iviansky 1977, 55, 56, 51). Again, the problem here is that those categories overlap, making it impossible to operationalize this typology. For example, "anarchist terrorism" could take place within the political context of violence against an existing regime. In that instance, is the terrorist act an act of "anarchist terrorism" or "terrorist warfare"? In fact, it could be either or both. Simply put, the question is, how can different types of terrorist groups be categorized?

Along similar lines, Dror develops a typology that denotes three predominant terrorism types found in democracies: "native," "imported," and "transient." In addition, two "secondary" types of terrorism are differentiated: group on group violence and extra-territorial terrorism. For Dror, "native terrorism" is indigenous terrorism, generated and sustained by political demands and aspirations including, but not limited to, social revolution. "Imported terrorism" is terrorism waged by "aliens" in support of a political agenda at odds with the existing regime. "Transient terrorism" is a third classification to encompass terrorism waged "by aliens and against aliens" in a democratic political arena. Lastly, Dror describes group on group violence and "extraterritorial terrorism," namely "... attacks against external representatives, persons, properties and symbols of democracy" to be "secondary" terrorism types (Dror 1983, 69). Like Wilkinson and Iviansky's work, Dror's typology would benefit from further theoretical refinement. For example, "transient terrorism" and "terrorism against groups and entities within a democracy but not directed against the state or government" (i.e., group on group violence) seems duplicative. Further, Dror's work would profit from a discussion about terrorism's causal variables.

66. Johnson 1978, 276. In much the same style, Alexander and Gleason construct a typology that also differentiates six terrorist group-types. Alexander and Gleason's categories include "ethnic, religious or nationalist," "Marxist-Leninist," "anarchist," "neo-fascist and extreme right wing," "ideological mercenaries," and "pathological." The authors explain that groups like the IRA comprise the "ethnic, religious or nationalist" group type, while groups like the Basque Separatist Sixth Assembly fall under the "Marxist-Leninist" group type heading. West Germany's "Red Cells" are examples of "anarchist groups," whereas groups like Mussolini Action Squads are placed in the "neo-fascist and extreme right-wing" category. Terrorist groups "for hire," such as the Japanese Red Army that attacked Lod Airport in Israel, are classified as "ideological mercenaries" by Alexander and Gleason. Lastly the "pathological" group-type is comprised of terrorist groups such as the Symbionese Liberation Army (Alexander and Gleason 1981, xiii-xiv).

In a similar vein, ideology forms the foundation of Burton's terrorist group typology. His group-types include "anarchist," "Moscow-oriented communists," "nationalist groups" (driven by "sectional chauvinism"), "composite and eclectic," "Maoist-Peking oriented splinter groups," "black racist," "New Left," "Castroite," "Trotskyist," and "right wing reaction." In each instance, Burton lists the theoretical background of the group-types. For example, he explains that the writings of Bakhunin, Marx, and Lenin inspire "anarchist" and "Moscow oriented communists," respectively. Alternately, culture, language, and history generate and sustain "nationalist groups." In contrast, "composite and eclectic groups" like the Tupamaros of Uruguay are influenced by a marriage of nationalism and socialism. Meanwhile, we are told that "Maoist-Peking oriented splinter groups" draw on the works of Mao Zedong and General Giap of Vietnam, while "Black racist" groups draw on Fanon. The author maintains that "New Left" groups are motivated by Marcuse, Fanon, and Bakhunin, whereas "Castroite" and "Trotskyist" groups draw on inspiration from Guevara and Debray on the one hand, and Trotsky and Guillen on the other. Finally, Burton asserts that "right wing reaction" groups are sustained by national history and a perceived threat to the integrity of the majority by emergent groups (Burton 1975, 246-247).

Rubenstein also focuses on the ideological differences between terrorist groups. He distinguishes between "anarcho-communists," "leftist nationalists," and "far right terrorist organizations" (Rubenstein 1987, 89-128). For Rubenstein, "anarcho-communists" wage war against their own ruling elite. "Anarcho-communists," reports Rubenstein, "share with the rest of the far left, a vision of a classless, stateless world society that has eliminated poverty, inequality and war" (Rubenstein 1987, 94). From Rubenstein's perspective, the most striking difference between "anarcho-communists" and the "leftist nationalists" is "situational" (Rubenstein 1987, 111). Lastly, "far right-organizations" are characterized by their capacity to elicit generally recognizable support and sympathy from allies and states who may act as sponsors of terrorism. Rubenstein's typology seems overly simplistic and fails to capture the subtleties, nuances, and complexities of terrorism. At the most basic level, it seems a gross oversimplification to simply assert that the primary difference between "anarcho-communists" and "leftist-nationalists" is "situational." For example, there seems to be tremendous ideological space between the Baader-Meinhof gang, which wages war against capitalism in general, and the Basque Fatherland and Liberty (ETA) that seeks to create an autonomous, most likely Marxist state in the Basque region of Spain (USDOD 1988, 61, 35; National Foreign Assessment Center, hereafter NFAC 1979, 3). Finally, the category "anarcho-communist" seems to be ill-conceived. Plainly, that category needs to be skillfully broken down to be consistent with what has happened in the world of terrorism. For example, there are Marxist-Leninist groups such as the Popular Front for the Liberation of Palestine (PFLP) and the Democratic Front for the Liberation of Palestine (DFLP) that more closely resemble nationalist groups rather than anarchist groups. In addition, there are terrorist groups that could be classified under this scheme as anarchist, such as the Posse Comitatis, or the "Phineas Priests" in the mid-western United States, that are about as far removed from Marxist-Leninist ideology as they can be (Gurr 1989, 19; Brown 1989, 49-50; Toy 1989, 144-145; Gurr 1989, 208; *Klan Watch Intelligence Report* 1996a, 1-3; *Klan Watch Intelligence Report* 1996b, 1, 4).

Nef differentiates between various types of terror based on what he calls the "functional perspective" of terrorist groups (Nef 1978, 13). For Nef, "repressive terror" is carried out to generate and sustain the extant regime, while "insurgent terror" is undertaken to change the substantive nature of "a domestic or international 'order'." Nef explains that "insurgent terror" takes three forms: "nationalist-irredentist," "radical revolutionary," and "radical reactionary" terrorism. Over and beyond the scope of political terrorism, Nef describes two additional terror types from a functional point of view. Those include "criminal terror" that is done to ensure the economic well-being of the terrorist organization and "psychotic terror" carried out as a result of pathological behavior (Nef 1978, 13). With respect to scope, Nef's classification scheme is broader than other classification schemes that have been considered thus far. Nef's typology suggests there are relevant connections between political terrorism and other forms of violence like "criminal terror" that elicit feelings of terror (Nef 1978, 13). That seems an ill-conceived notion. The best part of Nef's typology is his concise breakdown of "insurgent terror." Nef breaks down that category into three sub-components. "Nationalist-irredentist terrorists" seek self-determination or independence for part of a population under the jurisdiction of another polity. "Radical revolutionary terrorists," by contrast, seek fundamental structural change of society. Lastly, "radical reactionaries" use terrorism to preserve the status quo of an existing regime when faced with a direct and immediate challenge from forces that seek to reform society or transform it outright (Nef 1978, 13).

Mickolus denotes several types of terrorist groups including "group-types" for criminal activity and psychopathic behavior. Those categories include: "separatists/irredentists" (e.g., Corsicans, IRA), "fedayeen" (e.g., al-Fatah and PFLP), "ultra-left anarchists" (e.g., the Baader-Meinhof group), "Latin guerrillas" (e.g., the Tupamaros), "criminal gangs" (e.g., "La Cosa Nostra"), "psychotic individuals" and "hoaxes" (Mickolus 1976, 1317-1318). One problem that Mickolus's work has that is not found in the Nef typology concerns the redundancy of group-type categories. For example, the group-type "fedayeen" is repetitive since terrorist groups like al-Fatah and PFLP are motivated by nationalist-irredentist and/or separatist sentiments. In addition, the group-type "hoaxes" remains puzzling since it makes little if any conceptual sense.

Along similar lines, Bell constructs a more elaborate typology that designates six fundamental types of terror: "psychotic," "criminal," "endemic," "authorized," "vigilante," and "revolutionary." Furthermore, the category "revolutionary terror" is broken down into six component parts: "organizational," "allegiance," "functional," "provocative," "manipulative," and "symbolic." For Bell, "psychotic terror" is terrorism undertaken by persons who manufacture political reasons to mask psychopathic behavior. Perhaps the quintessential example of that is the Unabomber (Dr. Theodore Kaczyinski), whose "manifesto" that railed against the looming calamity of technology clearly masked profound and lasting mental disease. At a more systemic level, "endemic terror" is terrorism that flourishes largely as a result of wide-spread anomie found in certain societies. Alternately, terrorism carried out by government agencies against political opponents and/or the general population is "authorized terror." Lastly, "vigilante terror" is mounted by persons who act to implement a political agenda without any legal authority to do so (Bell 1975, 10-15). Within the framework of "revolutionary" terror, "organizational terror" is undertaken within the terrorist group with the aim "… of maintaining internal discipline, inhibiting penetration, and punishing errant members" (Bell 1975, 15). In order to garner support from the general population, terrorist groups employ "allegiance terror" such as extortion and assassination. Terrorist activity against the enemy is called "functional terror" because the targets they seek out perform roles or "functions" in society (Bell 1975, 15-17). "Provocative terror" is revolutionary terror that elicits profound and lasting responses that shape the contours of the political struggle. At a more functional level, "manipulative terror" is used to resolve a predicament that involves negotiation such as a hostage-taking situation. Bell asserts that "... manipulative terror extends the drama of the deed while it seeks a functional gain in terms of freed prisoners or ransom...." Finally, "symbolic terror" is revolutionary terror carried out against targets that embody the essence of the weltanschauung and/or political ideology of an opponent (Bell 1975, 17-19). Bell should focus on parsimony. He does not make the case persuasively that all six sub-components of "revolutionary terror" are necessary. For example, the categories "functional" and "provocative" terror do not seem to contribute to the overall quality of Bell's work. At the same time, some of the same problems that afflict in the typologies that have been discussed before are found in Bell's typology. For example, none of the categories that Bell creates are mutually exclusive and, as such, they cannot be made operational. Similarly, Bell's typology would benefit from some discussion about explanatory variables for terrorist group behavior. Schlagheck chronicles similar categorical distinctions in her discussion about terrorism categories (1988, 5-7).

Ronchey's rather sparse typology breaks down terrorism into three types. The bulk of Ronchey's discussion focuses on "ultra-left" and "fascist" and/or state terrorism, but there is only passing mention of terrorist campaigns that, "... all have radical, atavistic-religious, nationalist and separatist rather than revolutionary characteristics" (Ronchey 1979, 150, 151).

Long constructs a terrorism typology that differentiates between "nationalist or ethnic organization" on the one hand and "doctrinal organizations" on the other (Long 1990, 29-30, 31). For Long, ethnic or nationalist terrorist organizations pursue the political objectives of autonomy or outright independence for the nationalist or ethnic groups they represent. Alternately, "doctrinal organizations" are terrorist groups that rationalize their use of terrorism by drawing on real or perceived political, economic, or social issues that warrant increased attention on the part of the ruling elite. Long suggests that "nationalist or ethnic organizations" and "doctrinal organizations" are distinguished from one another based on constituency and the arsenal of terrorist tactics at their disposal (Long 1990, 30). He reports that "nationalist-ethnic groups" are characterized by rather large constituent groups and a wide array of terrorist methods. At the other extreme, most "doctrinal groups" such as the Baader-Meinhoff Gang, for example, are smaller in size and have smaller constituency groups. We are told, "that is particularly true of such utopian New Left groups such as the Red Army Faction and the Red Brigades" (Long 1990, 30). Interestingly, Long talks freely about the drawbacks implicit in his terrorist taxonomy. Like many other classification schemes discussed thus far, the categories that Long develops are not mutually exclusive and as such are not especially useful for this study. For example, we are told, "Hizbollah is predominately a doctrinal group (Shi'a Islam) but it is also ethnic in composition, rooted in the Shi'a confessional community in Lebanon" (Long 1990, 29-30).

The typology Selth constructs evokes the typologies of Wilkinson and Shultz. Selth differentiates between four major types of terrorism: "domestic terrorism," "international terrorism," "state sponsored terrorism," and "state terrorism" (Selth 1988, xxiv-xxv). We are told that "domestic terrorism" describes terrorism undertaken by groups within a nation that wage terrorist campaigns against political or economic institutions or the populace of that same nation (Selth 1988, xxiv). "International terrorism," by contrast, is widely used to refer to terrorism that moves over and beyond national boundaries and is, at the same time, actively supported by foreign governments (Selth 1988, xxiv). Selth correctly subsumes "state sponsored terrorism" within the "international terrorism" category. For Selth, "state-sponsored terrorism" is international terrorism where the threat or use of force is used "by agents of a state or the employment of more or less independent terrorist groups by a state to pursue its foreign policy aims ..." (Selth 1988, xxiv). What seems significant here is that Selth makes a quantitative distinction based on intensity and effect between low level "agitational" terrorism used by the vast majority of terrorist groups and the enormous levels of terrorism wielded by government agencies of totalitarian regimes such as that in post 1944 Brazil, Samoza's Nicaragua, the Third Reich, and the USSR under Stalin (Selth 1988, xxiv-xxv). That is an important distinction to make because, not withstanding state terrorism, most terrorist activity is relatively "low level" in terms of numbers of deaths and casualties and amount of property damage caused. Clearly, that is an underlying theme that permeates the work of many specialists who write about terrorism (Long 1990, 1; Flemming 1992, 164, 180, 194-195, 203-204; Gurr 1988, 45-46; Mickolus 1988, xxii-xxiii). In fact, the looming catastrophe that terrorism promises, along with its enormous capacity to shift from one site to another in an almost haphazard manner, is what the essence of terrorism is all about.

Perry's typology is another example of work that holds promise but would greatly benefit from further elaboration. In a discussion about Macedonian liberation movements, Perry distinguishes between state terrorism, terrorism used by "guerrilla forces," and political organizations that embrace terrorism in pursuit of political gain (Perry 1988, 185). While Perry's classification scheme may be useful for historical analysis, it is not especially useful for this study. At a theoretical level, an important distinction between guerrilla movements that commit terrorist acts and justifiable insurgency should be made. To be sure, that underlying issue is discussed at length in the earlier part of this chapter. At a functional level, it seems overly simplistic to describe so complex a phenomenon as terrorism as something that sometimes has "sectarian hues," at other times is "an urban phenomenon," and at other times still is "based on political and ideological considerations as in Nicaragua" (Perry 1988, 185). Such descriptions do not shed any light at all on the factors that generate and sustain terrorism.

Flemming develops a terrorist typology that differentiates group-types on the basis of distinguishing characteristics such as political ideology, constituency, and goals (Flemming 1992, 94-95). He also discusses the role of explanatory variables in terms of terrorist behavior in an effective and sustained way. Flemming distinguishes between three terrorist group-types that operate in Western Europe. The first category is "Euroclass," which is comprised of terrorist groups that carry on anti-imperialist and/or anti-capitalist struggles. The second terrorist group type category is "Europrimordial." "Europrimordial" terrorist groups wage war against the ruling elite as a result of aspirations for autonomy (Flemming 1992, 96-98). The third category constructed is "Palestinian nationalists." That category is comprised of Palestinian terrorist groups such as the Black September Organization that waged war against Israel and the West and that operated in Western Europe (Flemming 1992, 95, 98, 105).

67. Russell, Banker, and Miller 1979, 31-32.

68. Shultz 1978, 9-10.

69. Ibid., 10.

70. Ibid.

71. Ibid., 12

72. Ibid., 10-12.

73. Merari 1978, 333, 331.

74. Ibid., 331-334.

75. Ibid., 332-335.

76. Ibid., 332, 340-343.

77. Fattah 1981, 22.

78. Fattah 1981, 24, 22, 23, 25.

79. Ibid., 25, 27, 21-24.

80. Ibid., 28-29.

81. Crenshaw-Hutchinson 1978, 36-39.

82. Ibid.

83. We are told, "The Algerian terrorists have apparently found no difficulty integrating themselves into the post revolutionary society. Zohra Drif, for example became an attorney and is the wife of Algeria's minister of transportation, Rabah Bitat" (Crenshaw-Hutchinson 1978, 35). Also, see Schmid, Jongman, et al.'s description of Crenshaw-Hutchinson's work in "Chapter 1: Terrorism and Related Concepts: Typologies" (1988).

84. Friedman 1990; Hoffman 1984, 10-15.

85. Falk 1988, 170-173, 174-179.

86. Ibid., 76-79.

87. Ibid., 77.

88. Falk 1988, 76. Holton distinguishes between three types of terrorism also based on the type of activity carried out. For Holton, "Type I" terrorism consists of acts committed by persons acting individually or in collaboration with

others "to impose terror on other individuals or groups and, through them, on their governments." The author reports that "Type I" terrorism almost always fails to secure political goals (Holton 1978, 96, 97). In contrast, "Type II" terrorism is the infliction of terrorism on indigenous or foreign groups by governments. Conversely, "Type II" terrorism almost invariably succeeds. Holton states that "... from Mussolini's bombing of the Abyssinians to the 'Christmas bombing' of Hanoi in 1972 ... [such acts] have largely succeeded in their avowed aims" (Holton 1977, 97, 100, 101, 103-104). Lastly, "Type III" terrorism is a blending of "Type I" terrorism and "Type II" terrorism in the contemporary world. To be specific, "Type III" terrorism is the recruitment and use of terrorist groups by a nation-state to carry out illegal activity that would be shunned by the community of nations if committed directly.

Elliot's work is another example of a typology that classifies terrorist groups according to the outward appearance of terrorism. The author distinguishes three types of terrorism: "international," "transnational," and "urban guerrilla warfare." For Elliot, international terrorism is "... carried out by individuals or groups controlled by sovereign states." In contrast, transnational terrorism is "... carried out by basically autonomous non-state actors, whether or not they enjoy some degree of support for sympathetic states" (Elliot 1977, 7). The author presents the thesis that "terrorism has been a catalyst" responsible for the transformation from "urban guerrilla warfare" to "transnational terrorism." In a continuously evolving technological environment, terrorism reaches its most refined stage—"international terrorism"—as a result of technological advance-ment (Elliot 1977, 9). As with other works previously mentioned, Elliot's work could be improved in two ways: place more attention to explanatory variables of terrorism; make conceptual distinctions between terrorism and justifiable insurgency. That problem is evident when the author claims "terrorism is a basic form of guerilla warfare and, in itself, is not a new weapon. Terrorism is simply a good deal easier to apply these days" (Elliot 1977, 10). In the end, Elliot makes the mistake of confusing ends (*jus ad bellum*) with means (*jus in bello*) in much the same way as the well-worn colloquialism "one man's terrorist is another man's freedom fighter." Chalmers Johnson (1978, 271, 273) suggests that point in his discussion about the pitfalls associated with attempts to define terrorism.

89. Kellett, Beanlands, and Deacon 1991, 290, 418, 419, 425, 429, 430.
90. Waugh 1982, 56.
91. Ibid.
92. Ibid., 60.
93. Ibid., 63.
94. Ibid., 53, 56.
95. Ibid., 80.
96. Pluchinsky 1981, 71.

97. Ibid., 71, 48.

98. Ibid., 71, 52.

99. Ibid., 71, 60.

100. See Ted Robert Gurr's discussion about "relative deprivation" theory. Gurr's "relative deprivation theory," which was crafted during 1970, asserts that group violence is the foreseeable product of a discrepancy "between a group's value expectations and the political system's value capabilities" (Rubenstein 1989, 308-309; Graham 1989, 334-338).

101. Pluchinsky 1981, 71; Parry 1976, 543; Waugh 1982, 57; Schul, Dean, and Maurice 1968, 1, 6).

102. Perlmutter 1969, 52-53.

103. Goldaber 1979, 21-23.

104. Post 1984, 243, 241, 254.

105. Ibid., 247-248.

106. Ibid., 241, 243, 254.

107. In addition, certain methodological problems seem to plague some of the studies that are mentioned by Post to support this approach. For example, we are told that Bollinger interviewed captured "left wing" terrorists about their family background which "... suggest[s] a link between certain personality attributes and group behavior" (Post 1984, 246). That argument is spurious because their incarceration turns out to be an equally likely reason why emphasis is put on "bad childhoods" to explain deviant behavior (Campbell and Stanley 1963, 7). Similarly, Post reports that Schmidtchen's study of 227 "left wing terrorists" suggests that an "incomplete family structure" is a pivotal reason why people become terrorists. Schmidtchen's study seems to ignore the basic fact that the vast majority of people from "broken homes" do not become terrorists in the first place (Post 1984, 244). In a sense, there is a similarity between my way of thinking about the making of terrorist group activists, an alignment of explanatory factors, and Diamond, Linz, and Lipset's notion of "coincidental cleavages" in society, that in certain cases align themselves to increase the likelihood and/or intensity of ethnic conflict happening between groups of persons (Diamond, Linz, and Lipsett 1990, 380). For a comprehensive treatment of "social fissures" in several political landscapes, see Theen and Wilson 1996. To be sure, Reiss and Roth's "matrix," when applied to terrorist assaults, seems a fine theoretical concomitant to several works on ethnic conflict.

108. Kaplan 1978, 245.

109. Ibid., 247.

110. Ibid.

111. McKnight 1974, 13. Seen from a slightly different angle, Lifton's notion of "doubling" is, I think, a useful way to think about this issue. Lifton, who focuses special attention on the "state terrorism" of Hitler's Third Reich (1933-1945), really articulates a condition in which certain individuals are able to compartmentalize, thereby in effect making it possible to block out through

some rationalization process (e.g., "... Jews as the world's 'fundamental evil'";
Lifton 1986, 424), the unspeakable horrors perpetrated against victims. For
Lifton, "doubling is an active psychological process, a means of *adaptation* to
extremity" (Lifton 1986, 422). It is, the author tells us, "the division of the self
into two functioning wholes, so that a part-self acts an entire self" (Lifton 1986,
418). This is an intriguing idea that is as applicable, as Lifton suggests, to the
likes of Dr. Baruch Goldstein of Kiryat Arba as it is to Nazi doctors performing
experiments on Jewish victims of the Holocaust. Unequivocally, Lifton tells us,
"... Nazi doctors' behavior resembles that of certain terrorists and members of
the Mafia, of 'death squads' organized by dictators or even of deliquent gangs"
(Lifton 1986, 423). It also resonates with the Reiss and Roth "matrix"
applications that follow in this work (Reiss and Roth 1993).

    112. Parry 1976, 78-91, 365-394, 449-468, 223-233, 203-220, 131-202,
488-506, 496.

    113. Ibid.

    114. Ibid, 35.

    115. Ibid., 21, 23, 32.

    116. For example, see Nef 1978, 19-20. Crenshaw-Hutchinson (1972) is
another writer who accepts the rationality assumption with respect to the
decision-making of terrorist leaders. Also see Bremer 1988, 2. The term
"crazies" which I use comes from Hacker (1976).

    117. Rosemary Harris alludes to this point in her work on Northern Ireland
(Harris 1989).

    118. Laqueur and Alexander 1987, 380-381.

    119. Blakesley 1992, 56.

Chapter Three

Explanatory Variables for Terrorist Group Behavior and the Role of Prevailing Ideology

The purpose of this chapter about explanatory variables and the relationship between the Middle East region and terrorism is twofold. First, the work will explore and chronicle the explanatory variables for target selection that widely-recognized writers in the field deem important. That is essential because any hypothesis this study tests about terrorist group behavior needs to trace an arc to previous work about explanatory factors for terrorism. In a broader sense, any set of hypotheses under consideration needs to be well grounded in works that come before, thereby in effect summarizing the overall direction of the literature and revealing gaps in knowledge that deserve the increased attention and devotion of scholars.

Second, this chapter will describe why there may be terrorist assault patterns or variations in behavior among specific types of terrorist groups according to region. A close and careful scrutiny of "prevailing social ideology" in the Middle East presupposes and derives from works on the Middle East and Middle East terrorism and works on "diffusion of war" and "contagion effects" that have, among other things, been used to explain regional similarities in violent behavior.

Political Ideology and Target Selection

Several well-known specialists on terrorism cite the importance of ideology with respect to its influence on target selection. Those writers include, but are not limited to, Crenshaw (1983), Friedland (1992), Ronchey (1978), Bassiouni (1978), Aston (1980), Flemming (1992), Smart (1987), Mickolus (1976), Harris (1989), Della Porta (1985), Martin (1987), and Rapoport (1987).

Crenshaw reports that ideology is one of several critical explanatory variables that affect target selection. We are told, "ideology also makes a large difference, when it dictates forms and targets. Modern revolutionary-socialist terrorists self-consciously strike out at capitalists and imperialists; to choose working class victims would be contrary to the tenets of their beliefs. On the other hand, the philosophical convictions of fascists or neofascist terrorists include mythic affirmations of the value and necessity of violence for its own sake."[1]

Similarly, Friedland points to ideology as intrinsic to the target selection process. For Friedland, "... political terrorism is usually perpetrated by organized groups whose members have a clear group identity—national, religious or ideological. Furthermore, group processes are evident in terrorists' selection of targets. Those attacked are usually singled out according to group or class characteristics rather than on the basis of individual attributes."[2]

Ronchey also makes a connection between the ideology of a terrorist group and target type. In his discussion about terrorism in Italy, he reports that "fascist terrorism, which used mainly explosives, was blind, indiscriminate and impersonal; it lacked a social base or 'cover'. The terrorism of the ultra-left, which can be described as an anomalous partisan movement at war with democracy, chiefly uses pistols, strikes at precise symbolic and individual targets and tends to infiltrate street riots...."[3]

Bassiouni suggests that the actions of terrorists, inclusive of target choice, are driven by ideological considerations rather than profit motives. For Bassiouni, "It is commonly accepted that a terrorist is an ideologically motivated offender, a person who engages in acts of terror-violence not for personal gain but to accomplish a power outcome. Such a person rejects in whole or in part the social, political or economic system of the society of which he is a part."[4]

In his discussion about the nature of terrorists, Aston also suggests a relationship between ideology and the targeting behavior of different terrorist groups. For Aston, "it can be stated as axiomatic that not all terrorist groups aspire to the same goals, nor are they driven by the same primary motives and cannot therefore be assumed to engage in hostage taking for the same reasons nor, for that matter, be counted on to respond in the same ways. In fact ... terrorist groups can be classified according to ... criteria such as ideology...."[5]

Aston asserts that terrorist groups which are committed to waging war against an undesirable political system may be more inclined to target a symbol of that system. The author tells us that "an attack against one of those individuals ... symbolic leaders, such as royalty or leading figures in the commercial or industrial sectors ... is essentially an attack against the system itself."[6]

In a similar vein, one of Flemming's conclusions is that European terrorist groups that are involved in ideological struggles and embark on anti-capitalist or anti-imperialist campaigns are likely to limit the intensity of terrorist attacks in terms of casualties and deaths. Flemming classifies European terrorists that engage in anti-imperialist struggles as "Euroclass" terrorists. We are told that "Euroclass groups target people (11.8%), property (76.1%) and both (12.1%)."[7]

Smart expands on the relationship between targets and the agenda of terrorist groups. "For obvious reasons," Smart reports, "the targets and objectives of terrorism are linked. Those who are to be subjected to violence or the threat of violence, sometimes described as the terrorists 'instrumental' targets, must have some relation to the desired political reaction. Both targets and objectives nevertheless stretch over a very long spectrum."[8]

Mickolus also points to ideology as a variable of major importance in terms of terrorist group behavior and/or target selection. In his analysis of "the flexible response" standpoint on counter-terrorism policy, Mickolus tells us that terrorist groups "differ in ideology and purpose in their choice of terrorism. What we are dealing with is a group of people who have chosen a common tactic. We cannot infer from this that their motivations are commonly held."[9]

Although Harris does not refer to any direct influence of ideology on terrorist group behavior, she asserts that the norms and values of constituent groups do affect the nature and scope of terrorist attacks and targets. Harris compares and contrasts the protracted conflicts in Northern Ireland and Sri Lanka and points to fundamental differences in constituent group ideology to explain different terrorist group behavior patterns.

To be specific, Harris argues that Catholic and Protestant constituency groups have a restraining effect on the intensity of communal conflict in Ulster, presumably because of underlying Judeo-Christian concepts of "just" and "unjust" targets. Conversely, the author suggests that this restraining effect is largely absent among Sinhalese and Tamils. "Given the brutality of some of those involved in Ulster's Troubles," she claims, "I think we have to assume that it is because they have to reckon with a public opinion moulded by an ideology different from that of Sri Lanka that, willing enough as the hit men are to gun down a man out with his wife and children, Belfast murderers very seldom deliberately kill the wife and children also. In many cultures they would, but in Ulster the gunmen on both sides have to take account of public opinion antagonistic to such cruelty."[10]

Della Porta makes the tantalizing suggestion that the pathways of effect between explanatory variables may be more complex than the seemingly direct interconnections between them. Della Porta suggests that ideology may serve as an intervening variable of sorts, hampering or facilitating a particular type of terrorist act. Della Porta tells us that, "Rather than as causes of collective behaviors ideologies seem to operate as facilitating factors, resources or constraints in the making of an actor and in the definition of strategies."[11]

Some authors have written about the important role that ideology plays with respect to conflict in the Middle East in general. For example, Martin suggests how profoundly important religious cleavages are for the emergence of competing political ideologies in the region. In his discussion about the distinction between believers and unbelievers in Islam with respect to the doctrine of jihad (Holy War), Martin tells us that all other distinctions, including political and "human distinctions," are irrelevant. From a contemporary, albeit radical Muslim standpoint, "if non-Moslems reject Islam or *dhimmi* status, then 'fighting *(qital)* is the only remaining response under the circumstances'."[12]

Martin cites Sayyid Qutb of the Muslim Brotherhood, a widely recognized radical Muslim revivalist who was executed by the Nasser regime in 1966, to underscore that important point. Sayyid Qutb's conception of jihad is "[God] has established only one cause for killing—when there is no other recourse and that is striving for the sake of God *[jihad]*. He has defined the aim of the believer in a clear and decisive manner: 'Those who believe fight for the sake of God. And those who disbelieve fight for the sake of idols. Fight then, the followers of Satan surely the guild [sic, guile] of Satan is feeble'."[13]

To recapitulate, the notion of distinguishing between different groups based on religious differences is a long standing and time honored tradition in the Middle East. In fact, the durability of the Ottoman Empire presupposed and derived from the extraordinary capacity of the Ottoman rulers to devise and coordinate a grand strategy of subtle and not so subtle distinctions and interconnections between different religious groups within the overarching framework of the "millet system."[14]

In turn, Rapoport suggests that fundamentalist terrorist groups in the Middle East in general, including Jewish fundamentalist terrorist organizations, may be more at ease with the idea of targeting non-combatants because of the messianic nature of fundamentalist groups. Rapoport asserts that terror, defined here as "extra-normal or extramoral violence, a type which goes beyond the conventions or boundaries particular societies establish ...," is appealing to messianic movements precisely because it moves over and beyond the conventions and boundaries of pre-existing systems.[15] The author reports "for that reason, [terror] represents a break with the past, epitomizing the antinomianism or complete liberation which is the essence of the messianic expectation."[16]

Summing up, it seems possible that the political ideology of certain fundamentalist Islamic terrorist groups in the Middle East may be more tolerant of lethal violence against "unbelievers" or even encourage violence outright where political obstacles, such as the State of Israel, are commonly perceived to pose a serious challenge to the development of an overarching Pan-Islamic authority in the Middle East. It follows that Islamic fundamentalist terrorist groups which profess to stand up for Islamic ideals may be more inclined to target "unbelievers" who are non-combatants and view that as an acceptable practice because that would be consistent with the prevailing ideology of those terrorist organizations.

Recent events in Israel seem to substantiate that idea. For example, on March 2, 1993, an Islamic Jihad activist armed with a military style knife killed two Israelis and injured nine other Israeli civilians in Tel-Aviv. After the attack, Islamic Jihad reportedly declared that the attack was the result of "arrogance and haughtiness and international contempt for our people."[17]

On March 23, 1993, an Arab terrorist, carrying a Koran in one hand and a knife in his other hand, attacked five students and their principal at a Jerusalem vocational high school.[18] On April 9, 1993, Israeli security forces apprehended eighteen Hamas activists who were about to detonate a bomb-filled van in a Tel-Aviv shopping mall during Passover.[19]

What conclusions can be drawn from this discussion about the connections between political ideology and terrorist behavior? For one thing, what seems significant here is that focus by the foregoing authors on the link between goals and means seems to support the increasingly familiar notion that most terrorists, certainly among established and long standing terrorist organizations, are rational thinkers and not "crazies" if we define rationality, as Nef does, to be the recognition of a logical connection between means and ends and the effective marshalling of resources in pursuit of those objectives. In other words, the rationality assumption, so frequently written about with respect to leaders of state actors, seems in most cases to apply to terrorist leadership as well.[20]

Terrorist Group Size and Target Selection

A second variable that can affect target selection is terrorist group size. Several authors that refer to terrorist group size as an important determinant of terrorist group behavior include: Crenshaw (1983); Russell, Banker, and Miller (1979); Smart (1987); Oots (1984). Crenshaw reports that group size is one of an assortment of variables that determine the political outcomes of terrorism. The author tells us, "several factors are useful in explaining the political results of terrorism: properties of the terrorist group, including size, organization, leadership, intensity of political commitment, techniques of violence and goals; characteristics of both the domestic and international, situation ... and the government response...."[21]

Russell, Banker, and Miller also cite group size as one of several characteristics that influence terrorist group behavior. The authors tell us that "chief among them [basic characteristics] remain motivation and constituency; group size and make-up, the effects of countering effects and techniques; and attempts to acquire technical expertise via recruitment, coercion or education."[22]

Similarly, Smart reports that size serves to facilitate or constrain the types of activities undertaken by terrorist organizations. Smart tells us that "small numbers also limit terrorist options because the groups concerned rarely have sufficient fully committed supporters to build and run an effective infrastructure for communication, control or logistic supply."[23]

Oots's work stands out as perhaps the most comprehensive analysis of the influence of terrorist group size on terrorist activities. Oots distinguishes between three levels of difficulty, "excluding events occurring only once, threats, hoaxes, conspiracies and acts of an unknown type...."[24] At the most basic level, Oots tells us that terrorist acts can be grouped into "simple acts." Those acts consist of "bombings (all types), sniping, theft or break-in, sabotage, and shootouts with police."[25] At an intermediate level of difficulty are terrorist acts that Oots describes as "moderately difficult." Those acts include "armed attacks (with missiles or other weapons), hijacking, and takeovers of non-aerial transports."[26]

"Difficult" acts for Oots are comprised of "kidnapping, barricade and hostage, [sic] and facility occupation."[27] Oots elaborates further on this classification scheme by reporting that "the classification of the above types of acts is based on the amount of planning and resources which each type of action would normally entail."[28]

Oots's analysis tests several hypotheses about group size and the characteristics of terrorist operations. For definition purposes, Oots asserts that a successful act takes place where the terrorists are "able to carry out the act and were not stopped before the act was completed."[29] Oots's findings report that (1) "difficult" terrorist acts tend to be carried out by large groups (2) small groups are least likely to carry out a terrorist act successfully (3) deaths as a result of terrorist acts are most likely when small and intermediate size groups carry out the operation (4) the largest average number of deaths result from terrorist operations carried out by intermediate size terrorist groups and "lone wolf" terrorists (5) property damage is a more frequent outcome of terrorist acts committed by large terrorist organizations.[30]

Terrorist Group Age and Target Selection

The age of a terrorist group has been cited in the literature as an explanatory variable for terrorist group behavior and, by extrapolation, for how targets are selected. The writers who focus special attention on the relationship between terrorist group age and terrorist group behavior include: Flemming (1992); Long (1990); Karber and Mengel (1983). Flemming tells us that the age of a terrorist group under consideration is related to a broad or narrowly based repertory of terrorist techniques at a group's disposal.

Flemming reports that "the older a terrorist group is, the more experience it will have had in mounting successful operations. Terrorist groups such as the Provisional IRA for instance, are after years of campaigning, experienced enough to perpetrate a wide assortment of terrorist acts."[31]

Long goes a step further to suggest that a positive relationship between the age of a terrorist organization and the degree of violence that results from the act exists. We are told, "Groups generally resort to violent acts gradually over time. They do not spring up overnight as fully developed terrorist organizations but rather adopt increasingly violent tactics as the group itself develops cohesion."[32] Interestingly enough, Long points to "group psychology" to explain the transition from less to more violent behavior. He tells us that "the dynamics of the shift have been linked to the psychological climate of the group more than to the external reality facing the group...."[33]

In their discussion about the relationship between "political and economic forces" and terrorism, Karber and Mengel describe distinct phases of terrorist group growth and development that evoke particular patterns of terrorist group behavior. For example, the authors suggest that younger terrorist groups carry out terrorist assaults that are less severe and more "symbolic" than older terrorist groups.

For Karber and Mengel, "initial attacks are usually of low intensity and against undefended, discriminate and symbolic targets. The frequency of attacks is also low, the group waiting and wanting a positive response from the government."[34] As we shall see, the findings of this study are consistent with Karber and Mengel's explanation but do not differentiate between the authors' conclusions and other propositions.

One of the underlying themes of Karber and Mengel's work is the relationship they suggest between younger terrorist groups and "discriminate" terrorism on the one hand and older terrorist groups and "indiscriminate" terrorism on the other, where older terrorist groups seem to move in the direction of "indiscriminate" terrorism with the passage of time. For the authors, "lack of a positive response to terrorist acts generally causes an increase in both the frequency and intensity of attacks. Not a 'wave' of terrorism at this point, the group still recognizes the need to gain publicity for its agenda through attacks on targets...."[35] Again, the findings of this work are consistent with Karber and Mengel's interpretation of factors that underlie change in terrorist assault "frequency" and "intensity," but the empirical results do not preclude other possible interpretations to explain the relationships between explanatory variables.

Location and Target Selection

A fourth variable that is cited in the literature as likely to affect the target selection process is location. An underlying theme of several writers who cite location as an explanatory variable for terrorist group behavior revolves around the central idea that key factors which oftentimes converge create a favorable climate for terrorism at a particular site. The following authors describe the relationship between terrorist group behavior and the variable location: O'Neill (1978); Osmond (1979); Flemming (1992); Shultz (1978); Waugh (1982); Merari, Prat, Kotzer, Kurz, and Schweitzer (1986). O'Neill suggests that a decision to engage in transnational or intranational terrorism is influenced by the political landscape over which terrorist leaders make tactical decisions. To be specific, he suggests that the capacity of state apparatus to thwart terrorist operations and the presence of indigenous groups sympathetic to the cause can influence the choice of location for terrorist acts.[36]

Osmond explores the connection between the level of frustration among inhabitants of particular locations and the amount of terrorism carried out. He applies Gurr's "relative deprivation theory" to examine whether or not it can explain what causes terrorism to happen.[37] The theoretical proposition Osmond investigates "... is that terrorism in a state varies directly in magnitude with the intensity of relative deprivation in that state."[38]

For the dependent variable the author substitutes "a specific measure of level of terrorism by nation-state" "... for Gurr's Total Magnitude of Civil Strife (TMCS) measure."[39] Osmond uses Gurr's independent variables that operationalize various types of deprivation to perform multiple regression analysis on data for several nations.[40]

Osmond's findings suggest that "relative deprivation theory" is not a persuasive explanation for the causes of terrorism. He reports that "The weakness of the results suggest that the terrorism phenomenon is ... [not] a function of relative deprivation ... since the Gurr model does not explain terrorism, perhaps the error is that terrorism is not related to relative deprivation; the explanation must be sought elsewhere."[41]

Flemming makes a more direct connection between the site of terrorist activity and the underlying factors that facilitate successful completion of the terrorist act. In his discussion about theater of operations, Flemming tells us that, "in addition to locating sympathizers in foreign states, those terrorist groups that do not operate at home must contend with foreign governments on a routine basis."[42] Flemming points out that government tolerance of terrorist activity varies greatly, thereby in effect creating relative "safehavens" for terrorists.[43]

In his discussion about which variables cause political terrorism, Shultz tells us that "environment" is a critical explanatory variable. Shultz tells us that, "conceptualized on the basis of geographical spheres, these environmental variations may be broadly classified into internal environmental [within the nation-state] and external environmental [global, or systemic levels] categories."[44] O'Neill's work could be a specific application of Shultz's conceptualization. O'Neill tells us that, "from the Palestinian perspective, internal means Israel, the West Bank and the Gaza Strip [Palestine] whereas external means outside of this configuration."[45]

Waugh places a somewhat different emphasis on the variable location, using it to help define different types of terrorist group behavior in general. Waugh talks about different "permutations of international terrorism" that are based in large part on whether the location of the act is internal or external from the standpoint of the government that reacts to the event.[46] Those "permutations" are the underpinnings of Waugh's international terrorism taxonomy.[47]

Merari et al. also suggest that location is one of several key factors which explain terrorist group behavior. For the authors, that is the case in large part because of the presence or absence of constituency groups and differences in national legal sanctions with respect to terrorism. "Western Europe," the authors assert, "has proven particularly attractive to Middle East terrorists for several reasons including geographical proximity, ease of entry and of crossing national boundaries between European Community countries, the existence of large Middle East emigrant guest worker and student populations and the leniency with which many European countries treat captured Middle East terrorists."[48]

Political Events

Seen from a slightly different angle than the foregoing discussion about terrorism, political events, and analytical constructs of conflict, several writers on terrorism describe the relationship between the variable political events and terrorist group behavior. Some writers approach that issue with a discussion about the enormous capacity of political events to give shape to the stratagems or tactics of terrorist groups. Others underscore the salience of political events for terrorism by means of special focus on counter-terrorism challenges and opportunities or the effects on the growth and development of terrorism that presuppose and derive from various political frameworks. The authors under consideration include: Fattah (1980); Ronchey (1978); Aston (1980); Crenshaw-Hutchinson (1978); Charters (1994); Karber and Mengel (1983).

In a broader sense, Fattah suggests that political events themselves evoke a strategy for terrorist groups that emphasizes either terrorist assaults against government targets or terrorist assaults against civilian targets. On the one hand, Fattah suggests that if the aim of terrorism is government destabilization or to tarnish the authority of government, then terrorist assaults against government targets (e.g., "symbolic" targets) is an effective tactic. On the other hand, Fattah suggests that if the aim of terrorism is to augment "riots, revolts and civil disturbances," terrorist assaults against civilian targets seems the prudent method of choice.[49] For the purpose of this study, it is relatively easy to envision specific political events invoked by government that help frame a mindset among terrorist chieftains where different types of terrorist assaults are considered and then carried out.

In his discussion about terrorism in Italy, Ronchey really suggests that political events in both the domestic and international spheres had a profound and lasting influence on the intensity of Italian terrorist assaults during the 1970's. For Ronchey, many Italians were experiencing an economic malaise that when coupled with the "'revolutionary' thought" among some persons produced a framework of thinking where some no longer looked askance at the use of terrorism. Ronchey tells us of "contagion effect," where international political events like the Vietnam War and protracted conflict in the Middle East generated and sustained this "revolutionary thought."

Ronchey explains that, "in Italy, the conscious spread of psychological and ideological aversions that regard as debilitating and repugnant any form of debate with an 'enemy', insofar as he represents a form of absolute evil, can be traced back to the '60's, when 'revolutionary' thought was molded by the emotional influence of distant conflicts (Vietnam, South America and the Middle East), the social disorders caused by the economic boom, and the rise of the youth movements."[50]

The author states, "at the beginning of the '70's, partly because of the 30-year stalemate between the major political parties that made it impossible to achieve any real change in government, it became clear that a shift from an extremism of 'ends' to an extremism of 'means' was taking place."[51] Clearly, Ronchey's suggestion that domestic and international political events in the Italian political context of the 1970's had an interactive effect with the psychological make-up of particular types of persons that gravitate towards terrorism resonates deeply with underlying themes of this study and Reiss and Roth's propositions.

Aston suggests some type of relationship between terrorism and political events exists, and he focuses special attention on counter-terrorism negotiation postures and the lurking prospect of different terrorist assaults elicited as a response to particular ways of thinking about counter-terrorism. The author chronicles three counter-terrorism negotiating positions ranging from a policy of "no concessions" to a cookie cutter policy of government surrender to terrorist demands.

In the case of full-blown compliance with terrorist group demands, Aston asserts that "outright capitulation to demands may succeed in saving the lives of the hostages but may also serve to invite future operations against the same government."[52] In the case of a "more flexible approach," Aston suggests that terrorists can manipulate the situation thereby in effect making counter-terrorism military personnel resort to force that in turn, can have profound and lasting influence on how "the struggle" is perceived. That manipulation of counter-terrorist measures really presupposes and derives from the strategic considerations of terrorist group chieftains. Although those important interconnections between negotiation strategy and subsequent terrorist assault frequency and intensity are not explored in this study, the relationship between various types of government initiatives and targets of Middle East terrorist assaults is examined.

In her discussion about Algeria after the Second World War, Crenshaw-Hutchinson also makes the linkage between terrorism and government policy, namely French counter-terrorism operations. Faced with the lurking catastrophe of FLN terrorist assaults against non-Algerians, Crenshaw-Hutchinson tells us how the French government crackdown against terrorism was so fierce that it more than offset any political advantage made. For Crenshaw-Hutchinson, "Europeans, maddened by FLN terrorism and tense with fear and horror, called for violence against Algerians to halt terrorism. But government repression contributed directly to the continuation of terrorism."[53]

In turn, some writers underscore the importance of political events by writing on terrorism from the vantages of counter-terrorism or structural factors of political systems. In his discussion about the comparative effectiveness of counter-terrorist programs in place in various nations, Charters underscores the important influence of political events on terrorism when he links highly effective counter-terrorism organizations with a keen understanding of the political subtleties and intricacies at work in the process.

Equally important, Charters understands the enormous capacity of political events in the plane of international politics to influence terrorist assaults. For Charters, "the Italians probably had the most sophisticated conception of the problem, which set international terrorism in the context of Italian foreign policy and drew distinctions among the different origins, objectives and targets of such terrorism."[54] What seems significant here is that acumen for understanding political context and the inevitability of change is essential not only for a meaningful understanding of terrorism but also for highly effective counter-terrorism measures.

Finally, Karber and Mengel highlight the interconnections between particular types of government policy, terrorism, and the opportunity for political demands and aspirations to be met by government. The authors place emphasis on the structure of political frameworks within which political events happen. The authors construct a schema that depicts how greater or lesser degrees of "totalitarianism," "authoritarianism," and "democracy" correlate with terrorist activity.

On the one hand, we are told that well entrenched democratic systems and "more authoritarian" systems are most proficient with respect to the suppression of terrorism.[55] On the other hand, the authors assert that "weaker" democratic systems with what Huntington might call makeshift or incomplete "political institutionalization" have a harder time tackling the problem.[56] What seems important here is the assertion that structural political frameworks influence the type of political events that occur in the system, thereby in effect contributing to the frequency, intensity, or type of terrorism happening in response.[57]

Prevailing Ideology and Region

The Middle East is a region where political and economic institutions and, in some cases, structural political change are primarily based on religious rather than socio-economic cleavages. As mentioned earlier, the Muslim Middle East has a long-standing tradition of making distinctions between groups based on religious affiliation.[58] It follows that one fundamental issue revolves around the central idea that this set of social and political configurations might have some effect on terrorist group behavior or terrorist assault characteristics.

At a theoretical level, there is some justification for that way of thinking about culture, region, and terrorism. Starr and Most have done extensive work on "diffusion of war" and "contagion effect" as processes that relate to the outbreak of war. In one work, the authors examine "a global sample" and determine that nations with a "warring border nation," as compared to a peaceful neighbor, are some three to five times more likely to become "a war participant" over five years.[59] Starr and Most seem to suggest if a prevailing pattern of warfare is in place, there is a good chance that pattern will spread with the passage of time. In the case of the region of Africa, another study demonstrates similar findings that showcase what Starr and Most call "positive spatial diffusion" of conflict.[60]

One can draw on Starr and Most's work on war and look instead at cultural dissemination of conflict patterns to argue that if, within a region, one prevailing ideology such as Islam dominates, violent acts in the guise of terrorism committed by minority groups may resemble terrorism assaults committed by Islamic groups because of a *cultural* "positive spatial diffusion" of social and religious ideology that would shape the modus operandi of non-majority (e.g., Christian) terrorist groups to resemble the modus operandi of majority Arab/Islamic terrorist groups.

Seen from a different angle, it is possible to reflect in a broader sense on the allure of "charismatic leadership" and its capacity to pull at the heartstrings of emotion for those with religious or ethnic backgrounds or, by extrapolation, political ideologies that are somewhat antithetical to the prevailing social ideology of a particular region. For example, it is commonplace to note that some "charismatic leaders" of Middle East terrorist groups are Christians or members of Islam minority or "offshoot groups." Charismatic leaders who fit that description and who can also recruit significant numbers of minority group activists include Dr. George Habash of the Popular Front for the Liberation of Palestine (PFLP), Nayif Hawatamah of the Democratic Front for the Liberation of Palestine (DFLP), and Sabri al-Banna (Abu Nidal), himself an Alawite.[61]

Clearly, one underlying issue is how to cluster together charismatic leaders from non-charismatic ones in a way conducive to making categorical distinctions to classify empirical data. In terms of leadership, Weber tells us that it can be broken down into two types: charismatic and non-charismatic. For Weber, "in the case of charismatic authority, it is the charismatically qualified leader as such who is obeyed by virtue of personal trust in him and his revelation, his heroism or his exemplary qualities so far as they fall within the scope of the individual's belief in his charisma."[62]

Indeed, Long suggests that the charismatic leader of a terrorist group plays a pivotal role in terms of that group's capacity to evoke generally recognized feelings of loyalty and commitment from followers.[63] What seems critical here is Long's idea that there is a direct connection between religious cleavages in the region and terrorist group affiliation. For example, the author reports that many followers of Marxist-Leninist terrorist groups led by charismatic leaders are non-Muslims. "Their Marxist ideology," Long asserts, "can be explained at least in part, in terms of a crisis of Christian identity in a largely Muslim Arab culture."[64]

Bearing in mind that "crisis of Christian identity" in the Muslim world, there are some "realpolitik" ("power politics") issues that may dovetail nicely with the foregoing discussion of religious and ethnic fissures in the Middle East. It is commonplace to note that leaders in general must develop and nurture a set of interconnections with other political actors in the interest of political solidarity, accommodation, and the economic accouterments that follow. Consequently, it seems plausible that leaders of terrorist groups with religious and social ideologies somewhat antithetical to Islam might encourage their terrorist groups to act in ways more like other terrorist groups that are more in sync with the prevailing social-political ideology, to acquire "perks," be they economic or political in nature.[65]

In a similar vein, it seems plausible that charismatic leaders of terrorist groups which embrace the prevailing social ideology may serve to amplify widely shared and generally recognized propositions. For example, a charismatic leader of an Islamic fundamentalist terrorist group is able to focus almost single-minded attention on the idea that Israelis are non-believers who must be confronted and overcome by force because they do not accept Islam's mantle of authority. The issue is relatively clear cut in that case, with religious fissures being reinforced by existing distribution of power issues in a region where politics, as Nye suggests, is generated and sustained by realist thinking.[66]

If "cultural diffusion" and "cultural contagion" are effects that seem plausible, it is possible to make the case that charismatic leaders of non-Islamic terrorist groups may spur those groups on to act in ways more in line with terrorist groups that embrace Islam or, in the case of Islamic terrorist groups, ways that enhance Islamic tenets. Furthermore, it is possible to reflect on how terrorist groups might behave without charismatic leaders. It is reasonable to suggest that in the absence of a charismatic leader, terrorist groups that view their struggle as one primarily against a "world system" structure like advanced capitalism would place less emphasis on violence against civilians and more emphasis on government targets.[67] Conversely, it is plausible that terrorist groups that use the individual as the unit of analysis to frame the struggle, thereby suggesting that those who do not subscribe to prevailing social ideologies are legitimate targets, would place more emphasis on violence against civilians and less emphasis on government targets.

Finally, in the case of Middle East terrorist groups that place more of an emphasis on nationalist sentiment and self-determination issues, terrorist incidents should still result in a substantial amount of violence directed toward civilians. That is because intrinsic to nationalist ideology is the notion that an outside group of *individuals* inhabit land they do not own.

Jewish terrorist organizations in general and Jewish fundamentalist terrorist groups in particular ought to present a radically different configuration of targeting practices. At the heart of the matter is the fact that Jewish terrorist organizations operate in the United States or Israel and the Occupied Territories under Israeli suzerainty. That fact ought to have two basic consequences for Jewish terrorism. First, the Jewish terrorist groups under consideration should target ordinary civilians and Israeli political figures who are opposed to their political agenda. Second, it is reasonable to expect that Jewish fundamentalist terrorist groups led by charismatic leaders would attack targets with less intensity in order to maintain some degree of legitimacy among segments of the population and avoid a severe crackdown by Israeli authorities.

Conclusions

The discussion in this chapter about explanatory factors for terrorist group strategies or tactics really leads to the fundamental question of what has been learned about the literature on terrorism that describes explanatory variables for terrorist group behavior. Regrettably, one acute problem with the literature is its highly fragmented nature with no clear starting point among authors or much in the way of attempts to streamline or integrate discussion.

In a similar vein, much of what is discussed about explanatory factors for terrorism is mainly descriptive, with precious little in the way of attempts

to establish pathways between variables or interconnections between
different levels of analysis. While generally correct in their underlying
assumptions, a common thread that laces together works that discuss the
relationship between target selection, political ideology, terrorist group size,
terrorist group age, location, and political events is in fact the absence of
any meaningful analytical ties or conceptual relationships between them.

The underlying problems associated with an abundance of theoretically
unrelated work within a given discipline have already been recognized.[68]
For example, Zinnes suggests that the single most predominant goal of
research is for it to be "integrative" rather than simply "additive" in nature.[69] For Zinnes, additive cumulation is a process whereby a storehouse
of knowledge is filled with many "scattered bits and pieces of intriguing …
findings."[70]

Zinnes suggests that ideally, a study should inextricably tie together
previous works and place them in a context that explains their contributions,
which thereby in effect highlight what the study has to offer.[71] While
occasionally a study on terrorism will add something new that is a substantive contribution to the literature, there is, to use Zinnes words, very little
"integrative cumulation" in the literature about explanatory variables for
terrorist behavior. The end result of that condition is there is virtually no
rigorous analysis of fundamental explanatory variables for terrorism that
would determine if the variables some writers cite, almost capriciously at
times, actually do affect terrorist group behavior.

A cursory treatment of the "prevailing social ideology" of Islam in the
Middle East and the possible effects this ideology has on terrorism practices
of certain "minority" terrorist groups has been offered. An underlying
theme of that discussion is that religion, and in some cases ethnicity (e.g.,
Iranian Shi'ites), are cornerstones and shibboleths of life in the Middle East
and remain guideposts in terms of where individuals, and groups of
individuals, rank in Middle East society. The powerful effects of religion
and ethnicity reverberate in the Middle East and function to generate and
sustain a society very different from society in the United States and much
of the industrialized world, in which socio-economic divisions between
classes predominate, thereby in effect exerting a powerful pull on self-
identification, self-esteem, and how others perceive a particular person or
group.[72]

The context and effects of a "prevailing ideology" are articulated here,
drawing on works that have come before which focus attention on "diffusion
of war" and "contagion effect." The single most dominant theme is that
there is the potential for regional tendencies with respect to terrorist assault
characteristics. In addition, this study delves deeper to explore the role of

"charismatic leadership" in this context, its allure for potential recruits, and the capacity for charismatic leaders to shape the behavior of terrorist group activity. The foregoing lays a keel for discussion about the terrorist groups that comprise the terrorist group-types under consideration and analysis of the sources and origins of some of those groups.

Notes

1. Crenshaw 1983, 29.
2. Friedland 1992, 82.
3. Ronchey 1978, 150.
4. Bassiouni 1978, 523.
5. Aston 1980, 76, 77.
6. Ibid., 70.
7. Flemming 1992, 149, 146, 157, 161.
8. Smart 1987, 5.
9. Mickolus 1976, 1317
10. Harris 1989, 95, 89-90, 92, 86.
11. Flemming 1992, 70.
12. See Martin 1987, 64, 63. Amon elaborates on this way of thinking when he asserts that "revolutionary and terrorist ideologies usually fall into a messianic, gnostic and apocalyptic genre. They claim to represent, here and now, the attributes of the world to come, to know the nature of this ideal world and quite often even who its 'messiah' is. This knowledge stems from a conviction they have 'seen the light' and are therefore the only 'enlightened' people" (Amon 1982, 69). From a historical perspective, Benjamin Braude, an authority on the Ottoman Empire, suggests that in the Muslim world of antiquity, the single, most predominant distinction between groups was based on religious affiliation. For Braude, "In Muslim law and practice, the relationship between the Muslim state and the non-Muslim communities to which it extended its tolerance and protection was conceived as regulated by a pact called dhimma: those benefiting from it were known as ahl-a-dhimma, people of the pact, or more briefly dhimmis" (Braude and Lewis 1982a, 5, 12, 22, 29, 30, 32; Norton 1988, 13-14).
13. Martin 1987, 64.
14. For definitional purposes, Roderic H. Davison explains that the most common usage of the term "millet" was to describe "a community of people, a collection of individuals, who get their identity from a common religious affiliation." See Davison 1982, 320, 321, 327-328, 331.

Kemal H. Karpat states that religion and ethnicity were the cornerstones of the structure of the millet system. He reports, "The millet system was based on a socio-cultural and communal framework based, firstly, on religion and, secondly, on ethnicity which in turn often reflected linguistic differences. Religion supplied to each millet a universal belief system while ethnic and linguistic differences provided for divisions and subdivisions within each of the two Christian millets. The [millet] system provided on the one hand, a degree of religious, cultural and ethnic continuity within these communities, while on the other hand, it permitted their incorporation into the Ottoman administrative, economic and political system" (Karpat 1982, 141-142, 143-144, 145-169).

For a definitive account of the Ottoman Empire, see Lewis 1979, especially pages 334-347. For a definitive account of Ottoman reforms during the mid-late 19th century, see Maoz 1968, especially pages 186, 203, 216; Kedourie 1992, 19-20, 44-47, 71, 77, 226; Braude 1982, 69-83; Khalaf 1982, 117, 121, 123, 124; Maoz 1982, 92-103; Skendi 1982, 244-245, 255; Inalcik 1982, 437-438; Barsoumian 1982, 171-172, 175-179, 181-183; Clogg 1982, 185-186, 188, 190, 191, 192, 207; Bosworth 1982, 37; Bardakjian 1982, 90, 92-103; Cohen 1982, 7-15; Issawi 1982, 261-270, 272-278, 278-279; Philipp 1982, 169-180; Ahmad 1982, 404-406; Findley 1982, 344; Hacker 1982, 117, 121, 123-125; Turgay 1982, 287-318. The underlying influence of Ottoman rule with its basic power configurations endures in a profound and lasting way throughout the Middle East. Undoubtedly, the fusion of "church" and "state" dominions remains an underlying theme in the contemporary Arab world. One leading authority on Middle East politics asserts that Israel's ruling elite has used the Ottoman blueprint as a guide for the development and preservation of Israel's polity. According to Safran, "as of today Israel continues the millet system by allowing all religious communities to maintain their judicial institutions and follow their own laws in matters of personal status" (Safran 1978, 202-203; 200-202; 204-219). Freudenheim (1967, 85-87) makes a similar argument. For a useful analysis of the development of Israel's political structure, see Horowitz and Lissak 1978.

    15. Rapoport 1987, 73.
    16. Ibid., 85.
    17. Marcus 1993, 1.
    18. Hutman and Immanuel 1993, 1.
    19. Rotem 1993, 1.
    20. Nef 1978, 19-20; Hacker 1976; Bremer 1988, 2.
    21. Crenshaw 1983, 26.
    22. Russell, Banker, and Miller 1979, 34.
    23. Smart 1987, 10.
    24. Oots 1984, 63.
    25. Ibid.
    26. Ibid.
    27. Ibid.
    28. Ibid.
    29. Ibid., 65.

30. Ibid., 104, 86, 89, 90, 105, 91, 97.
31. Flemming 1992, 231.
32. Long 1990, 24.
33. Ibid.
34. Karber and Mengel 1983, 29.
35. Ibid., 30.
36. O'Neill 1978, 40, 25.
37. Osmond 1979, 115, 118.
38. Ibid., 58.
39. Ibid., 57, 115, 90-93, 101-102.
40. Ibid., 117, 118, 142-143.
41. Ibid., 145.
42. Flemming 1992, 91.
43. See Flemming 1992, 91-92. Gal-Or (1985, 91-92, 125) makes the same point in her discussion on terrorism from an international law point of view.
44. Shultz 1978, 10.
45. O'Neill 1978, 34.
46. Waugh 1982, 53.
47. Ibid., 56.
48. Merari *et al.* 1985, 6.
49. Fattah 1980, 29.
50. Ronchey 1978, 152.
51. Ibid.
52. Aston 1980, 81.
53. Crenshaw-Hutchinson 1978, 32.
54. Charters 1994, 218.
55. Karber and Mengel 1983, 38, 35.
56. Huntington 1968.
57. Ibid., 38.
58. Norton 1988, 13-14; Anderson, Seibert, and Wagner 1998.
59. Starr and Most 1976, 110-111.
60. Starr and Most 1983.
61. Seale 1992, 58.
62. Parsons 1964, 328, 358-363, 363-386.
63. Long 1990, 18-19, 211.
64. Long 1990, 22, 211; Schiller 1988, 96-97.
65. An underlying fact of Middle East life is that religion permeates political and social institutions and has a profound and lasting effect on political outcomes. The reasoning here is that Christian leaders of terrorist groups may feel pressure to act in ways that ingratiate them to their Muslim counterparts, thereby in effect solidifying the set of political interconnections between them.

about the role of religion with respect to terrorist group behavior. For example, John W. Doob, Neal E. Miller, O.H. Mowrer and Robert R. Sears construct a theory of "frustration aggression" where "the 'we group' and hostility against the 'other group' seem to be correlated factors.... Instead out-groupers are, as it were, blamed for the frustrations which are actually incident to group life; and a host of aggressive responses are displaced to them." See Dollard et al. 1939, 89; see also Gal-Or's discussion about Dollard et al. and "Frustration-aggression theory" (Gal-Or 1985, 14).

Harold D. Lasswell suggests the distinction between Dollard's "we group" and "other group" is reinforced by members of the collective group who develop and transmit for consumption normative images of society. For Lasswell, "The Mythology of great or superior worth is stereotyped in pattern.... Many collective Symbols emphasize the location of the group 'between' other people, and define the historic mission of the culture...." (Lasswell 1935, 107, 37).

In addition, Louis Coser and Gordon Allport discuss the role of the image of "outer enemy" and "outgroup" with respect to cohering a group within the context of group conflict (Coser 1956, 110; Allport 1954, 145, 244-245).

66. Nye 1993.

67. I am using Wallerstein's terminology to describe this phenomenon. See Wallerstein 1974. For a discussion of "charismatic leaders" of nation states in the Middle East, see Anderson, Seibert, and Wagner 1998, 202-226.

68. Flemming describes "the rather variegated fashion in which terrorism research has been approached ... at the expense of developing a common set of concepts, measurements and themes by which several studies can be related to each other" (Flemming 1992, 20).

69. Zinnes 1976a, 161; Zinnes 1976b, 1-19.

70. Zinnes 1976a, 163.

71. Ibid., 162.

72. Gordon 1964.

Chapter Four

Explanations for Terrorist Group Formation and Evolution

The purpose of this chapter is to provide a framework to explore the terrorist groups that comprise the terrorist group-types under consideration in this study. As previously mentioned in Chapter One, one way Middle East terrorist organizations that comprise those terrorist group-types are distinguished is whether or not they are led by a charismatic leader. Empirical investigation of the larger world of action demands that such distinctions be made, for there are viable terrorist groups whose leaders remain murky, perhaps even shrouded in mystery, while other terrorist groups coalesce around a leader who evokes a visceral response by followers, and gives structural shape to the political fray.

The framework that is developed will provide description of terrorist leaders and followers for several terrorist groups under consideration and chronicle the political context for those terrorist groups. One of the underlying themes of this work is use of Reiss and Roth's "risk factor" analysis of violent outcomes in the domestic sphere in an applied setting for Middle Eastern terrorism, to make interconnections between key players and political events, thereby in effect shedding light on terrorist group formation processes and evolutionary phases that may include "structural shifts" in terms of targeting behavior or target selection.

Before turning to the analysis, however, let us pause and again mull over the structural shape and contents of Reiss and Roth's taxonomy. The authors tell us, "the columns in the matrix classify risk factors by their proximity to a violent act: from left to right, as *predisposing factors and processes, situational elements* or *triggering events.*"[1] In other words, one way of thinking about that scheme is the authors' skillfully breaking down long-haul, middle-range and short-run explanatory factors that we will apply to Middle East terrorist group formation, group development, and group behavior.

Looking at the Reiss and Roth taxonomy horizontally "from left to right," we see rows of what the authors call "social and individual description" factors broken down into "social" and "individual" levels. In turn, those levels are each broken down into the subcategories "macro-social" and "microsocial," and "psychosocial" and "biological," respectively. For Reiss and Roth, the "macrosocial" realm includes "... societies and communities ...," while the "microsocial" realm, by contrast, is inclusive of "... encounters among pairs or small groups either as individuals or as members of gangs or families."[2] Posited within the taxonomy are short descriptive characteristics of what the authors call "relevant factors" that result from the intersection of "social" and "individual" factors with what can be seen as long term ("predisposing"), middle range ("situational") and short-run ("activating" or "triggering") factors. The "interplay" between variables and levels of analysis introduces a flexibility into the taxonomy that lends itself well to an application to Middle East terrorist group formation and Middle East terrorist group behavior.

To be specific, descriptive characteristics like "oppositional culture" and "flawed opportunity structure," for example, are a good fit with "oppositional cultures" in the Middle East or in the United States (e.g., Shi'as, Alawites, Christians, Jews), and forms of economic and political disenfranchisement found in certain locales. The "psychosocial" and "biological" sublevels articulate well some of the processes and ways of assimilating information that may be hallmarks of those who carry out terrorist assaults. Those processes and ways of assimilating information include misreadings or misinterpreting historical events (e.g., Holocaust readings, "al-Nakbah" readings) and making spurious connections between events.

To be sure, there are many relatively straightforward applications for several of Reiss and Roth's descriptive characteristics found at different levels, such as "access: weapons, emergency medical services," "accumulated emotion," and "impulse" that really resonate in the Middle Eastern political-social context. The emergent reality is that a host of Middle Eastern political events, germane to terrorist group "splitting" or "offshoots," dovetail nicely with what Reiss and Roth depict as "predisposing,"

TABLE 1 Reiss and Roth's Risk Factors Matrix

Matrix for Organizing Risk Factors for Violent Behavior

Units of Observation and Explanation	Proximity to Violent Events and Their Consequences		
	Predisposing	Situational	Activating
Social			
Macrosocial	Concentration of poverty Opportunity structures Decline of social capital Oppositional cultures Sex-role socialization	Physical structure Routine activities Access: Weapons, emergency medical services	Catalytic social event
Microsocial	Community organizations Illegal markets Gangs Family disorganization Preexisting structures	Proximity of responsible monitors Participants' social relationships Bystanders' activities Temporary communication impairments Weapons: carrying, displaying	Participants' communication exchange
Individual			
Psychosocial	Temperament Learned social responses Perceptions of rewards/penalties for violence Violent deviant sexual preferences Cognitive ability Social, communication skills Self-identification in social hierarchy	Accumulated emotion Alcohol/drug consumption Sexual arousal Premeditation	Impulse Opportunity recognition
Biological	Neurobiologic[a] "traits" Genetically mediated traits Chronic use of psychoactive substances or exposure to neurotoxins	Transient neurobiologic "states" Acute effects of psychoactive substances	Sensory signal-processing errors Interictal events

[a]Includes neuroanatomical, neurophysiological, neurochemical, and neuroendocrine. "Traits" describes capacity as determined by status at birth, trauma, and aging processes such as puberty. "States" describes temporary conditions associated with emotions external stressors, etc. Authors Reiss, Albert J. Jr., and Jeffrey A. Roth, 1993 *Understanding and Preventing Violence*. National Academy Press (NAP). Reprinted with the kind permission of NAP.

"situational" and "activating" events at both "social" explanatory levels and "biological" ones. Another underlying theme of this study that draws from Reiss and Roth's work is that a complex set of interconnections that resonate with one another exist between those different levels of analysis, where in the case of the few who become terrorists rather than constituent supporters, "individual factors" amplify existing "macrosocial" and "microsocial" factors.

Equally important, analysis of various terrorist groups and the continuously evolving political context that serves as their seedbed may help to isolate and identify some explanatory factors more typical of the origins of so-called religious, messianic, revivalist, or fundamentalist terrorist groups that are not as prominent, or absent outright in the case of secular terrorist groups.[3] Likewise, the analysis may help to group together a set of characteristics commonplace to note among charismatic leaders themselves, or it may point to political context as more of a determinant factor with respect to how character traits of "charismatic leaders" manifest themselves.

At a functional level, at least one terrorist group from seven out of the eight terrorist group-types under consideration will be analyzed in terms of an application of the Reiss and Roth analysis presented in Chapter One. Regrettably, precious little information is available about the Lebanese Armed Revolutionary Faction (LARF), and the Arab Communist Organization (ACO) to provide analysis of a non-charismatically led Middle East nationalist/irredentist terrorist group with Marxist-Leninist trappings (the ideo-ethnocentric terrorist group-type category).

Theocentric Groups

The theocentric group-type category is comprised of Muslim terrorist organizations without charismatic leadership that embark on campaigns that can be characterized as primarily religious, messianic, revivalist, or fundamentalist in nature. The world view of those terrorist organizations envisions a continuously evolving struggle against the West which is generally perceived as a provocateur in the Middle East and a threat to existing social and political institutions in the region.

The underlying aim of many of those terrorist organizations is to establish a Pan-Islamic state or confederation of Islamic states in the region. The creation of such a state or system of states will, following the reasoning, reaffirm time-honored Shi'a or Sunni tenets and result in the reemergence of an Islamic renaissance similar in breadth and scope to the Ottoman Empire at its zenith.[4] Consequently, the tactical goals of many theocentric group-type terrorist organizations include the destruction of the

State of Israel and the overthrow of pro-Western Sunni regimes in the region. The leaders of those regimes and other ruling elite are targeted because in addition to their pro-Western stance, many of them have thwarted the political ambitions as well as the political demands of Islamic fundamentalist politicians.[5]

Traditionally, theocentric groups only put a secondary emphasis on nationalist or nationalist redemptive aspirations. One characteristic that distinguishes that group-type in general is that Shi'ite populations, across national lines, can be a primary source of recruitment as a result of deep religious cleavages within Islam between Sunni and Shi'a movements.[6] Notwithstanding that basic distinction, there are exceptions as in the case of the Egyptian Muslim Brotherhood and its "offshoot" organizations, where a "Sunni revolution in Egypt," as Auda puts it, presupposes and derives from Sunni members.[7] Be that as it may, the theocentric group-type often represents a rather distinct segment of the population, be it defined in economic, religious terms or both, either in the nation it operates in, or the nation where it was spawned.

Several terrorist groups fall into the theocentric category. Those include "Kata'ib al Shahid 'Izz al-Dina Quassam'" which Abu-Amr translates as "Brigades of the Martyr 'Izz al Din al Quassam'," that is the military wing of Hamas.[8] Izzadine al Quassam ('Izz al-Dina Quassam') consists of some 80-90 armed activists who operate in the West Bank and Gaza.[9] Abu-Amr reports that Hamas itself is an acronym that stands for "Harkakat al-Muquawama al-Islamiya," otherwise known as "The Islamic Resistance Movement."[10] Hamas was originally founded by Shaykh Ahmad Yassin, Abdel Azziz al Rantisi and others in 1987, to serve as the Muslim Brotherhood's military branch in the Occupied Territories.[11]

The Muslim Brotherhood: Historical Antecedent and Blueprint for Action

Any meaningful discussion about Hamas and the Jihad Organization (Al-Jihad-Egypt) requires some discussion about the Muslim Brotherhood (Jam'iyyat al-Ikhwan al-Muslimin), that really is the parent organization for both groups. The Muslim Brotherhood was crafted in 1928 by Hassan al-Banna and it, in the words of Auda, had "... a quest ... [of] reform based on the teachings of Islam ... with emphasis on the reconversion of individuals to Islam."[12] For Auda, "reconversion" revolves around the central idea of the generally recognizable principle of "al-da'wa" or "the call."[13] In turn, Smith tells us, "the Muslim Brotherhood called also for drastic socio-economic reforms based on Islamic principles to redress the inequities that plagued Egyptian society."[14] In terms of composition, Auda, as previously mentioned, describes the Muslim Brothers as part of a "Sunni revolution in Egypt," and Anderson, Seibert and Wagner tell us that membership numbers were in the vicinity of one million as the 1930's passed into eclipse.[15]

In the broader sense, Anderson, Seibert and Wagner suggest that the revivalist Muslim Brotherhood, in contrast to its secular counterparts like the Liberal Constitutionalist and Wafd parties, really mirrored the underlying dichotomy of approaches to governance that was, and still remains a hallmark of the Middle East political landscape.[16] For the authors, "although the Wafd party had considerable influence with the middle class voting population, the Brotherhood laid out a straightforward message that appealed to the masses. The Muslim Brotherhood's strident message was feared by the establishment."[17] That condition, as described, provides a tantalizing clue that political ideology, defined in part in the Egyptian political context in religious terms and differences, may have powerful interconnections with socio-economic fissures, thereby in effect giving credence to the argument, put forward by some, that ideology partially masks other factors that cause rents, and even "violent outcomes," in society.[18] In essence, one aspect of this work is to apply the Reiss and Roth "risk factors" analysis to shed light on what some of these empirical observations in the Egyptian political context are all about.

Interestingly enough, Abu-Amr reports that Muslim Brotherhood "offshoot" influence in Palestine traces back to 1936, a period characterized by increased Jewish immigration and Jewish National Fund land purchase that really amounts to change in what Reiss and Roth might describe as "macrosocial and microsocial level" explanatory factors.[19] In fact, Allen tells us that it was during the continuously evolving environment in Palestine during the 1930's that profound and lasting anxiety about the inviolability of existing Arab social and political institutions began to reach its zenith. For Allen, "between 1931-1935 Jewish immigration showed a steady and startling increase. In 1935 it was more than fifteen times as large as in 1931."[20] Allen goes on to report, "... a peak of Jewish immigration, both legal and illegal was reached in 1935."[21]

One way of thinking about those demographic shifts is to view them from the vantage of Reiss and Roth's "macrosocial predisposing and situational factors."[22] In the case of the former, it is commonplace to note that Arab leadership in Palestine failed to capture an opportunity for some degree of local leadership because such a compromise with the British and Zionists offered makeshift and incomplete Arab control over Palestine.[23]

Schlagheck suggests that even with the affirmation of the Balfour Declaration in 1917, there was, from the vantage of Palestinian Arabs, enormous substantive distance between a "Jewish homeland" and a "Jewish state."[24] Regrettably, that lost opportunity would almost certainly result in a diminishing of "opportunity structures" for legitimate political empowerment and expression.[25]

With respect to "microsocial-predisposing factors," it is possible to make the case that the strains and tensions at the foregoing "macrosocial level" were closely mirrored by strains and tensions between parallel "community organizations." Those "community organizations," peppered heavily with political, religious, and social aspects, gave life to the religious and social tenets of each community.

Seen from the angle of a "macrosocial-situational" level of analysis, the fact that Jewish immigration grew apace increased the density of what Reiss and Roth might call the "physical structure" of interaction between Jewish and Arab groups, thereby in effect making ripe the opportunity for conflict. Perhaps the Arab Revolt of 1936-1939 can be seen as an "activating macrosocial event" that increased the influence and reverberations of the Muslim Brotherhood presence in Palestine.[26] Smith provides insight into the profound and lasting economic and political antecedents of the 1936 Arab Revolt when he describes a host of Arab "secret societies" and groups whose "raison d'etre" revolved around the central idea of social equality and political justice for Arab Palestinians.[27] Be that as it may, the underlying effects of the Arab Revolt in 1936 would pale in comparison with the full-blown volcanic-like eruptions of Israel's War of Independence of 1947-1948, nowadays still referred to by Palestinians and others as "al-nakbah" ("the catastrophe").

Hamas

Moving forward in time, the development of Hamas, itself an "offshoot" of the Muslim Brotherhood in the Occupied Territories, can be viewed within the theoretical construct of "failed macro-social opportunities" for nationalist expression, this time within the context of seemingly endless Israeli military administration of those areas.[28] As in the case of the 1936 Arab Revolt, economic factors also played some role in the formation of Hamas, and in the broadest sense, were some root sources of the Palestinian *intifadeh* ("uprising"), precisely because some parts of the Territories were no more than economic backwaters.

It is critical to recall the Israelis had taken Gaza and the West Bank from Egypt and Jordan respectively in 1967, and it appeared to many that remarkably little in the way of substantive resolution to the final status of those lands had been carefully reasoned out in twenty years. With that as a backdrop, Abu-Amr tells us that, to use Reiss and Roth's term, "the activating factor" for both the *intifadeh* and Hamas was a car accident involving an Israeli driver and Arab drivers in other cars.[29] O'Ballance goes into more detail when he reports, "the incident that sparked off the Intifada occurred on 8 December 1987 near the Jebaliyah refugee camp in Gaza, when an Israeli vehicle crashed into vehicles carrying Palestinians to work in Israel. It was soon alleged that this had been a deliberate act."[30]

In terms of chronological events, Abu-Amr tells us that Shaykh Ahmad Yassin, the single most predominant figure in what would become Hamas, met with an array of local leaders that included, "Dr.'Abd al-'Aziz al Rantisi, Dr. Ibrahim al Yazuri, Shaykh Salah Shihada, Issa al Nashshar, Muhammad Sham'a, and 'abd al-Fattah Dukhan."[31] Abu-Amr goes on to tell us that the emergent reality was Hamas. For Yassin, the underlying approach of Hamas is laser-like in its relatively single minded focus: "if the Zionists accuse us of being terrorists because we are seeking to liberate our country then we welcome this accusation, which will make us join the ranks of martyrs and righteous ones.... the gathering of Jews in the Promised Land has been decreed by God almighty so that they will be led to their end just as it is stipulated in the Holy Koran."[32] By the same token, that invective against Jews, over and beyond the vitriol aimed against Zionists or Israelis, is an underlying theme of other Islamic revivalist leaders in the political fray. For example, Gaffney tells us that an underlying theme of "fundamentalist preaching" in Egypt is the looming calamity of Jewry where, "... the Jews [Shaykh Ahmad] ... proclaimed, stood first on the list of enemies of Islam."[33]

Shaykh Ahmad Yassin certainly is "charismatic" in some sense, but Hamas is categorized as a terrorist group without charismatic leadership for two reasons. First, in his discussion about Hamas and Yassin, Abu-Amr suggests that the formation of Hamas could be described as a joint venture undertaking. The author states, "he [Yassin] was not a Khomeini, a Fadlallah, a Shari'ati, not an al-Banna or a Qutb. His prominence derived ... from his role within the political context of the Palestine issue."[34] Second, at a functional level, Yassin was arrested by Israeli authorities in 1989 and subsequently imprisoned until 1997, when freed by the Israelis as part of a deal to retrieve two Mossad agents caught in a "botched" Mossad operation in Amman, Jordan. As Abu-Amr puts it, after Yassin's arrest in 1989, "... it was a matter of necessity that the movement change its leadership style and rely on a more collective leadership."[35]

Hamas's interconnections to money funneling from outside sources underscores the fluidity of terrorist group growth and ties to other political actors. Hamas qualifies, according to Mickolus's definition, as an example of "international terrorism" because of financial and logistic support generated and sustained by Iran's leadership. O'Ballance reports that "financial help from Iran arrived in 1990, perhaps just before, and some Israeli sources said this amounted to at least $50 million for each of three years. Iran then began to provide arms as well as money, and it opened its training camps to Hamas guerrillas."[36] Further, Legrain reports that money from Saudi Arabia and Kuwait helps Hamas thrive in effective and sustained ways.[37] At a theoretical level, this raises a set of tantalizing issues that leads to the fundamental question, under which conditions does "transnational terrorism" become effective enough or otherwise significant, thereby in effect paving the way for support from a sympathetic patron-state. To be sure, that theoretically threadbare issue and others that relate to such terrorist group "patron thresholds" require empirical investigation in the future.

The Jihad Organization

Al-Jihad (Egypt) and Amal are two other prominent theocentric terrorist organizations. In the broadest sense, Auda tells us, "the Jihad Organization [was] a broad alliance of smaller groups [that] understood violence as part of a larger action and strategy, the Islamic revolution."[38] Auda tells us that the Jihad Organization presupposed and derived from a set of interconnections between Al-Jihad, created by Muhammad 'Abd al-Salam Faraj in 1979, and al-Jama'a al Islamiya al-Jihadiyya, under the aegis of Karam Zuhdi and Umar Abdul Rahman, who later became notorious world-wide for his full-blown role in the World Trade Center bombing in 1992.[39] In terms of recruitment patterns, Auda reports many al-Jama'a al Islamiya recruits were persons found shackled on the fringes of society. Apparently, it was Faraj himself who was the religious guidepost behind President Anwar el-Sadat's assassination at a military parade in Cairo on October 6, 1981.[40]

For Auda, "the Jihadist Islamic Jama'a is a grassroots organization emphasizing the recruitment of individuals on the margins of society—the unemployed, the poor, and the undereducated."[41] One claim made by Taheri is that al-Jihad is one of several noms de guerre used by the Qutbist movement in Egypt, which seeks to abolish Hosni Mubarak's Western oriented secular government and establish a religious fundamentalist regime in its place.[42] While the number of its armed activists remains shrouded in mystery, Taheri claims, "the Qutbists had a total membership of more than half a million...."[43] Al-Jihad also reportedly engages in terrorism under the name of Gama'a el Islamiya (the Islamic Group).[44]

Clearly, it is possible to view the Jihad Organization as an "offshoot" or "splinter group" that traces an arc to the Muslim Brotherhood. What seems significant here is that Auda, Piscatori, and Gaffney all suggest the emergent reality of The Jihad Organization and other Jama'ayyat can be explained, at least in part, by a host of economic afflictions that plagued Egypt in the 1970's and 1980's.[45] Auda tells us, "the Islamic movement of the 1970's was a sociopolitical expression of the contradictions and shortcomings of the modernization and transformation of state society relations under Gamal Abdul Nasser (1952-70) and Anwar Sadat (1970-81)."[46] For Piscatori, "second generation" Muslim organizations are really "... not so much a reaction to the failures of modernization, though that acute sense of disappointment is obviously present: but rather, a reaction to the failures of leaders—religious as well as political—to deal with these failures."[47]

An underlying theme of Gaffney's work is that the "peace and prosperity" promised to Egyptians that presupposed and derived from the "peace accord" with Israel never really materialized. Gaffney explains that "government spokesmen trumpeted assurances that peace would also bring prosperity, blaming the patent liabilities of a bloated and inefficient public sector and poor performance of agricultural cooperatives on the exigencies of the long standing 'war' with Israel, which had been institutionalized decades before. But the promised prosperity would elude most Egyptians ..."[48]

Again, macro-economic factors, here in the guise of Egyptian policy, fraught with shortcomings and their deleterious effects as described by Gaffney, resonate with Reiss and Roth's analysis of explanatory factors for violent outcomes. With respect to the development of recruitment pools for revivalist groups in general, Egyptian "opportunity structures" seem to have "failed" for segments of the population, and many persons in the Egyptian political and economic landscape found themselves on the fringes of society.[49] Compounding the problem even more was the absence of economic well being among many Egyptians that contrasted with the affluence acquired by many of their countrymen and others in the oil rich Gulf states. Gaffney reports that, "complicating the moral commentary from the mosques ... was the fact that so much of the petroleum was located in lands that had not been developed into modern secular societies. Many Egyptians saw a connection between this vast wealth and the maintenance of an explicit Islamic identity."[50]

To be sure, that muddled set of interconnections made by some between wealth and "Islamic identity" as Gaffney puts it, dovetails nicely with Reiss and Roth's "individual-psychosocial level" analysis where problems in terms of "cognitive ability" and "self-identification in social hierarchy" seem to be at work. It seems many Egyptians processed a linkage between wealth and "Islamic identity" that was spurious, but nonetheless, that interconnection evoked long-standing emotions among the disenfranchised in Egyptian society. All in all, the workings of several risk factors for violent outcomes, in this case the formation or growth of terrorist groups, seems to shed light on the allure that Islamic revivalism has on sectors of Egyptian society. Within the context of the growth and development of those "jama'ayyat" ("associations"), terrorist assaults were sometimes carried out by persons whose "psychosocial" or "neurobiological" make-up, in my judgment, amplified the explanatory factors described above.

Amal

Turning to Amal, it is important to recognize that meaningful discussion of both Amal and Hezbollah must be grounded in some description of the "confessional politics" of Lebanon, and the long-standing and time honored divisions between ethnic and religious groups.[51] Kramer tells us that the Lebanese political landscape revolves around the interactions of Lebanese Druzes, Maronite Christians, Lebanese Shi'as, Lebanese Sunnis, Greek Orthodox Christians and Armenians.[52] From a historical vantage, the social and political fissures between those groups were compounded even more by the practice among the Great Powers during the Ottoman Empire period, of adopting a "proxy minority group" to generate and sustain influence among high level Ottoman officials. For example, the French cloaked the interests of Maronite Christians under the aegis of France, while the Russians established a set of interconnections with Greek Orthodox Christians.[53]

Those profound and lasting social fissures, exacerbated by "great power machinations" to promote Great Power geopolitical interests, were the underlying reasons for Lebanon's "National Pact" of 1943, which Anderson, Seibert and Wagner tell us, "formerly recognized the religious and cultural heterogeneity of Lebanon, and divided the major governmental posts between the different groups who were to share power."[54] Nonetheless, as the authors point out, Lebanon's delicate set of interconnections, reified to some extent by "the understanding" of the National Pact, was disrupted by the political shock waves caused by Gamal Abdul Nasser's "pan-Arabist" movement. Plainly, the lurking threat of Pan-Arabism served as the basis for President Eisenhower's positive response to President Camille Chamoun's request to land US troops in Lebanon in 1958, within the context of United States Cold War "containment policy."[55] Anderson, Seibert, and Wagner suggest the ineluctable conclusion to the political strains and tensions in Lebanon was civil war, but somehow political stability and social unrest did not transform into in full-blown civil war until 1975.[56]

In the narrower sense, the Christian dominated government in Lebanon provided an economic and political framework that evoked long-standing feelings of discrimination and other similar sentiments among Shi'a Muslims in Southern Lebanon and elsewhere. Norton suggests the central leitmotifs of Shi'a political activism revolved around, "demands in the military, social, economic and political realms, including improved measures for defense of the South, the provision of development funds, construction and improvement of schools and hospitals, and an increase in the number of Shi'as appointed to senior government positions."[57] Norton suggests it was against that backdrop of "failed opportunity structures," as Reiss and Roth would put it, and "relative deprivation" both in economic and political terms, to use Gurr's phrase, that strains and tensions between Shi'as and other Lebanese groups inextricably grew apace.[58] Compounding the problem even more was another "macrosocial" factor, in this case "situational," in the guise of King Hussein's war against the Palestinians in 1970.

In 1970, a set of PFLP terrorist assaults that involved Swissair, TWA and BOAC jetliners served, as Brown tells us, as a catalyst to King Hussein's "Black September" war against the Palestinians.[59] In retrospect, both Norton and Kramer, as well as others, suggest the significance of King Hussein's capacity to defeat the Palestinians was partially offset by the "dislocations" for Shi'as that presupposed and derived from the Palestine Liberation Organization's move to Southern Lebanon. That profound and lasting demographic shift really caused change in the "physical structure" of Southern Lebanon in terms of how Shi'as would interact with newly uprooted Palestinians arriving in the country. The emergent reality was Shi'as as well as Palestinians were now exposed to the lurking catastrophe of Israeli air and ground assaults spearheaded against the Palestine Liberation Organization. As Norton tells us, "with the influx of thousands of fida'iyin in 1970 and 1971, following the bloody conflict in Jordan, the existing social and economic problems of the Shi'a were compounded by a rapidly deteriorating security problem in the South."[60]

It was in that political landscape that the fledgling Amal organization entered the Lebanese political fray. In 1974, Musa al-Sadr, himself an alluring figure of enormous physical stature, established Amal's precursor, "Harakat al-Mahrumim" ("Movement of the Deprived").[61] Amal, which means "Hope" in Arabic, and also "Afwaj al-Muqawama al-Lubnaniya" ("Lebanese Resistance Detachments"), evolved to fit a political landscape fraught with peril for Shi'ites.[62] Indeed, Kramer makes the important point that from the start, Amal was conceived of by Musa al-Sadr as a security organization designed to protect the Shi'ites. For Kramer, "Sayyid Musa sympathized with Palestinian aspirations because the Palestinians had been dispossessed, but he did not believe that the Shi'ites, alone among the Arabs, should bear the burden of their struggle."[63] Norton buttresses that viewpoint in his contention that Musa al-Sadr, "... was a reformer, not a revolutionary."[64] Interestingly enough, Norton tells us that Amal was originally trained by Fatah, which would later face off against Amal, pitting the interests of Shi'ites against Palestinians in pitched battles.[65]

Regrettably, Sayyid Musa al-Sadr's tenure as leader of Amal would be short lived. Musa al-Sadr most probably died at the hands of Colonel Muammar Quadhafi in 1978, and Norton provides several possible reasons for his disappearance.[66] Norton reports that Musa al-Sadr's "disappearance" revolves around the possibility that either the Shah or Khomeini had him killed because they viewed him as a political threat, that he died as a result of a plot between Khomeini, Quadhafi, and Assad of Syria, or that he died as a result of alienating Quadhafi, perhaps over money.[67] Be that as it may, Amal, which may have used the front name "Sadr Brigades," had some 1,500 activists even at its low point in 1975.[68] The death of a significant leader has profound and lasting effects, and Kramer makes the point that Musa al-Sadr's disappearance not only elevated his stature among Shi'ites, but also in effect paved the way for Hezbollah to consolidate its considerable influence in Lebanon. For Kramer, "the disappearance of Sayyid Musa, tragedy though it was, opened a gate of opportunity for Fadlallah and his message."[69]

Theocentric Charismatic Groups

The theocentric charismatic group-type is comprised of revivalist or religious fundamentalist Islamic terrorist organizations led by charismatic leaders. Theocentric charismatic terrorist groups are distinguished from theocentric groups by the heavy emphasis placed on recruitment from the followers of a particular charismatic leader. Followers of a charismatic leader are imbued with that leader's singular vision about the scope and shape of the struggle and the best ways to acquire political gain.[70]

Hezbollah

The best known of those groups is Hezbollah, otherwise known as Islamic Jihad, Party of God and the Organization for the Oppressed (On Earth), that was established in 1983 and has an estimated 500 armed combatants.[71] Hezbollah is an Iranian artifact, created by Ayatollah Khomeini and sustained by those who came after him. Its leader, Ayatollah Sayyid Muhammed Husayn Fadlallah, and the essence of that group's perspective remain inextricably bound up with the spiritual teachings of Ayatollah Khomeini and Iran's political elite. Interestingly enough, Jaber suggests the origins of Hezbollah presuppose and derive from the Israeli invasion of Lebanon in 1982. For Jaber, "when Israel launched its invasion in June 1982, Lebanon's leading Shia Muslim clerics were in Teheran, attending the annual Islamic Conference. Sheikh Subhi Tufeili and Sheikh Ragheb Harb had both attended the conference and were to be central figures in realizing Iran's initiative: Tufeili became the first leader of the new Islamic movement and Harb was to die fighting for its cause. Hezbollah had been conceived."[72]

Kramer suggests that a fundamental difference between Hezbollah and Amal revolves around the central idea of how to frame the struggle against interests antithetical to Islam.[73] It is important to recall that Sayyid Musa al-Sadr's emphasis was to address the ticklish political and economic demands, aspirations, and security concerns of the Shi'ite Muslims within the context of the tapestry that is Lebanon's political landscape. For Kramer, Fadlallah by contrast introduced flexibility and a much broader vision into the political system, whereby the struggle against "imperialism" that Shi'as should undertake would interlock nicely for Palestinians and others under the banner of Islam. Kramer reports that, "Shi'ites must act, Fadlallah wrote, because Islam was endangered by the threat of aggressive imperialism; Lebanon's strife was really a flash point in the global confrontation between Islam and imperialism."[74]

It follows that Hezbollah recruitment, in contrast to Amal's special focus and increased devotion to poorer Shi'ites in the South largely concerned with security matters, had an allure for a broader constituency ranging from poorer Shi'ites to intellectuals and students. To be sure, much of that support presupposed and derived from what Kramer calls Fadlallah's enormous capacity for oratory. Kramer's description of Fadlallah depicts a man with "a mastery of words" who was ever "the artful dodger," as he puts it, when a situation demanded vague, episodic and inconsistent responses about the interconnections between Fadlallah and Iran's political elites, and even Hezbollah itself.[75]

In his discussion about Hezbollah's origins and development, Kramer tells us about three pivotal events, two of which can be seen in the context of Reiss and Roth's framework of analysis. First is the Iranian revolution that Norton refers to as the "Iranian exemplar" that served as a "situational" guidepost and inspiration for those in pursuit of an Islamic state.[76] However, in the case of Lebanon, what seems significant here is that Fadlallah understood that an Iranian revolution transplant, without modifications, would be untenable due to the heterogeneity of the Lebanese political landscape.[77] Accordingly, Fadlallah's understanding of Lebanon's demography led to a continuously evolving approach to recruitment efforts that began to emphasize more positive roles for non-Muslims over and beyond dhimmi status.[78] A second pivotal event that, in my judgment, was an "activating factor" for Hezbollah growth, was the Israeli invasion of Lebanon in 1982 and the bombing of the French and American military barracks in Beirut that propelled Ayatollah Fadlallah onto a stage of worldwide proportions.[79] Finally, a third pivotal event that increased Fadlallah's allure was the disappearance of Sayyid Musa al-Sadr in Libya. It is commonplace to note Musa al-Sadr's enormous capacity to evoke an appeal that always enabled him to wrest some influence away from Fadlallah. Clearly, for Fadlallah the positive role of serendipity, itself somewhat removed from the Reiss and Roth's "risk factor" analysis, was a profound and lasting one.

Hezbollah/Palestine and Turkish Islamic Jihad

Other theocentric charismatic groups include Hezbollah/Palestine and Turkish Islamic Jihad. Hezbollah/Palestine probably began operations around 1991 and is reportedly made up of Palestinian religious fundamentalists in league with Hezbollah.[80] Cubert cites a French report that suggests Hezbollah/Palestine is one of several "rejectionist groups" in opposition to "autonomy talks" with the Israelis, and presumably with "more moderate" elements of Palestinians.[81] Turkish Islamic Jihad by contrast, is a fundamentalist organization that was active in Turkey by the late 1980's, and operates against US interests there.[82]

Ethnocentric Groups

The ethnocentric group-type category is composed of terrorist groups that spearhead terrorist campaigns characterized as primarily nationalist or irredentist in nature. Ethnocentric terrorist groups are distinguished from theocentric terrorist groups by their more secular orientation and political ideology. In the case of ethnocentric groups, the role religion plays in terms of a guide for political behavior is practically nil.

One characteristic that distinguishes nationalist or irredentist terrorist groups (i.e., ethnocentric) is they usually represent a relatively broad-based constituency.[83] In the case of the Arab nationalist groups that comprise the ethnocentric terrorist group-type, it is commonplace to note those groups select primarily US and Israeli targets. Bound up with this practice is the realization that Israel poses the most concrete political obstacle to fulfilling nationalist aspirations of partial or complete Arab control of Palestine. At the same time, the United States, with its decidedly pro-Israel standpoint, is perceived to play the role of provocateur in the Middle East since it provides Israel with a capacity to thrive in an effective and sustained way.

Al-Fatah

Terrorist groups that make up this category include al-Fatah, which among all Palestinian terrorist groups is the richest, most extensive and most venerable organization, claiming an estimated 6,000-8,000 activists.[84] At the same time, al-Fatah has conducted terrorist operations using front names presumably to conceal its identity. For example, Cobban tell us that following its creation in 1959, Fatah used the name "al-Assifa" ("The Storm") between 1964-1965.[85] We are told that al-Fatah also operated under the name "Black September Organization" from 1971-1974.[86]

The sources and origins of al-Fatah really presuppose and derive from Israel's War of Independence of 1947-1948 that, from the vantage of the Palestinian Arabs and others, is "al-nakbah" ("the catastrophe"). Safran tells us that some 700,000 Palestinian Arabs were displaced from their homes and the ticklish question of why is explained as a complex one where Palestinians, when faced with the looming catastrophe of defeat, "... were forcibly driven out by the Jews who sought, thereby to secure the advantage of a more homogenous population."[87] The "Palestinian Diaspora" present-ed a set of challenges and opportunities for leaders of fledgling nationalist movements interested in tapping into Palestinian communities in areas ranging from Gaza and the West Bank, Gulf States and other Middle East states, to Europe and the United States.

As Yaari tells us, "Fatah" is itself an acronym that is coded backwards to stand for the "Palestinian National Liberation Movement" ("Harakat al Tahrir al-Filastiniyya" or HATAF).[88] Fatah traces an arc to the pre-Fatah student activities of Yasser Arafat, a young engineering student in Cairo, and several of his coterie, many of whom would later hold leading positions in al-Fatah. For Yaari, "the university offered him an ideal stamping ground for his work. After the war of 1948 more and more young Palestinians left Gaza and the West bank and came to study in Egyptian universities seeking new fields of action."[89]

Arafat, also known by his nom de guerre "Abu Ammar," reportedly had a complex set of interconnections with the Muslim Brotherhood in Egypt that evoked hostility and other similar feelings from the Nasser regime, which made it necessary for Arafat to relocate. Livingstone and Halevy tell us, "in late 1956 or 1957 Arafat was arrested by Egyptian security services as a political agitator, allegedly because of his ties to the Moslem Brotherhood. He was released from jail several months later and along with Qadoumi and Abu Jihad, departed for Kuwait."[90] In Kuwait, Arafat, working in tandem with his long-standing associate Salah Khalaf (Abu Iyad) and others crafted the Fatah organization in 1959.[91]

At a functional level, Yasser Arafat was not known to be a leader with charisma. Yaari tells us, "his particular gift for command found its expression not before the masses, but in closed rooms. His power lies in conversations not speeches."[92] Livingstone and Halevy's description of Arafat supports Yaari's depiction of him as "an underground leader," when the authors report, "Fatah has been led in effect by Arafat since 1964, when he began to emerge as 'first among equals', although it was not until April 15, 1968, that he was appointed by Fatah's Central Committee the 'official spokesman and representative' of Fatah."[93]

An underlying theme for Arafat was that Palestinians, and not the leaders of Arab nation states, would be the gatekeepers for the liberation of Palestine. In his discussion of a PLO Palestinian National Council, Gresh tells us "Thus this fourth PNC saw Fatah's theses triumph: the Arab character of the liberation struggle was certainly not rejected but pride was given to its Palestinian aspect."[94] The threat or use of force was acceptable, nay desirable in the face of "Zionist occupation" and the lurking calamity of "Zionist aggression" in Palestine. Clearly, the accounts of Cobban, Yaari, Nassar, and Livingstone and Halevy all suggest that "al-nakbah" ("the catastrophe") qualifies as an enormous "activating" explanatory factor at Reiss and Roth's "macrosocial" level of analysis, with respect to the emergent reality of a Palestinian resistance movement (see Table 1).[95]

Arafat's emphasis on the Palestinian aspect of the struggle seems to presuppose and derive from two sources. Nowhere was the problem more acute than in the overwhelming defeat of Arab confrontation armies at the hands of the Israelis. Seen from a different angle, Nassar tells us that Arafat was influenced by the writings and actions of General Giap of North Vietnam, Mao Zedong, Che Guevara, and the ideas of French political theorist Debray.[96] Yaari suggests that Arafat's unconventional approach to "the struggle" presupposed and derived from Muslim Brotherhood terrorist assaults.[97] In short, we can extend the analysis to suggest that what Reiss and Roth might call an "oppositional culture" of conflict in the plane of international politics, in the guise of unconventional warfare against governments unable or unwilling to meet political demands and aspirations, was "in the air." This was the case precisely because of the activities of the foregoing luminaries, and concrete examples can be seen in the cases of Vietnam (1954), China (1949), Cuba (1959) and perhaps most significantly Algeria (1962).[98]

Compounding the problem even more was what can be thought of as an across the board deficiency of "macrosocial-opportunity structures" for Palestinian political demands and aspirations in Arab states. In fact, the common wisdom was that leaders of Arab states were freewheeling in style and substance, trying to avoid full-blown responsibility for the Palestinian cause. For example, Livingstone and Halevy tell us, "both Fatah and, later the PLO were set up ... as a way of channeling Palestinian frustrations away from the governments of Cairo and Damascus."[99] Plainly, Yaari goes farther when he tells us, "Nasser believed that he could awaken Palestinian nationalism from its slumber to serve him in his inter-Arab campaigns."[100] Be that as it may, there seems ample justification for suspicion on the part of Palestinians about the motivations of Arab states, thereby in effect evoking the Palestinian emphasis of the struggle for Palestine that was the hallmark of Fatah.

The analysis of Fatah is even more tantalizing at Reiss and Roth's "microsocial level" of analysis. Here, at the "psychosocial" level, in this case with respect to cognitive processing, a historical reading of "Diaspora history" may have introduced inflexibility into the Fatah world view epitomized best by Fatah's call for the destruction of the State of Israel, and Ahmad Shuquairy's now infamous clarion call "to drive the Jews into the sea."[101] For example, one can imagine an "al-Nakbah" interpretation of history that results in overstating the case, such as equating Zionism with racism or labeling it and Israel as "a bastion of imperialism," when in fact that United States has supported many "bastions of imperialism" in the region like Iran, Kuwait, and Saudi Arabia. In fact, as we shall see, this phenomenon is similar to historical readings of "Holocaust history" that contributes to "a stretch" in historical comparisons between Nazi Germany and more contemporary conditions like the persecution of Soviet Jews in the former Soviet Union.

With respect to recruitment, it is important to recognize that al-Fatah was able to tap the fountainhead of the Palestinian Diaspora in effective and sustained ways that other groups could only envy. Fatah was accepted as the mainstream expression of Palestinian nationalism, and consequently, it drew a groundswell of support from students, intellectuals and others, thereby in effect transcending national boundaries. For example, one account describes significant numbers of recruits as Palestinians who came from West Germany.[102] What seems significant here is that the timing of Fatah as the first ridge on the map of contemporary Palestinian nationalist groups, especially in the context of the failures of Arab leadership to provide authentic help for the Palestinians, gave Fatah an unprecedented opportunity to draw from a very rich and deep pool of recruits.

Al-Fatah "Offshoot" Terrorist Groups

In this study, Fatah affiliated organizations that carry out terrorist acts in the Occupied Territories such as the "Black Panthers," "Fatah Eagles," and "The Revolutionary Security Apparatus" are considered Fatah and coded accordingly.[103] In addition, terrorism carried out by al-Fatah's elite unit "Force-17" is coded as Fatah activity.[104] The linkage between those local terrorist organizations and Fatah is made explicit in several *Jerusalem Post* newspaper accounts.[105]

Cubert chronicles the origins of the Black Panthers within the context of the 1987 Palestinian *Intifadeh* ("uprising"), and he asserts this terrorist organization traces an arc to the acute problem, as seen from the vantage of the Palestinian resistance, of Palestinian "collaborators" coopted by the Israelis in the Occupied Territories. For Cubert, "the Fatah linked Black Panther organization, and its PFLP counterpart, the Red Eagle group, appear to have been formed initially to persuade Palestinian residents through intimidation and terror not to cooperate with the Israeli authorities."[106] The author reports that the Revolutionary Security Apparatus is a Fatah artifact that was crafted to partially offset the terror invoked by the Black Panthers and the PFLP supported Red Eagle group. Somewhat ironically, The Revolutionary Security Apparatus began willy nilly, to ape the behavior of the aforementioned terrorist groups at the expense of Palestinian residents living in the Occupied Territories. According to Cubert, "it was not long however, before the Revolutionary Security Apparatus began to mimic the very groups it claimed to oppose."[107]

What seems meaningful here is the sequence of political events that contribute to the emergent reality of how terrorist groups like the Black Panthers and the Red Eagles come together. For example, the *Intifadeh,* itself an "activating event" for the formation of those terrorist groups, was brought about by more entrenched factors associated with the Israeli administration of the Occupied Territories. In turn, the Revolutionary Security Apparatus was formed precisely because of the activities of the foregoing terrorist groups. From the vantage of qualitative analysis, that cycle seems to underscore the fluidity and evolutionary character of explanatory factors which themselves take on new, more long-term significance with the passage of time.

The Palestine Liberation Organization

The Palestine Liberation Organization (PLO) is another ethnocentric group that was established as an "umbrella" organization of various Palestinian groups in 1964. Its military arm, the Palestine Liberation Army (PLA), itself traces an arc to the fledgling PLO. Unequivocally, the PLO remains in the guise of the Palestinian National Authority, the primary sub-national actor in the Middle East political landscape. As such, its structural shape and political role are more elaborate than those of other terrorist groups under consideration.[108] Long estimates that some 15,000 people are active members of the PLO.[109]

Interestingly enough, the PLO was crafted in response to the emotionally laden matter of Israeli political leaders making efforts to construct a fresh water network that would serve as a gatekeeper for the Negev (Desert) to water pumped out of Northern Israel.[110] Yaariv tells us that Nasser, who looked askance at full-blown war with the Israelis over "the Israeli National Water Carrier," sought to partially offset this lurking catastrophe of war by crafting an organizational framework to include all Palestinian resistance members working in tandem with the Arab League. For Yaari, Nasser "... was interested in presenting the masses with substitutes that would not bring about war, but would create the impression that the Arabs were preparing for it."[111] What seems significant here is Nasser's deft action suggests a conscious attempt at political context manipulation that helped to take the wind out of the sails of those calling for war, thereby in effect precluding the construction of a water resource system from becoming an "activating" factor for a war fraught with peril for him.

At a functional level, the Palestine Liberation Organization was inextricably bound up with the struggle for Palestine even under the leadership of Ahmad Shuqairy, the first Chairman of its Executive Committee. That is the case precisely because Fatah, using the front-name "al-Assifa" ("the Storm"), began terrorist assaults against Israel in 1964-1965.[112] Nassar suggests that Shuqairy's misgivings about the use of irregular forces really presupposed and derived from his Pan-Arab emphasis with respect to how "the struggle" should be shaped and his role as

Palestine's representative to the Arab League.[113] The strains and tensions associated with differing perspectives on the struggle, one Pan-Arab in emphasis, the other Palestinian, reached its apex with the Six Day War of 1967 and the subsequent resignation of Shuqairy in December 1967.[114]

Perhaps the single most predominant change in PLO leadership thinking revolved around the central idea of moving away from a rigid doctrine of military conflict to one that introduced some flexibility into the Middle East conflict. As both Seale and Gresh report, Arafat's way of thinking about conflict with the Israelis changed after the October War of 1973 for he had reached, in his own mind, the ineluctable conclusion that Israel was too powerful in military terms to destroy, and equally important, that Nixon and Kissinger were interested in more even keeled negotiations between Israelis and Palestinians.[115]

It follows that an underlying theme of this continuously evolving PLO approach was to limit terrorist assaults to areas that included Israel, the West Bank and Gaza. For Melman, "Arafat decided to abandon international terrorism and to concentrate on political activity combined with an armed struggle against targets in the occupied territories and Israel itself."[116] We are told by the author that the PLO stopped its international terrorist assaults after an operation against the Saudi Arabian embassy in the Sudan in 1973.[117] What seems significant here is that political context, in terms of Arafat's appraisal of sustained Israeli military might and American interests, had changed, thereby in effect leading to change in strategy and tactics of PLO military operations. Plainly, that structural change in Arafat's tactics to restrict the geographical sites susceptible to PLO terrorist assaults can really be seen as a vehicle to sustain political negotiations through "constrained terrorism," and as an important reason why PLO "splinter group" activity happened.

Arab Organization of 15 May, the Arab Liberation Front, the Abu Musa Faction, Al-Saiqa, and the Popular Struggle Front

Another ethnocentric group used in this study is the Arab Organization of 15 May that was created in 1979 and has some 50-100 armed combatants.[118] The complex historical legacy of Arab Organization of 15 May is really a quintessential case study about how terrorist groups in the Middle East can coalesce and disintegrate with the death of a leader. It underscores the importance of a typology that can respond to the development of new terrorist groups in the region.[119] The framework for discussion involves Dr. Wadi Haddad, a Christian Palestinian who originally served alongside Dr. George Habash as the co-leader of the Popular Front for the Liberation of Palestine (PFLP).[120] After a series of personal clashes with Habash that culminated with Habash's decision to refrain from attacks against targets outside of Israel, Haddad broke ranks with him to form the Popular Front for the Liberation of Palestine Special Operations Group (PFLP-SOG) around 1974.[121]

Dr. Wadi Haddad's "charismatic leadership" spearheaded the operations of PFLP-SOG until his death from cancer in 1978.[122] One of the most notorious terrorist operations undertaken by Haddad's PFLP-SOG was the hijacking of a German Lufthansa jet to Mogadishu, Somalia in 1977.[123] In the wake of Haddad's death, three new terrorist groups emerged. Those groups were The Lebanese Armed Revolutionary Faction (LARF), the Popular Front for the Liberation of Palestine – Special Command (PFLP-SC) and the Arab Organization of 15 May.[124] What seems important to recognize is that one type of terrorist group can spawn others that have different defining characteristics. To be sure, the parent group, PFLP-SOG, was a nationalist-irredentist terrorist group that was Marxist-Leninist and led by a charismatic leader, while one of its offspring, LARF, is, by contrast, a Marxist-Leninist nationalist-irredentist terrorist group without charismatic leadership. In turn, the Arab Organization of 15 May can be described in a relatively straightforward way as a nationalist-irredentist terrorist organization.

Other ethnocentric terrorist organizations included in this study are the Arab Liberation Front (ALF), the Abu Musa Faction, al-Saiqa, and the Popular Struggle Front (PSF). ALF is an Iraqi creation that was established in 1969 in part to offset the influence of its Syrian equivalent al-Saiqa.[125] Nasr reports that the Iraqi artifact was "... headed by Dr. Abd al-Wahab al Kayalil, consisting of Palestinians allegedly working to liberate Palestine."[126] ALF claims to have some 500-800 members.[127] Even though ALF was spawned by an ostensibly Marxist-Leninist regime in Iraq, it is coded as an ethnocentric group.[128] Al-Saiqa, otherwise known as "Thunderbolt," the "Vanguards" organization, and the "Eagles of the Revolution," is a Syrian creation that was established in 1966 and has about 1,000 combatants under arms.[129]

Long tells us that Palestinians who reside in Syria comprise the bulk of al-Saiqa's membership.[130] The common wisdom is that al-Saiqa's almost singular purpose is to promote Syrian political influence within the Palestinian movement as it pursues nationalist objectives that, for one thing, call for the destruction of Israel.[131] Accordingly, al-Saiqa is coded as an ethnocentric group. The Abu Musa Faction, which reportedly operates under the front name "Arab Revolutionary Cells-al-Kassem Unit," is a pro-Syrian Fatah splinter group that was established in 1983 and has roughly 2,000 armed combatants.[132] Lastly, the Popular Struggle Front (PSF) was created in 1967 in the wake of the Six Day War, and has an estimated 200-500 members under the leadership of Dr. Samir Ghousha.[133]

Ethnocentric Charismatic Groups

The fourth category is composed of ethnocentric charismatic terrorist groups. Ethnocentric charismatic groups differ from ethnocentric groups in that they recruit primarily from the personal following of a charismatic leader who heads the group. Groups that make up that category include: The Palestine Liberation Front (PLF) that was established by Muhammed Abu al-Abbas in 1976 and has an estimated membership of 200 activists,[134] and Sabri Khalil al-Banna's Abu Nidal Organization (ANO).[135]

The Abu Nidal Organization

The ANO is generally recognizable as one of the most active and extensive terrorist organizations in the contemporary Middle East political landscape.[136] It was probably established in 1973 and has some 500-800 armed personnel.[137] Simultaneously, a description of the sources and origins of the Abu Nidal Organization reflects the fierce competition among groups of Palestinians between alternative ways to pursue the Palestinian struggle set against the backdrop of wide-ranging competition between Iraq and Syria about the influence exerted over the Palestinian resistance movement. "Abu Nidal," Seale reports, "also became the beneficiary of the endemic rivalry between Iraq and Syria, which dated back to the great Ba'ath Party schism of 1966, which over the years had hardened into enmity between the two Ba'athist states."[138] It follows that the descriptions to come about the sources and origins of the Abu Nidal Organization reflect dynamics that emanate from both vantages.

From the vantage of Palestinian group politics, recall that both Melman and Seale tell us that the "maximalist" position of Fatah-PLO to liberate Palestine in its entirety began to break up and pass into eclipse after the October War of 1973.[139] "Several strands," Seale asserts, "may be identified in Arafat's thinking at this time. He believed that after the October War, the United States genuinely wanted an even handed settlement in the region and that Henry Kissinger could deliver one.... Arafat now believed that with Israel overwhelmingly strong and the Arabs defeated and divided, guerrilla warfare could not possibly result in statehood."[140] Unequivocally, that "structural shift" in the continuously evolving Middle East political landscape sent earthquake-like shock waves throughout the Palestinian resistance movement, thereby in effect renting it apart into "moderates" and "hard-liners." In fact, we are told that the so-called "Rejectionist Front," crafted in 1974, traces an arc to that rent in the political fabric of the Palestinian resistance movement.[141]

It is against that backdrop that Sabri al-Banna (Abu Nidal), from his crow's nest as PLO representative in Baghdad, began to make his mark in the political landscape. For al-Banna, Arafat's "revisionist" approach to the Palestinian struggle was an anathema, compounded even more by the generally recognizable sentiment among some Arab leaders like King Hussein of Jordan that now the PLO "was the sole legitimate representative of the Palestinian people."[142] Equally troublesome, as both Seale and Melman report, was that Arafat had put on the robes of legitimacy with his 1974 address before the UN General Assembly, resplendent in a "kafiya," a gun belt wrapped around his waist, and able to evoke generally recognizable sympathy and other similar feelings with his offering of "the olive branch of peace."[143]

For the "rejectionists," the myopic-like Arafat, shackled with cowardice and branded as "a traitor," had to be confronted. From the vantage of politics at the nation-state level, Seale suggests the Iraqis were willing gatekeepers for al-Banna's efforts because of their interest in the acquisition of "a counterweight" force against Syria's "al-Saiqa," that would really augment the Arab Liberation Front (ALF), itself an Iraqi artifact created for that purpose.[144] Melman tells us of another geopolitical factor at work, namely that the Iraqis had antipathy for the Syrians because of Assad's "capitulation" to Israel with respect to cease fire terms over the Golan Heights in 1973.[145]

Within that context, both Melman and Seale chronicle the first terrorist assault by the Abu Nidal Organization against the Saudi Arabian embassy in Paris, France in 1973.[146] To be sure, Abu Nidal had already shown an enormous capacity for ferocious violence and terrorist assaults of great intensity. Indeed, Seale tells us that Abu Nidal, before his departure from Fatah, was able to generate and sustain support among PLO "hardliners" for the use of deadly violence against King Hussein as a payback for King Hussein's victory over the Palestinians in 1970.[147]

Melman tells us of the death sentence invoked against Sabri al-Banna by the PLO precisely because of an attempt by Abu Nidal to assassinate Yasser Arafat. "Sabri al-Banna's action," Melman explains, "caused tremors among the PLO leadership. While the annals of the Palestinians organizations are filled with stories of bitter fighting between factions, they had always been governed by one unwritten rule, that leaders were never allowed to be attacked."[148] Both Melman and Seale chronicle how Sabri al-Banna would later become inextricably bound up with President Hafaz al Assad of Syria and Colonel Muammar Quadhafi of Libya, thereby in effect acquiring a reputation, to use Seale's phrase, as "a gun for hire" for the commission of terrorist assaults.[149]

All of the aforementioned really leads to the basic issue of what explanatory factors can account for Sabri al-Banna's political inflexibility and generally recognizable hatred and rage that seems even to outpace the rage of many other terrorist group leaders in the Middle East. Interestingly enough, both Melman and Seale suggest, and I think correctly, psychological factors that really dovetail nicely with an analysis of Sabri al-Banna and the Abu Nidal Organization within the "risk factors" framework provided by Reiss and Roth.

The explanatory factors covered by both authors revolve around the central idea that Abu Nidal's *persona* was given structural shape from devastating childhood experiences and the calamity of al-Banna's inability to withstand them, that by extrapolation, amplified existing social and political conditions. In a tantalizing description that showcases al-Banna's idiosyncratic nature, Nasr reports "he jumped from idea to idea, sometimes talking calmly and persuasively, and at other times acting awkward and introverted. It seemed as if Abu Nidal never matured."[150] As previously mentioned, Seale points to Sabri al-Banna's somewhat scandalous Alawite background, that stemmed from his mother and father's relationship, as a source of personal insecurity and family antagonism.[151] Seen from a different angle, Melman tells us that Dr. Issam Sartawi, himself a prominent PLO official, explained that Abu Nidal's underlying rage, at least in part, presupposes and derives from Sabri al-Banna's mother's stature as one of Khalil al-Banna's eight wives.[152]

In a broader sense, Melman reports that the sudden loss of the al-Banna family's extensive wealth, precisely because the lurking calamity of war in Palestine happened in 1947-1948, had enormous repercussions for the young al-Banna.[153] It is probably no exaggeration to say the loss of the mansion that al-Banna grew up in, that provided the rarified air of stability and insulation from the outside world, evoked profound and lasting feelings of anger and depression that made the political and social traumas associated with the Israelis even more difficult to face.

What seems significant here with respect to recruitment is that those who demonstrated a similar political inflexibility and rage in a continuously evolving political landscape may have also had personal experiences comparable to al-Banna's in terms of "cognitive processing" or appropriate interpretation of political events and their interconnections with the inner self. At a functional level, Melman tells us that Abu Nidal's cookie cutter strategy of violence had allure for some Palestinian students who resided in Europe as well as some students and intellectuals in the Middle East.[154]

In his discussion about the Middle East, Melman asserts, "terrorists are not born, they are made, and nobody makes them better than the Palestinian refugee camps, especially those in Lebanon."[155] Imagine a situation replete with poverty and an absence of hope, and that condition ought to resonate powerfully with Reiss and Roth's notion of a "failure" of "opportunity structures" for many persons in society.[156] At a substantive level, Seale reports that Abu Nidal, "... was on the lookout for lively students, preferably very young ones, who were eager to get ahead and who also wanted to strike a blow for the Palestinian cause."[157] From an organizational vantage, Seale tells us that recruitment happened under the aegis of the Abu Nidal Organization's "membership committee" that would oftentimes engage in "poaching" recruits from different Palestinian terrorist groups, thereby in effect creating an ANO morality tale about how to pursue the struggle in effective and sustained ways.[158]

The Abu Nidal Organization (ANO) has operated throughout the Middle East under a variety of front organizations, some of which, Melman tells us, mirror the names Fatah has used in the past. We are told this is done precisely because Abu Nidal wants to tell the ANO morality tale that ANO bears the true standard of what Fatah stood for before 1973. "... Sabri al-Banna," Melman explains, "sees himself as carrying the torch of Fatah ideology, and all his opponents as betraying Fatah's aims."[159] The front organizations Abu Nidal has reportedly used include: Fatah Revolutionary Council (FRC), Black June, Black September Organization (BSO), Revolutionary Egypt or Egyptian Revolution, Palestinian National Liberation Movement (PNLM), Revolutionary Organization of Socialist Muslims (ROSM), Al-Iqab ("The Punishment") and Arab Revolutionary Brigades (RABO).[160]

Ideo-ethnocentric Groups

The fifth terrorist group-type category, ideo-ethnocentric, is composed of nationalist-irredentist terrorist groups with Marxist-Leninist trappings, but without charismatic leadership. Ideo-ethnocentric groups are nationalist groups that view the Palestinian movement within the context of the traditional Marxist-Leninist conception of the struggle between owners of capital and wage earners, and promote a Marxist-Leninist political agenda.[161] Groups that comprise that category include the Arab Communist Organization (ACO) and the Maronite Christian Lebanese Armed

Revolutionary Faction (LARF).

Arab Communist Organization and Lebanese Armed Revolutionary Faction

While the origins and composition of the Arab Communist Organization remain unclear, it is clearly a Marxist-Leninist organization whose stated purpose is to "destroy imperialist positions in the local bourgeois dictatorship and Arab reactionaries, the allies of imperialism and Zionism."[162] To be sure, many targets of ACO terrorist assaults seem to resonate as symbols of American or British influence in the region. At a functional level, when an ACO terrorist assault destroyed the offices of the National Cash Register Company, a communique was issued that announced the firm "... represents a form of imperialist exploitation of the area."[163] Regrettably precious little information is available about the Maronite Christian LARF, but the group was established in 1979 and is, according to one US government account, comprised of some twenty-five activists.[164]

The sixth terrorist group-type category, ideo-ethnocentric charismatic, is comprised of the same type of terrorist group described above, but the groups under consideration here are led by a charismatic leader. Ideo-ethnocentric charismatic groups differ from ideo-ethnocentric groups in that they recruit activists primarily from the personal followers of a charismatic leader who controls the terrorist group. Given the previous discussion about the "prevailing social ideology" of Islam, and social fissures in the Middle East that presuppose and derive from religious and ethnic differences between groups of persons, what seems significant here is that several ideo-ethnocentric charismatic groups share a Christian historical legacy. Indeed, several notable Middle East terrorist groups share that characteristic and fall into this category.

The Popular Front for the Liberation of Palestine

The Popular Front for the Liberation of Palestine (PFLP) was founded in 1967 by Dr. George Habash, a Greek Orthodox Palestinian, and claims some 1,000 armed activists.[165] Cobban suggests that the formation of PFLP was a continuously evolving process that in some sense could be seen as an incremental evolution involving several intermediary phases. That process traces an arc to the Arab Nationalist Movement (ANM) founded by George Habash and Hani al-Hindi in the 1950's, and to earlier student activities under their aegis in Beirut that generated and sustained support for their ideas about the Palestinian resistance. Cobban tells us that in those early days Habash and Hindi "... first won the elections to the Executive Committee of a key campus literary/nationalist association called Jam'iyat al-Urwa al Wathqa (the Society of the Firm Tie), and then transformed this Committee into the nucleus of a new secret nationalist organization: The Arab Nationalists."[166] Somewhat predictably, the author suggests that the Arab Nationalist Movement (ANM) was a response to the lurking catastrophe of Israel's war of Independence. As we have seen before, the earthquake-like shock waves of that war, and the massive number of Palestinian refugees it created, was the pivotal "activating" event for terrorist group formation at this time.

Cobban suggests that the Arab Nationalist Movement (ANM) had an "anticommunist" and "anti-socialist" flavor to it from the start, but what Gresh calls "Nasserism" became a generally recognizable hallmark of the movement. Gresh reports that, "the ANM later converted to Nasserism and adopted the views of the Egyptian leaders until the 1967 defeat...."[167] In more specific terms, Cobban tells us this set of interconnections with the Nasser government was interwoven precisely because a protest against the Eisenhower-Dulles Baghdad Pact at the American University of Beirut resulted in the deaths of several ANM activists at the hands of government officials.[168] What seems significant here is that important encounter is illustrative of how "micro" political events, such as a political protest handled badly, can become an "activating factor" with an enormous capacity in the context of Middle East politics to shape the evolutionary process of terrorist group formation and development.

Cobban suggests that the structural shape of the Arab Nationalist Movement (ANM) was brittle with an enormous capacity to break. The author tells us the Arab Nationalist Movement (ANM), which was inclusive of many Middle East locales and persons of differing backgrounds, had an inherent potential for political instability and unrest within it.[169] Keeping that in mind, an important "situational factor" for PLO "offshoot" development that is commonplace to note is the formation of the PLO in 1964, replete with, as former Israeli intelligence chieftain General Yariv puts it, "the blessing of Nasser."[170] Cobban suggests that the coalescence of the PLO in 1964 resulted in the creation of PFLP's direct antecedent, the National Front for the Liberation of Palestine (NFLP). Cobban suggests that pressures elicited by a call among some for the ANO to disband into a sea of pan-Arabism, coupled with pressures evoked by the genesis of the PLO, a plainly Palestinian organization, "... prompted Habash and Haddad to start forming a distinct Palestinian grouping within the ANM, and this move was endorsed by the May 1964 conference."[171]

The fragile condition of the elitist Arab Nationalist Movement (ANM), fraught with peril and uncertainty, was tailor made for disruption by an "activating event" that in this case was President Gamal Abdul Nasser's enormous defeat in the Six Day War of 1967.[172] It is commonplace to note in the literature that Nasser's defeat at the hands of the Israelis remains a tortured historical legacy for the Arab world.[173] As Cobban reports, the ANM's lack of cohesion, compounded even more by various interpretations about what the root causes of Nasser's defeat were all about, helped to create an environment ripe for terrorist group splitting. For the purposes of this study, one way of thinking about the Six Day War is its role as an "activating factor" for the eventual formation of the PFLP.

We are told that in the wake of the Six Day War debacle and the lurking catastrophe of confusion and recriminations that followed, Habash and Haddad made full-blown efforts to tie together powerfully several factions of the Palestinian resistance movement.[174] Illustrative of those efforts was that three resistance groups, namely, "the Palestinian Liberation Front" ("Jabhat al-Tahrir al-Filastiniyya"), "the Heros of the Return" ("Abtal al-Awda"), and Habash and Haddad's National Front for the Liberation of Palestine (NFLP), became inextricably bound together in the guise of the Popular Front for the Liberation of Palestine (PFLP).[175] Livingstone and Halevy tell us that PFLP's ideological cornerstones revolve around the central idea of a Pan-Arabist movement to combat and wrest power away from the imperialist West, the State of Israel, and pro-western Sunni regimes by means of effective and sustained terrorist assaults.[176] With respect to PFLP recruitment patterns, Livingstone and Halevy suggest an economic component at work that derives from a Marxist-Leninist interpretation of events because much recruitment is done in the oil-rich Gulf states and Saudi Arabia, presumably among political and economically disenfranchised persons on the fringes of society.[177]

The Democratic Front for the Liberation of Palestine

The Democratic Front for the Liberation of Palestine (DFLP) was created in 1969 by Naif Hawatamah as a result of severe political infighting among PFLP chieftains.[178] Within the context of the 1967 Six Day War debacle, Cobban tells us that there were profound and lasting differences among PFLP members about Nasser's legacy and suitability as a model for struggle, that in part derived from and certainly made for sharp distinctions between "first" and "second" generation PFLP activists. For Cobban, "the accusations that Nasserism was a 'petty bourgeois' phenomenon were voiced loudest by those very activists who had formerly idolized Nasser most strongly: the 'new generation' from the ANM, led by Muhsin Ibrahim and Nayef Hawatma."[179] Again, what seems significant here are the powerful reverberations of the Nasser defeat and its effect on making for even more terrorist group "offshoots." Cobban goes on to tell us that when the emergent reality of the PFLP "spin-off" group DFLP actually happened, there was an unequivocal lambasting of what the author calls "Arab 'nationalist' regimes."[180] Like Habash, Naif Hawatamah is also a Greek Orthodox Palestinian with a substantial Greek Orthodox following that has been estimated at 1,000 soldiers.[181]

Popular Front for the Liberation of Palestine-Special Operations Groups and Popular Front for the Liberation of Palestine-General Command

Two other significant ideo-ethnocentric charismatic groups are the Popular Front for the Liberation of Palestine-Special Operations Group (PFLP-SOG) and the Popular Front for the Liberation of Palestine-General Command (PFLP-GC).[182] As mentioned earlier, PFLP-SOG is now a defunct group that was led by Dr. Wadi Haddad, who Alexander and Sinai describe as a "Christian radical."[183] The PFLP-GC was created by Ahmad Jabril, a one-time Palestinian officer in Syria's army who split from PFLP in 1968.[184] Under the watch of Jabril, PFLP-GC has amassed an estimated 500 activists.[185]

Jewish Theocentric Groups

Background and Description of the "Gush Emunim Underground" (TNT)

Perhaps the most highly developed Jewish theocentric terrorist group was the "Gush Emunim underground," sometimes referred to as "Terror Neged Terror" or (TNT).[186] Clearly, TNT (Terror Against Terror) traces an arc to the Gush Emunim movement ("Block of the Faithful"), and therefore it is necessary to provide some discussion of the Gush Emunim "settler movement."[187] To be sure, it is useful to chronicle the emergent reality of Jewish fundamentalist terrorism against the backdrop of the fledgling Zionist movement. Sprinzak skillfully breaks down different strands of Zionism into four "'classical' schools" and relates them to Jewish revivalism. His "schools" include: the "Labour movement ... activists"; the "ultra-nationalist" approach of Brit Habironim, Uri Zvi Greenberg, and Abraham

Stern's (and Yitzhak Shamir's) Stern Gang; "the radical legacy of Vladimir Jabitinsky's" Revisionist "Betar" movement; "the messianic teaching of Rav Avraham Itzhak HaCohen Kook" (1865-1935).[188]

The Gush Emunim movement presupposes and derives from the Merkaz Haarav school of Rabbi Avraham Itzhak HaCohen Kook (1865-1935) and his son Rabbi Zvi Yehuda Kook (1891-1982).[189] What seems critical here are social fissures between Jews, in this case a religious one, namely the profound and lasting fissure between religious "anti-Zionists" on the one hand and "religious Zionists" on the other. At one level, Demant describes "the *haridim* (literally the God-fearing)" as non-Zionist religious Jews who seek isolation from the secular world and evoke hostility and other similar feelings toward the State of Israel and its leaders because, from their vantage, the establishment of Israel can only be "a divine" happening.[190] Alternatively, the Kookist approach acknowledges the legitimacy of the State of Israel as a vehicle to full-blown redemption, where the secular state, to paraphrase Engels, "will wither away" when faced with the emergent reality of a Jewish theocracy based on Torah law (*halacha*).[191]

Indeed, a comparison between the Kookist approach and a traditional Marxist way of thinking about a continuously evolving political environment seems close to the mark. Sprinzak tells us that the stage of "*Mashiach Ben Yosef*" (Messiah Ben Joseph), a period where Israel is powerful in military and economic terms, will pass into eclipse with the emergent reality of "*Mashiach Ben David*" (Messiah Ben David), the period of religious Jewish renaissance. For Sprinzak, "according to this distinction, salvation would come through two consecutive stages of redemption, material and spiritual. The first stage, that of Mashiach Ben Yosef, is manifested in material achievement of the nation. But this period is bound to pass and be superseded by Mashiach Ben David...."[192]

For Don-Yehiya, Rav Kook's conception of the fledgling Jewish theocracy can be seen as analogous to an egg hatching. Don-Yehiya reports, "how was it possible Rav Kook asked, for a secular movement to be the bearer of the very idea that paved the way to redemption? He resolved the problem by describing the expressions of secularism within Zionism and the Jewish community in general as a kind of outer, superficial, impermanent shell. As the process of redemption develops, the shell will crack and the inner spiritual light of the Zionist enterprise will be revealed as an expression of religious revival."[193]

Sprinzak suggests there is a certain post hoc analysis to Kookist thought that lends itself to rationalization of "good" and "bad" political events as part of the ineluctable tapestry of life. For example, the Six Day War (1967) was a watershed moment for Jewish revivalists, and a starting point for the period that spans 1967-1974, "the formative years" of Gush Emunim.[194] The enormous impact of the Six Day War on Jewish revivalists (and other Israelis) and its capacity to evoke feelings of near euphoria and closeness to the Almighty's divine plan cannot be overstated.[195] Conversely, the lurking calamity of the October 1973 War underscored the notion that Israel's progress toward redemption was more episodic and inconsistent than what God required.[196] What seems critical here is that there is an enormous capacity for "religious Zionists" to introduce political game-playing in the guise of political event ad hoc analysis, both within the Israeli *Knesset* (parliament) and elsewhere, in their pursuit of full-blown redemption.

Like their Islamic counterparts, change in political context in general and the inevitability of change in the Israeli political landscape in particular, had effects on contemporary Jewish terrorist group formation. In the broader sense, political change in Israel, nay fundamental political change inaugurated by Sadat's trip to Jerusalem, would not only happen quickly, but the pace of change itself would accelerate remarkably with the passage of time. The ratification of the Camp David Accords in 1978 evoked volcanic-like eruptions of shock and discontent among Jewish revivalists in general, and the Gush Emunim in particular, thereby in effect pitting the interests of Jewish revivalists against the interests of the secular Israeli government. Among segments of Israeli society, Prime Minister Begin was, in essence, lambasted as a "sell-out," and the political fray intensified apace, reaching its zenith with the ticklish showdown between the Israeli army and Jewish settlers at the Sinai settlement of Yamit in 1982. Here, some twenty thousand Israeli troops were confronted with a cacophony of voices and actions that showcased the enormous ideological distance between Israeli political actors for all to see.[197] Demant suggests one thing was crystal clear from the vantage of Jewish revivalism: any return of land, intrinsic to the "Israeli dove" notion of "land for peace" was, and remains, totally unacceptable, nay a violation of God's divine plan for redemption.[198]

Within that continuously evolving environment, the Gush Emunim underground was spawned. TNT (Terror Neged Terror) was an organization that became active in 1980 in large part as a response to the Camp David Accords that stipulated, among other things, that the Sinai peninsula be returned to Egypt in exchange for a peace agreement.[199] At the heart of the matter, the leaders of TNT, themselves bound up with the idea that the Jewish renaissance hinged on the building of the Third Temple in Jerusalem, believed fervently that the current agenda of the secular state of Israel was antithetical to the Jewish fundamentalist vision of a "Greater Israel."[200]

The essence of TNT's perspective revolved around the activities and military expertise of its leadership.[201] At a functional level, Sprinzak describes the "operational commander" of the Gush Emunim underground as Menachem Livni, a major in Israel's *Zahal* (army) reserve, and Yehuda Etzion as "the ideologist" and "dynamo" of the terrorist group.[202] Sprinzak goes on to report there is strong evidence that one of Gush Emunim's "hard-liners," Rabbi Moshe Levinger, was inextricably intertwined with the activities of TNT, thereby in effect acquiring the status of the "rabbinical authority" or gatekeeper of TNT's activities, even though his direct involvement with the terrorist group has never been proven.[203] After a series of terrorist assaults that included assassination attempts against the Mayor of Nablus, Bassam Shaka, and the Mayor of Ramallah, Karim Kahlef, and an aborted attempt to bomb several fully loaded Arab commuter buses, TNT was effectively dismantled by Israeli authorities in 1984.[204] By any standard of measure, TNT was an extremely small terrorist group. Some twenty-five persons, most of whom were residents of the West Bank and the Golan, were arrested in 1984.[205]

It seems possible to isolate and identify some of the explanatory factors that led to the genesis and evolution of the "Gush Emunim underground" if we devote attention to the "macro-social level" of the Reiss and Roth matrix. Reiss and Roth tell us the absence of "legitimate opportunities to achieve the purposes for which violence is used" is a characteristic of a "failing" macrosocial landscape.[206] Illustrative of those dynamics are the enormous feelings of betrayal and other similar sentiments felt by members of the Gush Emunim movement as a whole following the Camp David Accords of 1978. In turn, "situational" or middle range factors at the "macrosocial" level, namely "access to weapons," seem a factor in this case of terrorist group formation. It is commonplace to note profound and lasting concern about the enormous amount of Israel Defense Force (IDF) weaponry in the hands of Jewish settlers that was originally issued by the Israeli government with self-defense motivations in mind.[207]

It is possible to categorize explanatory factors in the sphere of Reiss and Roth's "micro-social factors." The religious invective to strive for a "Greater Israel" bound by *halacha* and the idea condoned by religious leaders to relegate the Palestinians to what Demant calls "dhimmi status" may make violent terrorist assaults easier to commit.[208] To be sure, that component of Jewish revivalism seems to meet the standard set by Reiss and Roth's explanation of "participants' social relationships," namely that "cultural and subcultural norms, such as the acceptance of behavior degrading to women or alienation among members of some ethnic categories against social control agencies managed by members of others, may reduce inhibitions to violence."[209] Again, in terms of "micro-social-situational" factors, the absence of what Reiss and Roth call "proximity of responsible monitors" (e.g., responsible government officials to oversee and establish limits to Gush Emunim activities such as marches through Hebron) as well as "weapons display" are at work here.[210] Finally, with respect to what Reiss and Roth call "activating events," terrorist assaults such as the murder of six Yeshiva students walking home in 1980, certainly qualify.[211]

Precious little is available about the "individual," "psychosocial," or "biological" attributes of TNT participants, but Sprinzak hints at some factors at these levels of analysis when he reports that, "Menachem Livni—an engineer and major in the reserves [was] probably the most balanced member of the group...."[212] Interestingly enough, Sprinzak's description resonates with some of Reiss and Roth's "psychosocial" or "biological" sublevels of analysis, when we are told, "Etzion ... is a man who talks and thinks in the language of this world but lives in another."[213] It is probably no exaggeration to say there were problems in terms of reconciling what Sprinzak calls "political reality" with the allure of a new Jewish renaissance.[214] It suffices to say that while TNT had its share of supporters sympathetic to the cause, if not to the means employed by the terrorists, the fact that Livni, Etzion, and others "acted out" really points to factors at the "individual" level of analysis that coincide with the other Reiss and Roth explanatory factors listed and described above.

Jewish Terrorist "Proto-Groups" and Other Groups

Illustrative of more contemporary Jewish revivalist terrorist groups without charismatic leaders are several other more loosely organized proto-groups and cohesive terrorist groups that engage in anti-Arab terrorism. Hence, proto-groups of the religious right in Israel, such as Jewish settlers in the West Bank, Yeshiva students and *Neturei Karta* members that periodically coalesce to commit terrorist acts, are considered Jewish theocentric terrorist groups.[215]

The proto-groups of the religious right in Israel present an interesting set of challenges and opportunities in terms of analysis because it is unknown to what extent those proto-groups and even the groups that make up this group-type are autonomous. It is entirely possible that some of those entities are front organizations for Jewish theocentric charismatic groups like Kach.[216] Compounding the problem is that the boundaries of those groups are permeable and interpenetrating, with the result that even if those groups were autonomous, members of Jewish theocentric charismatic groups could belong to Jewish theocentric groups thereby in effect influencing the decision-making process.[217]

Notwithstanding that, the Lifta Gang,[218] the Hasmoneans,[219] the Sicarii,[220] and Keshet[221] are coded as Jewish theocentric groups. Precious little information is known about any of those shadowy Jewish terrorist groups. Sprinzak tells us that the Lifta Gang was comprised of four persons who were criminal types or mentally unstable persons. Sprinzak asserts, "combining religious repentance with criminality, drugs and strange symbolism they had created a small messianic sect based on spiritual purification and on unmediated relation with God."[222] The author goes on to report that some Lifta Gang members were hospitalized or sent to prison, and one member went into hiding.[223] Interestingly enough, Lustick tells me that from the start the Sicarii terrorist organization really distilled down to the episodic and inconsistent terrorist assaults of one man, Yoel Adler, who is described as "an activist highly placed within the Tehiya Party."[224] Be that as it may, what we know is those groups claim responsibility for terrorist acts, and that there is no hard evidence to substantiate claims that any of those groups are front organizations for other terrorist groups.

Jewish Theocentric Charismatic Groups

The final terrorist group-type category is composed of Jewish terrorist groups that are led or guided by the spiritual teachings of a charismatic leader and recruit from that leader's followers. The groups include: the Jewish Defense League (JDL); Kach ("Thus" or "The Way") and Kahane Chai ("Kahane Lives"). In Chapter One, the Jewish Defense League is used as a case study to highlight how the Reiss and Roth "risk factor" matrix, when applied to the sources and origins of terrorism, provides insight into terrorist group formation and growth. That rather comprehensive treatment will be augmented here by discussion about why "structural shifts" in JDL strategy and targeting may have occurred.

The Jewish Defense League—Revisited

One issue that deserves increased attention is the evolutionary phase of the Jewish Defense League that involved a shift in focus from self-defense orientation, to terrorist assaults against Soviet targets. As previously mentioned, much of Jewish Defense League activity in earlier periods revolved around the central idea of self-defense against self-perceived "enemies" in Brooklyn, New York, and elsewhere. The aforementioned really leads to the fundamental question of why a "structural shift" in Jewish Defense League strategies and targeting happened.

One way of thinking about the matter is to look at change in American foreign policy that would have indirect but powerful reverberations for JDL perceptions of threats, enemies, and consequently, the marshaling of resources against them. Within the context of "détente" there was a "loosening" of what Nye would call the "tight bipolar" relationship between the United States and the Soviet Union that introduced flexibility into the international political system by means of arms control and improved diplomatic and communications interconnections. Brown tells us, "Nixon indicated that ongoing discussions with the Soviets were making progress in a number of fields—Berlin, SALT, the Middle East—and added pointedly that 'if the time comes, as it may come, and both sides realize this, then the final breakthrough in any one of those areas can take place only at the highest level'...."[225]

Those changes in emphasis in American foreign policy with respect to the Soviet Union can, in my judgment, be seen as a "macro-social-activating event" for a new shape to JDL activity. It is commonplace to note that "détente," within the context of the ticklish matter of Soviet abuses against its own Jewish citizens, really may, from the vantage of some Jewish-Americans, have amounted to a negative change in United States foreign policy. In fact, such a shift in the international political landscape seems analogous in effect to "political assassinations, killings by police officers, and controversial jury verdicts ... [as] catalytic social events" that Reiss and Roth describe in their discussion of domestic violent outcomes.[226] Clearly, with respect to the implications of "détente," JDL activists may have seen "a decline in legitimate opportunity" for expression that is an intrinsic part of what "macro-social factors" for violence, as Reiss and Roth describe them, are all about.[227]

Mergui and Simonnot tell us that, "Kahane was to find a new cause to espouse: the defense of Jews in Russia. He declared war on Soviet diplomats in Washington and New York, with the stated aim of provoking conflict between the USSR and the United States, so that as he said, 'the problem of the Russian Jews becomes Nixon's problem'."[228] At a "psychosocial-predisposing level," Kahane seemed to be processing the condition in the Soviet Union with readings of Holocaust history, with the emergent reality of Soviets as Nazis. Incidentally, that interpretation of the tortured historical legacy of the Jews in the twentieth century and before is not limited to Kahane. Indeed, as Helmreich tells us, this underlying theme of "holocaust history" reading and institutionalized anti-Semitism reading in general, was a guidepost in the thought processes of Era Rapoport, one of TNT's members convicted of the terrorist assault against Mayor Bassam Shaka of Nablus.[229] In summation, the application of Reiss and Roth's work to JDL activity seems a good fit with empirical events and underscores how shifts in the "macro-social landscape" can alter terrorist behavior that the foregoing explanatory factors help to determine. For the Jewish Defense League, membership figures are inexact, but Hoffman estimates some 15,000 members during the Jewish Defense League's halcyon days of 1972.[230] In terms of active combatants the actual number is almost certainly a fraction of that, and accordingly JDL is coded as a moderate size terrorist group.

Kach

Kach is a JDL offshoot that surfaced in Israel after Rabbi Kahane moved there in 1971. Hoffman reports that its mission was "to rid Israel and the Occupied Territories of its Arab population and promote Israeli settlement and annexation in the West Bank."[231] Sprinzak suggests that Kahane was "a one man show," whose exclusionary and racist ideology during his "Kach period" in Israel, was rather different from the underlying political emphasis of the Jewish Defense League in the United States.[232] The author explains that, "at the beginning of his career in the United States, Kahane had little to say about democracy and concentrated on self defense against ethnic hostility. In Israel, however, as his radical solution for the Arab problem crystallized, Kahane had repeatedly been accused of being anti-democratic."[233]

One aspect of the "Kach phenomenon" that is important to note is Kach was also a political party that was once a part of the Israeli Knesset (parliament), as well as a terrorist organization. To be specific, Kach generated and sustained enough voter support to propel Kahane into the Knesset in 1984. Precisely for that reason however, Israel's Central Election Committee passed an "anti-racist" amendment in 1985, thereby in effect allowing Israel's Supreme Court to help preclude an unrepentant Kahane from official participation in Israeli national elections of 1988.[234] Kahane's exclusionary message, when finally full-blown, railed against "Hellenized Jewry," the Arabs, and the Christian West, replete with its underlying political and legal frameworks. Hanauer relates that, "Kahane denied being a racist, however because he claimed that all his actions were justified by halacha—yet not one rabbi or halachic authority supported his interpretation of religious texts."[235]

It follows that one fundamental matter to consider is why Kach was able to garner support as a political force in the first place.[236] In the narrower sense, it is possible to use the Reiss and Roth analysis to explain the allure of Kach in the political fray that is Israeli politics. For one thing, Kach had a capacity to generate and sustain support among many Israeli Sephardim.

What seems significant here is that many Sephardic, or non-European Jews, were not as wealthy or as well represented politically, as many of their Ashkenazi counterparts. Indeed, with respect to Kach, Sprinzak reports, "Kahane knew his audience well. The Sephardi Jews have indeed suffered from a difficult absorption process, especially during the 1950's, and from cultural discrimination."[237] In a similar vein, Demant tells us, "... Kahanist forces, though still small, are spreading among oriental Jewish slums. Economic frustration might render them susceptible to its anti-Arab rhetoric, and breed a racism based on economic competition for scarce labor and resources...."[238]

Those accounts resonate with many of Reiss and Roth's "macro-social-predisposing factors" for violence that include "concentration of poverty" and "opportunity structures." At the "micro-social-predisposing" factor level, the effect of Sephardic "community organizations," as distinct from Ashkenazi ones, may amplify the effects of the "macro-social" factor "oppositional cultures," since Israel was largely culled out with the historical legacy of Jews from Central and Eastern Europe in mind. In short, a host of "predisposing" and "situational" factors, at both "macro-social" and "micro-social" levels of analysis seems generally recognizable here.[239] Those factors, when overlaid with particular "psychosocial" or "biological" patterns may help to explain the genesis of potentially violent persons who gravitated toward Kach terrorism.

Interestingly enough, Mergui and Simonnot make two important observations about Kach recruitment patterns that not only fit well in the Reiss and Roth framework, but also seem to provide insight into the allure of Rabbi Kahane as "a charismatic leader." First, Mergui and Simonnot report that many Kach recruits were "repentant leftists, often North Americans, in search of a new area of involvement."[240] To be sure, the authors suggest that factors at what Reiss and Roth term the "individual" level of analysis, are involved with this particular group of recruits.

Second, the authors tell us that many Kach supporters were Russians "who have brought from the USSR a bad habit of liking politicians who give clear-cut simple answers."[241] Again, assimilation difficulties with respect to "oppositional cultures," and "community organizations" factors at "macro-social" and "micro-social" levels of analysis and how they relate to new Russian émigrés in Israel, may contribute to a "failure" among those Russians that gravitate towards Kach. Certainly, that relatively straightforward "simple" way of thinking about politics and conflict resolution meshes well with the "black and white" Kahane approach to Israel and the complex set of challenges and opportunities that it confronts.

Kahane Chai

Kahane Chai is a Kach spinoff group that was formed after Rabbi Meir Kahane's assassination at a rally in New York City by a Muslim fundamentalist in 1990. Some written accounts suggest that el Sayyid al-Nosair, the killer of Kahane, while seemingly working on his own, was inextricably bound up with Shaykh Umar Abdul Rahman, formerly of Egypt's al-Jama'a al Islamiya al Jihadiyya, and then living in or near New York City.[242] At the most basic level, Kahane Chai and Kach pursue the same draconian political objectives that amount to resettlement of Arabs to promote a religious Jewish state.

According to a news account scripted in 1991, there was some free-wheeling discussion among Kach members about which person or group of persons would generate and sustain the "Kahane view" in the post Kahane world. Schlein of the Hebrew newspaper *Maariv* reports that for Kach chieftain Tiran Pollack, it was "... still unclear how the future leadership of the movement will appear, if one man or the leadership group is to be elected."[243] The emergent reality is that Benjamin Ze'ev Kahane, the son of the late Meir Kahane, put on the robes of Kahane Chai leadership and condoned, among other things, deadly violence against Prime Minister Yitzak Rabin in August 1995.[244] According to another account scripted in 1995, Schlein reports that "most of this group's members live in the settlement of Tapuah in Samaria."[245] Both groups are relatively small; Israel's Police Minister reported in 1994 that Kach and Kahane Chai each have less than 100 active members.[246] Accordingly, those organizations are coded as small size terrorist groups.

Conclusions

All of the aforementioned really leads to a set of basic questions about what has been learned about the sources and origins of certain Middle East terrorist groups, gaps in knowledge about those processes that deserve the increased attention of scholars, and why distinctions between terrorist groups led by a charismatic leader and terrorist groups led by a coterie of non-charismatic chieftains are significant. By the same token, it is important to understand that a meticulous, close-reading of the set of interconnections among explanatory variables and between "social" and "individual" levels of analysis is beyond the scope of this study. Hence, the underlying objective here is to make a first pass at some qualitative relationships that seem plausible intuitively and deserve empirical investigation.

In the broadest sense, it is probably no exaggeration to say that political terrorist group sources and origins presuppose and derive from a set of political demands and aspirations either perceived to be unmet or unmet outright in a particular political context. To paraphrase Baldwin, it is possible to think of a "political context" as establishing what he calls an established "baseline of expectations" with respect to challenges and opportunities for political accommodation or structural political or economic change.[247]

Imagine a situation in a given political context or, in other words, a defined political landscape where villagers live replete with low-level strains and tensions between groups, and within a relatively predictable, but politically unresponsive and economically impoverished system. To be sure, such a set of conditions may help to elicit terrorism against perceived enemies, but what seems crucial here is the analysis suggests that a political context bombarded by long term, middle range and short run changes develops strains and tensions that build to a threshold point, that when crossed, can evoke terrorist assaults.

While it is not possible to pin down exact mixtures of explanatory factor influence for terrorist group formation or to trace interconnections between explanatory variables by using the Reiss and Roth "risk factors" typology for violence, there are, in the broader sense, some points to be made. What seems significant here is that a particular group of explanatory factors at what Reiss and Roth call the "individual" level, such as "psychosocial" or "biological" factors, may work in certain persons to amplify existing political and social traumas and conditions, thereby increasing the chance for terrorist assaults. Those traumas and conditions may threaten political, economic, social, and cultural needs or demands and aspirations to the point where what Reiss and Roth call "an activating event" may put a cycle or cycles of terrorist assault violence into play.

With respect to Islamic revivalist or fundamentalist terrorist groups, an ideological appeal by means of religious orthodoxy seems to mask some important economic and political factors at work in the case of Hamas in Gaza and the West Bank among Palestinians, and Hezbollah and Amal in Lebanon. In the case of Hezbollah, the study chronicles how Hezbollah appeals to many Shi'ites who have traditionally been afflicted with economic and political disadvantages, while there is discussion of the sources and origins of Amal that largely presupposed and derived from poor security and economic conditions of Shi'ites in southern Lebanon. In the broader sense, the protection of cultural and religious institutions seems to be an underlying theme that looms large when thinking about conditions and processes in Lebanon, Gaza, and the West Bank.

In turn, variations of the long term explanatory factor influence described above are present in the sources and origins of many Islamic revivalist groups that have been the emergent reality in Egypt. In the case of Egypt, we have covered how those factors hinge on support given to organizations like al-Jihad by politically and economically disenfranchised persons. With respect to the historical legacy of Egypt, the study has highlighted works by Auda and Gaffney that point to the inability of Nasser and Sadat's modernization efforts to provide resources that "trickle down" to groups of disenfranchised persons. Equally important, as the authors suggest, is the perception of failure of the secular regime, thereby in effect leading persons on the fringe to search for alternate modes of political and economic inclusion.

In the case of Palestinian resistance terrorist groups, long-haul explanatory factors like increased waves of Jewish immigration to Palestine (making "aliyah," literally, "going up"), and Jewish National Fund land purchase, all within the broader conflict between modernity and traditional patterns of behavior, had a disruptive effect on political context. Compounding the matter even more were middle term explanatory factors, such as British offers of "devolution" to Arab and Jewish Palestinians that were accepted in a full-blown way by many Jewish officials and rejected outright by Arab Palestinian officials. Finally, with strains and tensions increasing apace, the 1936-1939 Arab Revolt can be seen as an antecedent "tremor" leading to terrorist assaults, while the full-blown conflict of the 1947-1948 war in Palestine is, in the end, the underlying reason for long-standing and sustained conflict between Israelis and Palestinians, and those who carry out terrorist assaults from both camps.

In the case of Palestinian resistance terrorist groups with Marxist-Leninist trappings, it is possible to isolate and identify the same set of long haul and middle term explanatory factors that make for change in the political context for Palestinian nationalist groups like al-Fatah and PLO. Clearly, the war of 1947-1948 remains the long term factor able to generate and sustain the most influence for terrorist assaults. What seems significant here with respect to PFLP formation is the middle level explanatory factor of the PLO's formation in 1964 and the "activating factor" of the 1967 Six Day War. The formation of the PLO helped to shape the continuously evolving political environment, and Habash and Haddad had to respond to this new Palestinian political player of enormous stature with a political and military artifact of their own in the NFLP. In terms of PFLP splinter groups such as DFLP, the underlying "activating event" was the Six Day War debacle in 1967, that pulled at the heartstrings of the Palestinian resistance movement and eventually tore it apart. Nasser's role as the guidepost of Pan-Arab efforts to liberate Palestine was tarnished beyond repair, thereby in effect leading to other efforts along Marxist-Leninist lines to confront the State of Israel, the West, and the pro-western Sunni regimes in the Middle East.

In the case of Jewish revivalist or fundamentalist terrorist groups, the conceptualization needs to be broken down into sub-categories in large part because of differences in locales that transcend national borders. For Jewish revivalist terrorist groups without charismatic leaders, and Jewish terrorist "proto-groups" that are more murky, we can only make conjecture about underlying explanatory factors at work. Having said that, it seems reasonable to think that the strains and tensions of the *Intifadeh* and the prospect of a negotiated peace between Israelis and Palestinians was compounded even more by long term desires for secular Zionism to pass into eclipse in the face of religious Zionism's ascendancy. In that context, any number of "activating events" would trigger terrorist assaults from particular types of persons who deal with rage, differences of political perspective and opinion, and differences in cultural background in violent ways.

In the narrower sense, the origins of the Jewish Defense League may be a reflection of the very sharp social, religious, and economic cleavages between ethnic groups in New York. In the broader sense, it is possible to view the militarization of small numbers of Jewish-Americans as a reflection of "oppositional culture" dynamics in a secular United States, where social factors such as the threat of assimilation and anti-Semitism may lead to a defensive but belligerent stand against outside threats. Again, it is quite conceivable that long-standing and time-honored memories or accounts of the Holocaust may have led to spurious comparisons between the Nazis and the perception of more contemporary threats to Jews.

In time, that political context "status quo" was influenced by "an activating political event" in the international sphere, namely "detente." In light of the continuously evolving relationship between the United States and the Soviet Union, Rabbi Kahane shifted terrorist group strategies and tactics to confront the Soviet Union, thereby in effect helping to bring the plight of Soviet Jewry onto a stage of world wide proportions. With Kahane's move to Israel in 1971, Kahane embedded himself into a new political context in which Arabs were the single most predominant threat, followed by Jewish "lefties" and "secular-types." Here in Israel, economic and political factors came into the mix because the Kahane message appealed to segments of Sephardic Jews and new Russian immigrants who had experienced considerable problems realizing political demands and aspirations.

An underlying theme of this study is the importance of making distinctions between terrorist groups led by a charismatic leader and terrorist groups that are led in "a collective fashion" by a coterie of individuals. At a most basic level, such a distinction is necessary because of what we see around us in the likes of Ayatollah Khomeini, Ayatollah Sayyid Muhammed Hussayn Fadlallah, Dr. George Habash, Dr. Waddi Haddad, Nayif Hawatamah, and Meir Kahane, just to name a few. What seems significant here is that in addition to what see we in the larger world of action, an examination of political context, for example in the world of Palestinian nationalist-Marxist-Leninist terrorist groups, enables the reader to trace real differences in political perspective and following among leaders who have different religious backgrounds but who share in a broader sense, a similar experience of violence and counter-violence with respect to Israelis, Arab regimes in opposition to the terrorist group under consideration, and the ferocious competition between nation states for influence over the Palestinian resistance movement.

For example, consider Yasser Arafat in the days of Fatah, with his penchant to eschew a formal ideology, as Nassar suggests, and his emphasis on violence as a vehicle for the liberation of Palestine. The amorphous texture of Fatah's ideology and Fatah's venerable reputation allowed Arafat to draw from a very broad pool of recruits, as compared with Habash, Haddad, or Hawatamah, who are Christian and by definition somewhat outside of the prevailing social ideology of Islam, and who are interested in a Marxist-Leninist interpretation to and context for the political struggle. Furthermore, it is commonplace to note that many Christian followers revolve around the political themes of those leaders.

In the broader sense, it is commonplace to note that besides Christians, members of other ethnic or religious minority groups like Shi'as in Lebanon, and Iran, or "Sunni revivalists" in Egypt, also revolve around the political-religious themes articulated by leaders who in the case of persons like Fadlallah, Khomeini, or Qutb are charismatic leaders. The alignment of religion, ethnicity, specific political approaches to "the struggle" and in many cases, the presence of charismatic leaders at the helm of terrorist groups, seems to suggest some correlation between those factors and terrorist group formation that requires further investigation. In making the case for distinctions between Middle East terrorist groups led by charismatic leaders and those that are not, we need to isolate and identify, among other things, empirical trends in Middle East terrorist assault data to explore that conceptualization. It is to that fundamental matter and to other trends in Middle East terrorist group-type behavior that we now turn.

Notes

1. Reiss and Roth 1993, 296.
2. Ibid.
3. Piscatori alludes to that idea in his discussion about Islamic fundamentalism (Piscatori 1994).
4. The importance of an "Islamic Empire" in the struggle against Israel is underscored by Dr. Saud Shawa of Gaza City. For Shawa, "Nothing will stop the Jewish state except an Islamic state, but not on the model we can see—Saudi Arabia, for instance, but along the steps of the original state of the prophet Mohamed. Everything of life and death was destroyed by our prophet—from personal life to international law" (Geyer 1995, 11).
5. Ayalon 1989, 72-73, 79; Dawisha 1986, 87.
6. Practitioners of Sunni and Shia Islam chronicle the significant religious distance between those traditions to different lineages that begin with the Prophet Mohammed. Kramer describes Shi'ite lineage as able to trace an arc to Hussein, son of Ali, and Imam 'Ali, who himself was the brother-in-law and cousin of the Prophet Mohammed (Kramer 1997, 85-86). Zvi Ankori, a leading authority on Jewish history in the Arab world, describes Sunni Islam as the "mainview" of Islam and Shi'ism as "sectarianism" (Zvi Ankori, classroom discussion, July 1976, Harvard University). In a similar vein, Bernard Lewis tells us that, "Shi'ism became essentially the expression in religious terms of opposition to the state and the established order, acceptance of which meant conformity to the Sunni or mainstream, Islamic doctrine" (Lewis 1993, 73). See also Bosworth 1982, 48, 63, Khalaf 1982, 116, 118, Lewis 1979, 405, 108.
7. Auda 1994, 380, 383-384.
8. Abu-Amr 1997, 240.
9. Yaari 1990; Seriphis 1990, 2; O'Ballance 1998, 168.
10. Abu-Amr 1997, 225.
11. Undoubtedly, Abdel Aziz al Rantisi, Shaykh Ahmad Yassin and the other leaders of Hamas are not charismatic leaders in the sense that Weber uses the term. See Seriphis 1990, 2; Sela 1989c, 1.
12. Auda 1994, 375; Anderson, Seibert and Wagner 1998, 75-76.
13. Auda 1994, 376.
14. Smith 1996, 161.
15. Auda 1994, 383; Anderson, Seibert and Wagner 1998, 76.
16. Anderson, Seibert and Wagner 1998; Auda 1997, 406 n10.
17. Anderson, Seibert and Wagner 1998, 76.
18. Dr. Frederic S. Pearson made this point at the Mediating Theory and Democratic Systems "Brown Bag" symposium "Understanding Terrorism," Center for Peace and Conflict Studies, Wayne State University, September 28, 1998. See Reiss and Roth 1993.

19. Abu-Amr 1997, 227; Reiss and Roth 1993, 297.
20. Allen 1974, 306.
21. Ibid., 310.
22. Reiss and Roth 1993, 297.
23. Allen 1974, 311; Smith 1996, 73-74; Sachar 1976, 199.
24. Schlagheck 1988, 111.
25. Reiss and Roth 1993, 297; Allen 1974; Auda 1994.
26. Reiss and Roth 1993, 297; Allen 1974; Smith 1996.
27. Smith 1996, 95-98.
28. Reiss and Roth 1993, 291-305.
29. Abu-Amr 1997, 235; Reiss and Roth 1993, 297.
30. O'Ballance 1998, 26.
31. Abu-Amr 1997, 235.
32. Jeddah 'Ukaz 1990, 16, Foreign Broadcast Information Service Translation (FBIS).
33. Gaffney 1997, 275.
34. Abu-Amr 1997, 252, 232.
35. Ibid., 241.
36. O'Ballance 1997, 167.
37. Legrain 1994, 423; Piscatori 1994, 367.
38. Auda 1994, 397.
39. Ibid., 382.
40. Auda 1994, 382-383; O'Ballance 1997, 26; *Jerusalem Post* 1990a, 3.
41. Ibid., 401.
42. Taheri 1987, 187, 188.
43. Ibid., 186.
44. See *Jerusalem Post* 1990a, 3. Since al-Jihad (Egypt) and Gama'a el Islamiya each take responsibility for terrorist acts independently, this study classifies those groups separately. With respect to how Islamic fundamentalists view non-believers, Taheri reports, "... Qutbism bases its view of the world on a cut and dried Manichean division of all phenomena into good and evil, and Islamic and anti-Islamic ..." (Taheri 1987, 186).
45. Auda 1994, 375; Gaffney 1997, 274.
46. Auda 1994, 375.
47. Piscatori 1994, 361, 362.
48. Gaffney 1997, 263-264.
49. Reiss and Roth 1993, 291-305; Gaffney 1997.
50. Gaffney 1994, 265.
51. Anderson, Seibert and Wagner 1998, 93-95.
52. Kramer 1997, 122-123.
53. Anderson, Seibert, and Wagner 1998, 66; Smith 1996, 12.
54. Ibid., 92.

55. Anderson, Seibert, and Wagner 1998; Brown 1994, 102-104.
56. Anderson, Seibert, and Wagner 1998, 92-93.
57. Norton 1987, 44.
58. Reiss and Roth 1993, 297.
59. Brown 1994, 264-267.
60. Norton 1987, 46.
61. Ibid., 47-48.
62. Ibid., 48.
63. Kramer 1997, 94.
64. Norton 1987, 42.
65. Norton 1987, 51.
66. Norton 1987, 46; Norton 1988, 16-17. It seems likely that "the radical Shi'ite Moslem group" known as the "Sadr Brigades" is, at the least, connected with Islamic Amal (*Jerusalem Post* 1984a, 1; *Jerusalem Post* 1985a, 1). Although Musa al-Sadr certainly was a "charismatic leader" for the Shia community in Lebanon in ways that conform to Weber's definition, it remains unclear whether or not his popularity transcended from the political into the realm of terrorism. For example, Dawisha reports only that "by 1978, through the systematic work of the HSIC [the Higher Shi'ite Islamic Council] and Amal, the Shi'ite community had developed an extensive political, social and military infrastructure" (Dawisha 1986, 93-94, 100, 124). In fact, Taheri, like Norton, suggests that military infrastructure was created for self-defense against the Palestinians. Taheri tells us, "over the years Palestinian guerilla groups established bases in the south, on the border with Israel, and by 1971 were virtual masters of the region, which is inhabited almost exclusively by Shi'ites" (Taheri 1987, 76-77). Bearing that in mind, and given that Musa al-Sadr probably died before many Shi'ite terrorism acts happened, Amal is classified as a theocentric group.
67. Norton 1987, 46.
68. Norton 1988, 16; Kedourie 1992, 242-243.
69. Kramer 1997.
70. Parsons 1964, 328, 358-363, 363-386.
71. See USDOD 1988, 15; Taheri 1987, 89. Taheri asserts that, "there are two key concepts in the organization of the Party of Allah. The first is leadership. The supreme leader, Ayatollah Khomeini, is no political leader in the ordinary sense of the term, but represents Allah's will on earth. He does not have to convey his orders through any official party hierarchy; if he makes his commands known in a radio of TV broadcast he will be instantly and blindly obeyed. He does not have to be specific in giving his orders; it is sufficient for him to give a hint, and the rest will be explained by his representatives and the mass'uls" (Taheri 1987).

Consider how that passage from Taheri's work dovetails perfectly with

Weber's description of "charismatic authority." Weber tells us, "The genuine prophet, like the genuine military leader and every true leader in this sense, preaches, creates, or demands new obligations. In the pure type of charisma, these are imposed on the authority of revolution by oracles, or the leaders own will, and are recognized by the members of the religious, military or party group because they come from such a source. Recognition is a duty. Charismatic authority is thus specifically outside the realm of everyday routine and the profane sphere" (Parsons 1964, 361). Other works that provide useful ways to look at leadership dynamics include Nutting 1923; Zeleney 1939; Jenkins 1947; Gibb 1947; Moore and Smith 1953; Stephenson 1954; Morris 1964 and Stogdill 1974. See also Rubin 1993, 2; Rotem and Rudge 1993, 2; Rotem 1993c, 2; Rotem 1993b, 2; Rudge 1991b, 1.

72. Jaber 1997, 47.
73. Kramer 1997.
74. Ibid., 98.
75. Ibid., 109, 106, 111.
76. Norton 1987, 57.
77. Kramer 1997, 122-123.
78. Kramer 1997.
79. Ibid., 108-109.
80. Rudge 1991a, 12.
81. Cubert 1998, 93 n23.
82. *Jerusalem Post* 1991, 4.
83. Long 1990, 30.
84. Alexander and Sinai 1989, 37; Cobban 1984, 23, 33, USDOD 1988, 12.
85. Cobban 1984, 33, 23.
86. USDOD 1988, 12; Jenkins 1988, 279.
87. Safran 1978, 62.
88. Yaari 1970, 29; Cobban 1984, 6; Livingstone and Halevy 1990, 67.
89. Yaari 1970, 16.
90. Livingstone and Halevy 1990, 65.
91. Ibid.
92. Yaari 1970, 25.
93. Livingstone and Halevy 1990, 68; Yaari 1970, 25.
94. Gresh 1983, 29.
95. Reiss and Roth 1993, 297.
96. Nassar 1991, 82-84.
97. Yaari 1970, 17-18.
98. Nassar 1991; Gresh 1983; Livingstone and Halevy 1990; Yaari 1970; Cobban 1984.
99. Livingstone and Halevy 1996, 142,
100. Yaari 1970, 31-32.

101. Gresch 1983, 32.

102. Yaari 1970, 40.

103. The linkage between those local organizations and Fatah is made explicit in several *Jerusalem Post* articles. For example, see *Jerusalem Post* 1992a, 2; Blitzer 1989, 12; Lahoud 1992, 18; *Jerusalem Post* 1993b, 2; Immanuel 1992a, 1.

104. USDOD 1988, 12; Cobban 1984, 96; Kaplan and Sela 1989, 1; Long 1990, 178.

105. *Jerusalem Post* 1992a, 2; Blitzer 1989, 12; Lahoud 1992, 18; *Jerusalem Post* 1993b, 2; Immanuel 1992a, 1.

106. Cubert 1997, 142-143.

107. Ibid.

108. See Long 1990, 193; Alexander and Sinai 1989, 29-49; Khouri 1976, 357-358; Cobban 1984, 29; Dawisha 1986, 80-85. Technically, while the PLO is composed of some "affiliated" terrorist groups that would fall into categories other than ethnocentric (i.e., PFLP is coded as ideo-ethnocentric charismatic) PLO is coded as ethnocentric because it is under the direct control of Yasser Arafat, who like Ahmad Shuqairy, was not a "charismatic leader." Moreover no "charismatic leader" of those terrorist groups belonged to the PLO Executive Committee or the Fatah Central Committee (DIA 1992).

109. Long 1990, 193.

110. Seale 1992, 76-77; Nassar 1991, 19; Cobban 1984, 28.

111. Yaari 1970, 44-45.

112. Livingstone and Halevy 1990, 68; Cobban 1984, 30, 33.

113. Nassar 1991, 53.

114. Nassar 1991, 53-54; Livingstone and Halevy 1990, 68-69.

115. Seale 1992, 94; Gresh 1988, 133-136.

116. Melman 1986, 97.

117. Ibid.

118. Alexander and Sinai 1989, 46; USDOD 1988, 8; Long 1990, 42.

119. USDOD 1988, 9; Long 1990, 42; Cobban 1984, 148, 140-141.

120. Cobban 1984, 140-141; Alexander and Sinai 1989, 41, 46-47, 159, 186, 189; Long 1990, 41-42; Dawisha 1986, 80.

121. Long 1990, 42.

122. Long 1990, 30-31; Cobban 1984, 148.

123. Alexander and Sinai 1989, 159.

124. USDOD 1988, 9; Long 1990, 42; Alexander and Sinai 1989, 47.

125. Alexander and Sinai 1989, 44; Directorate of Intelligence 1992; Cobban 1984, 163-164.

126. Nasr 1997, 91.

127. Directorate of Intelligence 1992.

128. The CIA (Directorate of Intelligence, CIA, July 1992) categorizes the Arab Liberation Front as a "PLO member group." Moreover, Long states that ALF's "Ideology/ethnic-national identification" is "Palestinian nationalist, Ba'thist" (Long 1990, 168).

129. Alexander and Sinai 1989, 44-45; Cobban 1984, 157-161.

130. Long (1990, 42) tells us that, "Saiqa (Thunderbolt) was formed under the aegis of the ruling Syrian Ba'th Party in October 1969, its members mainly drawn from Palestinians living in Syria."

131. USDOD 1988, 29-30.

132. See Alexander and Sinai 1989, 45-46. Alexander and Sinai's estimation of 2,000 armed combatants was used for the purposes of this study. On the other hand, CIA estimates that the Abu Musa Faction has an "approximate membership" of 500. See Directorate of Intelligence (1992). Unfortunately, there is no clear-cut choice to make about which of these two statistics to use. An unscientific comparison of data on several groups reveal that estimates vary greatly. In two cases, CIA estimates were somewhat low when compared to data from other sources. For example, in the case of DFLP, USDOD (1988, 10) estimates a membership of 500, Alexander and Sinai (1989, 42) estimate a membership of 1,000, Long (1990, 174) estimates 500 members, and Directorate of Intelligence (1992) assess membership at 300-350. Similarly, in the case of PLF, USDOD (1988, 22) estimates membership at 300, Alexander and Sinai (1989, 43) suggest membership is around 300, and Directorate of Intelligence (1992) puts the number at 200.

133. See Directorate of Intelligence 1992. In this instance, both the United States Department of Defense (1988, 28) and Long (1990, 195) have estimates of 200 and 100-200 respectively. These figures vary from the estimate provided by CIA. Nonetheless, all of those estimates categorize the Popular Struggle Front (PSF) as a "moderate" size group according to the scale used in this study. See Directorate of Intelligence 1992. In the case of the Palestine Liberation Front (PLF) estimates by the United States Department of Defense, and Alexander and Sinai were very similar. See USDOD (1988, 22). Alexander and Sinai (1989, 43).

134. See Directorate of Intelligence 1992. Other estimates were similar. Irrespective of which statistics are used, the Palestinian Liberation Front (PLF) is classified as a "moderate" size terrorist group.

135. See Alexander and Sinai 1989, 47-48. There is a general consensus on the appropriate size of the Abu Nidal Organization (ANO). See also USDOD (1988, 5); Directorate of Intelligence (1992).

136. USDOD 1988, 5.

137. Alexander and Sinai 1988, 47-48; USDOD 1988, 5.

138. Seale 1992, 96.

139. Melman 1986, 77; Seale 1992, 93.

140. Seale 1992, 94.

141. Melman 1986; Seale 1992.
142. Seale 1992, 93.
143. Seale 1992, 94, 160; Melman 1986, 98.
144. Seale 1992, 97, 95; Melman 1986, 103.
145. Melman 1986, 92.
146. Seale 1992, 91; Melman 1986, 83.
147. Seale 1992, 86.
148. Melman 1986, 102.
149. Seale 1992, 109, Melman 1986, 125-126, 94.
150. Nasr 1997, 91.
151. Seale 1992, 58.
152. Melman 1986, 63.
153. Ibid., 58-59.
154. Ibid., 85, 84.
155. Ibid., 85.
156. Reiss and Roth 1993, 297.
157. Seale 1992, 6.
158. Ibid., 197.
159. Melman 1986, 76.
160. Alexander and Sinai 1988, 49; Long 1990, 211 n11; Melman 1986, 88, 83, 195.
161. Peleg 1988, 541.
162. *Jerusalem Post* 1974a, 2.
163. Mickolus 1980, 483. With respect to the ACO's composition, it can be extrapolated from the few newspaper accounts that are available that the organization consists of a group of persons with differing backgrounds who share common Marxist-Leninist principles. Newspaper accounts of Syrian proceedings are informative and provide insight into ACO group dynamics. It is reported that "two other Palestinians, including a woman and a Syrian were sentenced to life imprisonment at hard labor, and a Palestinian and two Jordanians were sentenced to 15 years imprisonment at hard labor" (*Jerusalem Post* 1975c, 1; *Jerusalem Post* 1975d, 1; Pace 1975; *New York Times* 1975; *New York Times* 1977; Schmid and Jongman 1988, 669). Also see Schlagheck's description of how "symbolism" is inextricably bound up with terrorism (Schlagheck 1988, 2-3).
164. USDOD 1988.
165. USDOD 1988, 24; Alexander and Sinai 1989, 4041; Long 1990, 30, 41, 109, 115, 195; Cobban 1984, 140-152; Taheri 1987, 76; Schiller 1988, 99; TVI Report Profile 1989b, 10.
166. Cobban 1984, 140-141.
167. Gresh 1988, 35-36.
168. Cobban 1984, 141.

169. Ibid. 141-142.

170. Livingstone and Halevy 1990, 69.

171. Cobban 1984, 142; Livingstone and Halevy 1990, 69.

172. Cobban 1984, 142-143.

173. Cobban 1984, 140-153, 142; Anderson Seibert and Wagner 1998; Smith 1996.

174. Ibid., 145.

175. Ibid., 143.

176. Livingstone and Halevy 1990, 221.

177. Ibid., 143.

178. Alexander and Sinai 1989, 41-42; Long 1990, 22, 41-42, 173-174; USDOD 1988, 10; Cobban 1984, 152-157.

179. Cobban 1984, 142.

180. Ibid., 145.

181. Alexander and Sinai 1989, 41-42, 47; Long 1990, 22; Directorate of Intelligence 1992.

182. Alexander and Sinai 1989, 47, 42-43, USDOD 1988, 9, 26, Long 1990, 30-31, 42, 41, 109, 196; Cobban 1984, 148, 161-163; Dawisha 1986, 80, 82, 83, 114; Directorate of Intelligence 1992.

183. Alexander and Sinai 1989, 186.

184. Cobban 1984, 161; Alexander and Sinai 1989, 42, 51; USDOD 1988, 26-27; Long 1990, 41, 109, 196; Dawisha 1986, 82, 83, 114; Directorate of Intelligence 1992.

185. USDOD 1988, 26; Directorate of Intelligence 1992.

186. Long 1990, 30, 43; Lustick 1988, 67-71; Norton 1988, 7-8; Wilkinson 1986, 204-205; Lustick 1993, 368, 538 n41.

187. Sprinzak 1991, 290.

188. Sprinzak 1991, 296.

189. Sprinzak 1991, 298; Don-Yehiya 1994, 266-267.

190. Demant 1994, 1; Don-Yehiya 1994, 272.

191. Sprinzak 1991, 118, 228. Interestingly enough, AbuKhalil makes a similar analogy to Marxist-Leninism, and the structural shape of Hezbollah. See AbuKhalil,

192. Sprinzak 1991, 111-112.

193. Don-Yehiya 1994, 270.

194. Sprinzak 1991, 125.

195. Ibid., 300.

196. Ibid., 64; Helmreich 1996, 8.

197. Sprinzak 1991.

198. Demant 1994, 6; Helmreich 1996, 8.

199. Sprinzak 1988, 197-198, 200, 213, 214.

200. Sprinzak 1988, 194-216; Wilkinson 1986, 204-205; Lustick 1988, 67; Merkel 1986, 25; Peri 1983, 98, 99, 268-272; Smooha 1978, 231-237, 406.

201. Sprinzak 1988, 200, 199.

202. Sprinzak 1991, 96-98, 156.

203. Sprinzak 1991.

204. Sprinzak 1988, 200, 199; Sprinzak 1991, 97.

205. *Jerusalem Post* 1984b, 5; Sprinzak 1988, 200, 194, 214; Rosenberg 1984a, 1, 2; Rosenberg 1984b, 1, 17; Rosenberg 1984c, 1, 2; Rosenberg 1984d, 1, 10, *Jerusalem Post* 1983c, 1, 2; *Jerusalem Post* 1983b, 1, 2; Richardson and Rosenberg 1984, 1, 8; Wilkinson 1977, 204-205.

206. Reiss and Roth 1993, 303.

207. Sprinzak 1991.

208. Demant 1996, 7.

209. Reiss and Roth 1993, 303.

210. Ibid., 297.

211. Ibid. In fact, Helmreich, who draws on Smelser's work on "social movements" actually labels this particular terrorist assault as a "precipitating event" (Helmreich 1996, 6).

212. Sprinzak 1991, 96.

213. Ibid., 257.

214. Ibid.

215. "The Neturei Karta," Moshe Keren reports, is "an ultra-orthodox Jewish sect whose members do not recognize the State of Israel ..." (Lustick 1980, 115). *Jerusalem Post* 1978, 2; *Jerusalem Post* 1979, 2; Rosenberg 1983, 1; *Jerusalem Post* 1983a, 2.

216. Brilliant 1982b, 2; Brilliant 1982a, 1, 12.

217. Ibid.

218. Yudelman 1984, 1; *Jerusalem Post* 1984a, 1.

219. Immanuel 1992b, 3.

220. Sela 1989a, 2; Sela 1989b, 1; Izenberg 1989, 1; Sprinzak 1991; Lustick 1998, personal correspondence; Lustick 1993, 411, 554-555 n47.

221. Friedler 1989, 1; *Jerusalem Post* 1989a, 1.

222. Sprinzak 1991, 283.

223. Ibid., 284.

224. Lustick 1993, 411, 554-555 n47; Lustick 1998, personal correspondence, August 7. Letter from Dr. Ian S. Lustick, Department of Political Science, University of Pennsylvania. That information raises some interesting questions about the permeability between particular Israeli political parties and terrorist groups that requires further investigation.

225. Brown 1994, 248.

226. Reiss and Roth 1993, 300.

227. Ibid., 303.

228. Mergui and Simonnot 1987, 16.

229. Helmreich 1996, 6.

230. Hoffman 1984, 13, 15 n14, 11.

231. Hoffman 1984, 13, 15 n14, 11; Keinon 1993, 3.

232. Sprinzak 1991, 211, 214, 218.

233. Ibid., 227.

234. Ibid., 245, 5, 211, 305.

235. Hanauer 1995, 262.

236. Sprinzak (1991, 84) tells us some 26,000 Israelis voted for the Kach Party in 1984.

237. Ibid., 242.

238. Demant 1994, 20.

239. Reiss and Roth 1993, 297.

240. Mergui and Simonnot 1987, 27.

241. Ibid.

242. O'Ballance 1997, 19-20; Sprinzak 1993, 250; McKinley Jr. 1990, L29; Kifner 1990, B1, B4.

243. Schlein 1991, 8, 91840117A MA'ARIV, JPRS-NEA-91-011 5 February 1991.

244. Judean Voice in English (internet) FBIS-NES-95-169 31 August 1995, 37.

245. Schlein 1995, 5 MA'ARIV (HAYOM supplement) 11 September 1995 - FBIS-NES-176 12 September 1995, 40.

246. Nelan 1994, 39-41; Hutman 1994, 1; *Jerusalem Post* 1992b, 1; Keinon 1993, 3; Schacter and Rotem 1990, 1; Haberman 1994.

247. Baldwin 1971; Baldwin 1985.

Chapter Five

Middle East Terrorism 1968-1993: An Empirical Analysis of Terrorist Group-Type Behavior

The study of political terrorism demands that research begin to move over and beyond theoretically threadbare accounts of what happened and where, toward more rigorous and scientific efforts. This analysis uses empirical data to establish what some parameters of Middle East terrorism are, thereby in effect providing fresh insight for scholars and policymakers into what terrorism is all about.

An underlying theme of some important works on terrorism is that the rationality assumption in decision-making is as valid for terrorist tacticians as it is for the political leadership of nation-states.[1] What seems significant here is to understand that the terrorist who straps pipe bombs around his or her waist and boards a bus may in fact be acting rationally.[2] Taken one step further, this way of thinking about terrorism means that terrorist group activity and, in the narrower sense, terrorist group targeting practices, are based on much more than chance and opportunity.

Eight Middle East terrorist group-types are crafted for study that are differentiated according to ideology, the presence or absence of a charismatic leader, and hence, recruitment. Plainly, this classification scheme draws from empirical observations of the political landscape, like Dr. George Habash's Popular Front for the Liberation of Palestine (PFLP),

Naif Hawatmah's Democratic Front for the Liberation of Palestine (DFLP), Sabri al- Banna's Abu Nidal Organization (ANO), Dr. Wadi Haddad's Popular Front for the Liberation of Palestine-Special Operations Group (PFLP-SOG), and Rabbi Meir Kahane's Jewish Defense League (JDL), as well as from authoritative works on Middle East terrorism and "charismatic authority."[3]

The dependent variable is target, while the independent and intervening variables tested include: political ideology, terrorist group size, terrorist group age, location, and political events. Several theoretical propositions about the major roles those variables play in determining terrorist group behavior are explored. Those hypotheses about Middle East terrorist group-types share a set of interconnections that are twofold in nature. At a basic level, they serve to flesh out the fundamental characteristics of Middle East terrorism by group-type, moving from suppositions to detect differences in targeting patterns, to suppositions that help to provide a more complete picture about the intensity of terrorist acts (i.e., number of deaths, wounded, and level of property damage). At a theoretical level, those hypotheses furnish analytical constructs that make it possible to breathe life into the underlying theme of this study, namely that meaningful distinctions can be made between varieties of "structuralist" and "non-structuralist" Middle East terrorist group-types in terms of target choice.

Typology Construction

In the broadest sense, those group-types and hypotheses presuppose and derive from a Middle East terrorist group-type typology that is based on three defining characteristics: ideology, goals, and recruitment patterns. It is critical to recognize that terrorist group defining characteristics and attributes are not necessarily interchangeable. When defining characteristics are the basis of group-types, no terrorist group should be able to fall into more than one group-type category. For example, many religious fundamentalist terrorist groups are rather recent creations. Nonetheless, age is not a defining characteristic because it does not make it possible, for example, to categorize a group that resembles Hezbollah in ideological terms but was formed before 1980, a time when many Islamic fundamentalist groups were not a part of the Middle East political landscape. In a similar vein, size is not a defining characteristic because larger and smaller groups abound in many of the eight terrorist group-types that are constructed.

On the other hand, ideology, goals, and recruitment patterns are defining characteristics between group-types that are useful for the construction of a functional terrorist typology. In its role as a key explanatory variable for terrorist group behavior, political ideology has been discussed in depth in Chapter Three. What seems significant here is that ideology differs fundamentally between religious groups, nationalist-irredentist groups, and Marxist-Leninist groups with profound and lasting implications for creating a framework for terrorist activity.

A second characteristic that distinguishes between terrorist group-types is goals. Goals, which presuppose and derive from the ideology espoused by a terrorist group, are necessarily different for different terrorist group-types. An underlying theme of this typology is the considerable conceptual distance between ideology and goals, the latter really amounting to tactical alternatives, like in the case of Islamic revivalist terrorist groups (theocentric terrorist groups), a single Islamic state, a confederation of Islamic states, the destruction of Israel, or the destruction of contemporary Sunni regimes.

In this typology, the strategic goals for different terrorist groups can be broken down into four categories of "utopia" state types. Those state types include: an Islamic state in Palestine and/or at other locations in the Middle East; a secular Palestinian state; a Marxist-Leninist state in Palestine and/or at other locations in the Middle East; a religious Jewish state in Israel. The construction of utopian types that are then incorporated into a terrorism typology is a concept that is neither new nor original. In the broader sense, Schmid and Jongman tell us that, "typologies are ideal type classifications, not 'true' reflections of the real world which include impure cases and exceptions."[4]

A third defining characteristic that distinguishes between terrorist group-types is recruitment patterns. For example, in the case of religious fundamentalist terrorist groups led by a charismatic leader, recruits are drawn from the ranks of followers who view their leader as the guidepost for the struggle. In the case of Hezbollah for instance, new recruits are drawn by the spiritual teachings of Ayatollah Sayyid Muhammed Hussayn Fadlallah, and ultimately by the spiritual teachings of the late Ayatollah Ruhollah Khomeini of Iran. Interestingly enough, that pattern of charismatic leadership by one man over the group dovetailed with recruitment relatively narrow in scope, seems to be replicated at lower levels of organization. Corporate authors of a prominent journal in the field of terrorism studies report that "the smaller terrorist organizations within Hizbollah may consist only of the relatives of a single extended family or the personal following of a particular leader."[5] AbuKhalil suggests the same idea when he reports that Hezbollah power structures are divided into certain districts where "... an *alim* in a certain district presents to the people the required actions and their general outline. The manner in which a certain act is executed is left to the initiative of the people provided the *alim* intervenes when it is necessary. The *alim-quid* presumably Khumayni in the thought of Hizballah, only presents the outline of the path of action."[6]

Recruitment patterns are also distinctive for religious fundamentalist terrorist groups that have operated under the tutelage of non-charismatic leadership irrespective of whether those groups are Muslim or Jewish. In many cases, recruitment is more narrowly based, drawing on a clan, which for definition purposes, is a close-knit group whose members share common interests and/or values and a common historical legacy.[7] For example, Amal has operated without a charismatic leader since Sayyid Musa al-Sadr vanished mysteriously in 1978 during a trip to Libya.[8] Recall that Norton tells us that Amal recruits from Shi'ites in Lebanon who are interested in making structural political and economic change there to create opportunities for the Shia community.[9] That recruitment pattern seems to hold for the Jewish "Gush Emunim underground" organization known as "Terror Against Terror" or "TNT." When that organization was disbanded by Israelis authorities in 1984, some twenty-five persons from settlements in the West Bank and the Golan Heights who all shared the Jewish fundamentalist vision of a "greater Israel" were arrested.[10]

In the case of Palestinian nationalist groups without charismatic leadership like al-Fatah, recruitment seems to favor Palestinians who "... come from low income backgrounds ... most are recruited from refugee camps."[11] By contrast, in the case of Palestinian terrorist groups with charismatic leaders that espouse Marxist-Leninist ideology, recruits are drawn over and beyond national boundaries, but, in the narrower sense, presumably share their charismatic leader's vision of a Marxist-Leninist approach to "the struggle." For example, with respect to the PFLP, we are told that in addition to Palestinians, many of whom are still in school, "... non Palestinians (Japanese, Europeans, Germans, Scandinavians and Iranians)" have been inducted.[12] In the case of the PFLP-GC, recruitment also transcends national boundaries, resulting in "current membership ... [that includes] Libyans, Eritreans, Syrians and Tunisians."[13]

This typology, which draws on Starr and Most's work on third world conflicts, is a three dimensional cube with the characteristics ideology, goals, and recruitment, each posited along one axis.[14] Since there are four possible goals available, three types of recruits and three ideology types, the structure of the typology is a 4X3 three-dimensional cube. Consequently thirty-six combinations of terrorist group-types are possible, even though it is clear that not all these possible combinations exist in the real world.[15]

It is possible to extract eight terrorist group-types to study from the three-dimensional terrorist typology cube. Those terrorist group-types include: theocentric, theocentric charismatic, ethnocentric, ethnocentric

Figure 1   A 3-Dimensional Typology Cube of Middle East Terrorist Group-Types

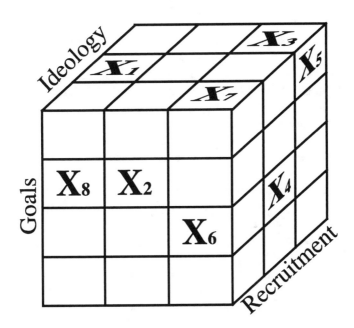

X_1 = Theocentric
X_2 = Theocentric charismatic
X_3 = Ethnocentric
X_4 = Ethnocentric charismatic
X_5 = Ideo-ethnocentric
X_6 = Ideo-ethnocentric charismatic
X_7 = Jewish theocentric
X_8 = Jewish theocentric charismatic

Source: Chasdi, Richard J. 1995.
"The Dynamics of Middle East Terrorism 1968-1993:
A Functional Typology of Terrorist Group-Types."
Ph.D., dissertation, Purdue University.

charismatic, ideo-ethnocentric, ideo-ethnocentric charismatic, Jewish theocentric, Jewish theocentric charismatic. For definitional purposes, theocentric terrorist groups are Islamic fundamentalist or revivalist terrorist groups, ethnocentric terrorist groups are nationalist-irredentist terrorist groups, and ideo-ethnocentric groups are nationalist-irredentist terrorist groups driven by Marxist-Leninist ideology. Those categories are constructed so as to capture, as broadly as possible, the qualitative distinctions between terrorist groups.[16] Moreover, the categories are clearly defined with the aim of making them as mutually exclusive as possible. It should be self-evident where groups, even those relatively similar in nature, should fall in the schema. For example, the Abu Musa Faction and al-Fatah are ethnocentric groups, while the Abu Nidal Organization (ANO) and Muhammed Abu al-Abbas' Palestine Liberation Front (PLF) are ethnocentric charismatic organizations.

Precisely for those reasons, this study eschews more traditional classification schemes that seem to focus on one distinguishing characteristic like ideology, at the expense of others. The theoretical omissions implicit to that approach provide an incomplete picture of the underlying differences between groups that in turn cause operational problems with the group-type categories. In addition, a typology scheme based on the acts a terrorist organization commits is shunned as well since the modus operandi of a terrorist organization can change over time.[17]

Nonetheless, choosing the right terrorist groups to include in a study that uses descriptive statistics is critical. Attention must be focused on terrorist organizations that represent broad differences with respect to ideology, goals, and recruitment patterns. At the same time, those terrorist organizations must represent the broad spectrum with respect to political ideology, group age, group size, and location of the incident because those are independent variables under scrutiny in this study.

What seems significant here is this terrorist group-type typology is "functional" in the sense that it makes it possible to isolate and identify patterns of terrorist group behavior that distinguishes one group-type from another. Another advantage of this typology is that it can accommodate the dissolution of terrorist group-types and the formation of new ones, in contrast to those typologies that classify terrorist groups according to location of incident, or the type of terrorist activity undertaken.

Theoretical Framework and Definition of Terrorism

The theory that drives this study is conceived of as a continuum, with structuralist terrorist group-types at one axis and non-structuralist group-types at the other. In the case of Islamic and/or Arab terrorist group-types, it is proposed that the more "structuralist" a group-type is (i.e., the more the political struggle is viewed as one against a "world system" like capitalism and/or imperialism), the more emphasis is placed on government targets. Conversely, the more "non-structuralist" a group-type is (i.e., the more the political struggle is viewed as one waged against individuals), the more emphasis is placed on civilian targets.[18] It is also proposed that the influence of a charismatic leader ought to increase the intensity of terrorist attacks committed by groups in sync with the prevailing social ideology of Islam and increase the intensity of attacks committed by Arab terrorist groups that embrace alternate systems like Marxism-Leninism.[19] It is expected that Jewish fundamentalist groups should present a radically different picture of terrorist group behavior. To be specific, Jewish fundamentalist groups should attack targets with less intensity than their Islamic counterparts. That is the case because Jewish fundamentalist terrorist groups operate predominately in so-called "friendly" areas such as Israel, the Occupied Territories, and the United States.[20]

For operational purposes, any of the following is considered political terrorism: the threat, practice or promotion of force to influence the political attitudes or policy dispositions of a third party and used against: (1) non-combatants; (2) military personnel in non-combat or peacekeeping roles; (3) combatants, if the aforementioned violates juridical principles of proportionality, military necessity and discrimination; (4) regimes which have not committed egregious violations of the human rights regime that approach Nuremberg category crimes.[21]

Data Collection

A data base for this research was compiled from two sources: *The Jerusalem Post* and Mickolus's data base chronology, *Transnational Terrorism: A Chronology of Events 1968-1979.* Accounts of terrorism from that English daily newspaper make up the vast majority of the data base chronology. Reports of terrorism from January 1, 1978 to December 1993 were taken directly from that newspaper, while entries from January 1968 to August 1978 for sixteen terrorist groups were taken from Mickolus's work.[22] Known acts of "independent" state terrorism (i.e., non-reactive events without interconnections to what some writers call "insurgent terrorism") were excluded from the analysis. It follows that terrorist assaults that happened in the "security zone" in Southern Lebanon were excluded from the data base because, all too frequently, the fundamental question of whether or not a terrorist assault was really an act of state terrorism remained unclear.

So to ensure data compatibility between entries extracted from Mickolus's work and articles drawn from the *Jerusalem Post,* I was careful to use Mickolus's entries on terrorist assaults as a guide to find matching reports whenever possible for the 1968-1978 period. It follows that descriptions of terrorist incident attributes such as numbers of dead and wounded, and property damage, were taken from the *Jerusalem Post* when available. Otherwise, data provided in Mickolus's accounts were used. Plainly, it is clear that my data set, while comprehensive, does not represent nor claim to represent every terrorist assault undertaken for the period of time under consideration. Undoubtedly, several acts of terrorism have been omitted because of the selective nature of accounts for the 1968-1978 period, the extremely large number of unclaimed and uncompleted terrorist assaults, and human error (e.g., doublecounting, miscoding bits of terrorist event information, wrongful inclusion of "terrorism" events).[23]

The Jerusalem Post was chosen as the predominant centerpiece of this data base on Middle East terrorism for several compelling reasons. For one thing, it provides in depth accounts of terrorist assaults inextricably linked to Middle East politics that happen in the Middle East and throughout the world. Those *Jerusalem Post* reports provide descriptions, sometimes very rich, of the players involved, and the political context within which those terrorist assaults take place. Equally important, *Jerusalem Post* accounts chronicle, in extensive and sustained ways, terrorist assaults that did not cause deaths, injuries or property damage or were otherwise thwarted. Regrettably, it is probably no exaggeration to say that the degree of coverage that major U.S. and European papers devote to Middle East terrorism depends in large part on the physical devastation that occurs.

Plainly, my use of *Jerusalem Post* accounts might, for some, raise the generally recognizable issue of source bias. I recognize that some terrorist incidents might not be reported in the *Jerusalem Post* for national security reasons, or lack of access to or interest in low intensity terrorist assaults that happened in other parts of the Middle East. At the same time, it is critical to recall that each assault reported had to dovetail well with the foregoing definition of terrorism before it was included in the data base I constructed. Simply put, that definition served as a gatekeeper: some assaults chronicled in the *Jerusalem Post* as "terrorist acts" were excluded from the data base (e.g., assaults against military personnel on active duty) while other assaults, (e.g., specific incidents of vandalism) with generally recognizable political undercurrents were put in the data base.

Interestingly enough, some newspaper accounts published in the Middle East seem to suffer from source bias, a problem that might presuppose and derive from protracted battles between pro-Western Sunni regimes and Muslim fundamentalist groups. One indication of this, in my judgment, is that many English newspaper accounts describe the all too familiar reality of Muslim fundamentalist terrorist assaults with milque toast descriptions.[24] Compounding the matter further, it seems that some Arabic newspapers share the same underlying problem with respect to accounts about assaults perpetrated by Islamic fundamentalist terrorist groups.[25] Be that as it may, what seems significant here in terms of data gathering, is that newspaper accounts like the foregoing, provide insufficient coverage of Middle East terrorism assaults to be useful for this study.

Coding Scheme and Framework of Analysis

The basic structure of the coding conceptualization consists of "government urban or government rural targets" (coded "govt. targets"), "non-government urban or non-government rural infrastructure" (coded "infrastructure"), and "civilian targets." The first category includes government buildings such as courthouses, military administration and recruitment centers, non-combatant troops such as U.N. and U.S. peacekeepers, and senior military personnel in non-combatant roles. Other "government targets" include major political actors, religious figures (e.g., the Pope), heads of state, parliament members and police officials. The category "non-government urban or non-government rural infrastructure" includes, but is not limited to, energy facilities, oil pipelines, oil tankers, television and radio stations, bridges, and highways. Alternately, "civilian targets" include schools, civilian hospitals, commercial airliners, commuter buses, and marketplaces. The foregoing coding scheme makes it possible to code primary and secondary targets if necessary, by putting together the basic framework components listed above.[26]

With respect to perpetrators, an overwhelming number of terrorist events in this data base were carried out by groups or "proto-groups," and those terrorist assaults were either claimed by terrorist groups, or attributed to them by the governments of Israel, the United States, other governments, or *Jerusalem Post* sources. In the case of "lone assassins," when attribution was not made by the aforementioned sources, I used "contextual analysis" (e.g., the presence or absence of a disclaimer of responsibility for the terrorist assault under consideration) to classify events as to such criteria as motivations of lone assailants and their interconnections, if any, to terrorist organizations. I did look for general corroboration, if possible, from more than one *Jerusalem Post* report in such cases. Other terrorism specialists have used "contextual analysis" to make coding decisions and, in my judgment, have probably found themselves, from time to time, in a position of having to make "judgment call" decisions.[27]

It is probably no exaggeration to say that military and religious events that take place in the Middle East or are otherwise connected with it, have profound and lasting political implications for terrorist groups. Accordingly, political events, as I have defined them, are inclusive of military and religious events such as the Six Day War, the Yom Kippur War, the Lebanon War, Tish B'eav, Yom Kippur, Ramadan, Passover and Rosh Hashanah. Turning to the matter of how causal relationships between "political events" and terrorist group assaults were established, several measures were used, including *Jerusalem Post* attribution (e.g., *Jerusalem Post* sources and/or Israeli police/military sources, attribution made by other governments), terrorist group claims of responsibility as reported in the *Jerusalem Post,* Mickolus's attributions, occasional attributions made by other scholars, and "contextual analysis."

In the case of "contextual analysis" some connections were relatively straightforward, such as the calamitous death of Emil Greenzweig at a "Peace Now" rally in 1983, and terrorist assaults happening on or a few days before Tish B'eav, Land Day, and the Balfour Anniversary, while others involved making interconnections between the terrorist event under consideration and widely known political events that preceded the terrorist event. For example, several Americans and Germans were kidnapped in Beirut in 1987, all within a few days, against the backdrop of articulated opposition by Arab extremists to U.S. policy with respect to the looming prospect of Mohammad Hamadi's extradition to the United States by West Germany and the emergent reality of U.S. backing for Iraq against Iran.[28]

The framework of analysis involves a discussion about broad trends in the behavior and the influence of each independent and intervening terrorism variable under consideration. Specifically, the analysis involves crosstabulation analysis where relative percentages and frequencies for terrorist group-types are presented along with relevant significant test coefficients. The Pearson chi square statistic, degrees of freedom and p values are presented.[29] With respect to this study of Middle East terrorism, the usefulness of crosstabulation analysis is threefold. First, it makes it possible to determine whether or not a statistical association exists between terrorism variables under consideration. Second, because it is a presentation of observed rather than predicted values, crosstabulation analysis is able to isolate and identify empirical trends in those data that will be used to test several hypotheses for validity. Third, crosstabulation analysis serves as a springboard for more sophisticated analysis of terrorism.

At a functional level, in the bar charts and tables on Middle East terrorism to come, the number of missing cases may differ for four possible reasons. First, a missing bit of information in a terrorist assault entry (e.g., level of property damage) would result in exclusion of that entry from analysis of the variable under consideration. Second, in the case of "political events" analysis, the category "reaction to religious events," with two terrorist assaults, was deleted because of conceptual overlap with the category "commemoration of religious holidays." In the case of the distribution of terrorist assaults by group, the group "Palestine Liberation Army (PLA)," with two assaults attributable to it, was removed because of overlap between PLA and the Palestine Liberation Organization (PLO).[30] Third, collaborator killings were excluded from the crosstabulation analysis because such assaults would skew the results. It is commonplace to note very little variation in numbers of deaths, numbers of injuries, and property damage when collaborator killings happen. Fourth, terrorism event entries from January 1968 to August 1978 were excluded from the test to determine frequency by year because of the non-randomness associated with the way those events were extracted from Mickolus's compilation.

For definition purposes, "percent" indicates the percentage of the frequency of a value, like "0 injury," for the total number of terrorist event entries (e.g., Figure 7., 776/1237 or .6273). In turn, a "valid percent" is the percentage of terrorism cases for a value, like "0 injury," with respect to the working data set for a particular test under consideration (e.g., Figure 7., 776/1180 or .6576). "Cumulative Percentage," by contrast, is an aggregate percentage of the valid percent of a value, like "1-50 injuries," coupled with the valid percents of values that came before. For example, the "cum percent" of the value "1-50 injuries" in Figure 6, is 98.2%, the sum of the valid percents 65.8% and 32.5%, taking "rounding off" into account. In turn, "cells with expected frequency less than 5" is a measure presented with some of the crosstabulation analysis findings that describes the percent and number of cells with expected values of less than five observations.[31] Finally, the minimum expected frequency figure presented with some crosstabulation tests under consideration, really serves as a threshold marker for the minimum value of the chi square necessary to appraise, in a meaningful way, whether or not statistical associations exist between "terrorism variables."[32]

Some General Observations about Middle East Terrorism

Relative Frequency of Incidents By Year

For the fifteen year period between 1978 and 1993, the data is comprised of 973 incidents of domestic, transnational, and international terrorism carried out by terrorist groups that either operate or originate in the Middle East and/or are bound up with Middle East politics. It is evident that Middle East terrorism of the sort described is characterized by distinct cycles of activity. That pattern is consistent with the findings of several studies.[33]

With respect to the range of incidents, the greatest number took place in 1993 when 143 occurred (14.7%). The smallest number of incidents happened in 1982 when 28 incidents (2.9%) were carried out (see Figure 2). The "peak years" for Middle East terrorism that occurred between 1978 and 1993 were the years 1978, 1985, 1989, and 1993. Fifty-nine incidents (6.1%) took place in 1978 as compared to 1985 when 84 terrorist incidents (8.6%) were carried out. In 1989, 119 terrorist acts (12.2%) occurred, while 143 incidents (14.7%) took place in 1993. Clearly, there has been a general increase in the frequency of Middle East terrorism from 1978 to 1993.

Terrorist Acts By Group-Type, Group and Location

A breakdown of terrorist incidents by group-type reveals which types of terrorist groups have carried out the greatest number of incidents between 1968 and 1993 (see Figure 3). The data show that ethnocentric terrorist groups carried out the largest number of acts with 204 incidents (18.1%) while the second largest number of acts was carried out by ideo-ethnocentric charismatic groups with 108 incidents (9.6%). Theocentric groups carried out the third largest number of acts with 101 incidents (9.0%). At the other extreme, the fewest number of incidents were committed by ideo-ethnocentric groups with 19 incidents (1.7%).

Among Islamic fundamentalist terrorist groups, theocentric groups carried out 101 acts (9.0%) while 92 incidents (8.2%) were attributable to theocentric charismatic groups. Among Jewish fundamentalist terrorist groups, 61 terrorist acts (5.4%) were attributed to Jewish theocentric charismatic groups while 55 incidents (4.9%) were carried out by Jewish theocentric groups. Terrorist incidents that were thwarted by government agencies or aborted by the group itself amounted to 119 incidents (10.6%). What stands out here is that the single, largest number of terrorist incidents

Figure 2: Relative Frequency of Middle East Terrorist Attacks by Year, 1978-1993

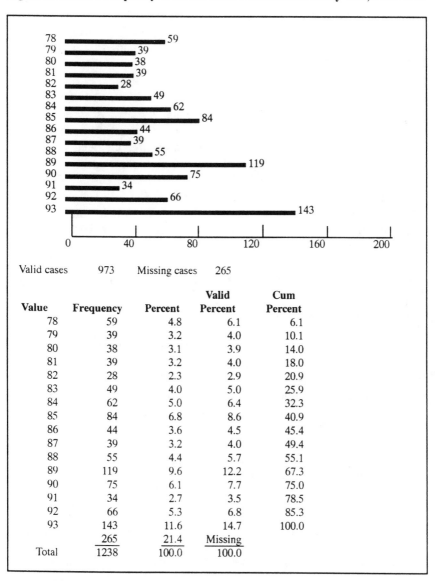

Value	Frequency	Percent	Valid Percent	Cum Percent
78	59	4.8	6.1	6.1
79	39	3.2	4.0	10.1
80	38	3.1	3.9	14.0
81	39	3.2	4.0	18.0
82	28	2.3	2.9	20.9
83	49	4.0	5.0	25.9
84	62	5.0	6.4	32.3
85	84	6.8	8.6	40.9
86	44	3.6	4.5	45.4
87	39	3.2	4.0	49.4
88	55	4.4	5.7	55.1
89	119	9.6	12.2	67.3
90	75	6.1	7.7	75.0
91	34	2.7	3.5	78.5
92	66	5.3	6.8	85.3
93	143	11.6	14.7	100.0
	265	21.4	Missing	
Total	1238	100.0	100.0	

Valid cases   973   Missing cases   265

Source: Chasdi, Richard J. 1995. "The Dynamics of Middle East Terrorism, 1968-1993: A Functional Typology of Terrorist Group-Types." Ph.D. dissertation. Purdue University.

were unclaimed acts (311 acts or 27.7%).

If the analysis is directed toward particular terrorist groups it becomes clear which groups carried out the greatest and the fewest number of terrorist acts from 1968 to 1993 (see Figure 4). Among Arab and/or Islamic fundamentalist groups, the most prolific group was al-Fatah, which carried out 118 acts (15.6%). Following closely behind, the Popular Front for the Liberation of Palestine (PFLP) and Hezbollah committed 94 acts (12.5%) and 88 acts (11.7%) respectively. The least dynamic group among Arab and/or Islamic fundamentalist groups was the Popular Front for the Liberation of Palestine - Special Operations Group (PFLP-SOG) which carried out two incidents (.3%). Other low activity terrorist groups include the Arab Organization of 15 May, which carried out seven acts (.9%), the Popular Struggle Front (PSF) which engaged in three incidents (.4%), and the Arab Liberation Front (ALF) which committed three incidents (.4%).

Among Jewish terrorist organizations, the Jewish Defense League (JDL) was most active, having carried out 38 incidents (5.0%). The second most active organization was the JDL offshoot Kach, which carried out 27 incidents (3.6%). The least dynamic Jewish terrorist organizations include the Hasmoneans with one incident, the Lifta Gang with one incident, and Kahane Chai with two incidents.

An analysis of terrorist incidents by location reveals where the largest number of acts have occurred between 1968-1993 (see Figure 5). The largest number of terrorist attacks took place in Israel where 436 incidents (35.4%) happened. The second largest number of incidents occurred in the Occupied Territories with 368 incidents (29.9%). Somewhat ironically, the number of terrorist acts perpetrated by Middle East terrorist groups in Europe (155 incidents or 12.6%) was almost equal to the number that happened at other Middle East locations (195 incidents or 15.8%). The smallest number of terrorist attacks took place in the United States with 59 incidents (4.8%).[34]

Terrorist Act Characteristics: Fatalities, Injuries, Property Damage, Target Preference

A widely shared belief by scholars and policymakers is that terrorism does not cause large numbers of fatalities and injuries or a substantial amount of property damage.[35] That notion is supported by the analysis. For example, only 377 incidents (31.0%) out of 1,215 resulted in the deaths of between one and fifty persons. In fact, eight hundred and thirty-four incidents (68.6%) that took place between 1968 and 1993 did not cause any deaths (see Figure 5). Further, the number of terrorist incidents that resulted

Figure 3: Relative Frequency of Middle East Terrorist Attacks by Group-Type, 1968-1993

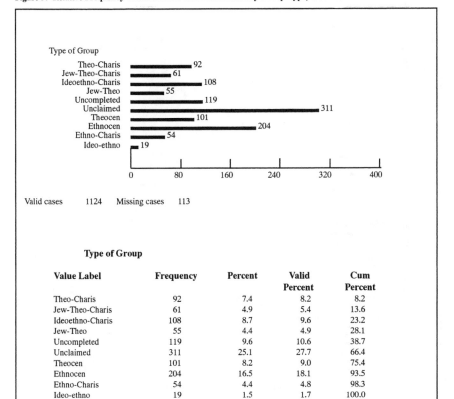

Type of Group

Value Label	Frequency	Percent	Valid Percent	Cum Percent
Theo-Charis	92	7.4	8.2	8.2
Jew-Theo-Charis	61	4.9	5.4	13.6
Ideoethno-Charis	108	8.7	9.6	23.2
Jew-Theo	55	4.4	4.9	28.1
Uncompleted	119	9.6	10.6	38.7
Unclaimed	311	25.1	27.7	66.4
Theocen	101	8.2	9.0	75.4
Ethnocen	204	16.5	18.1	93.5
Ethno-Charis	54	4.4	4.8	98.3
Ideo-ethno	19	1.5	1.7	100.0
	113	9.1	Missing	
Total	1237	100.0	100.0	

Source: Chasdi, Richard J. 1995. "The Dynamics of Middle East Terrorism, 1968-1993: A Functional Typology of Terrorist Group-Types." Ph.D. dissertation. Purdue University.

Figure 4: Relative Frequency of Middle East Terrorist Attacks by Terrorist Group, 1968-1993

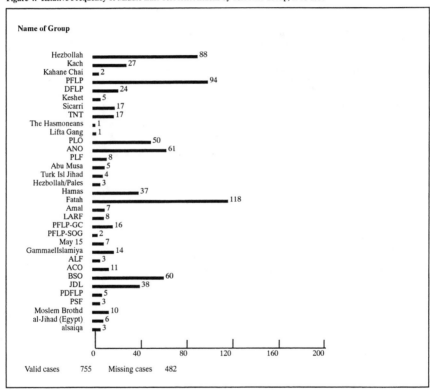

Source: Chasdi, Richard J. 1995. "The Dynamics of Middle East Terrorism, 1968-1993: A Functional Typology of Terrorist Group-Types." Ph.D. dissertation. Purdue University.

Figure 4: (Continued)

Name of Group					
Value Label	**Value**	**Frequency**	**Percent**	**Valid Percent**	**Cum Percent**
Hezbollah	1	88	7.1	11.7	11.7
Kach	2	27	2.2	3.6	15.2
Kahane Chai	3	2	.2	.3	15.5
PFLP	4	94	7.6	12.5	27.9
DFLP	5	24	1.9	3.2	31.1
Keshet	6	5	.4	.7	31.8
Sicarri	7	17	1.4	2.3	34.0
TNT	8	17	1.4	2.3	36.3
The Hasmoneans	9	1	.1	.1	36.4
Lifta Gang	10	1	.1	.1	36.6
PLO	11	50	4.0	6.6	43.2
ANO	12	61	4.9	8.1	51.3
PLF	13	8	.6	1.1	52.3
Abu Musa	14	5	.4	.7	53.0
Turk Isl Jihad	15	4	.3	.5	53.5
Hezbollah/Pales	16	3	.2	.4	53.9
Hamas	17	37	3.0	4.9	58.8
Fatah	18	118	9.5	15.6	74.4
Amal	19	7	.6	.9	75.4
LARF	20	8	.6	1.1	76.4
PFLP-GC	21	16	1.3	2.1	78.5
PFLP-SOG	22	2	.2	.3	78.8
	23	*(PFLP-SG omitted on account of overlap with Group 22 PFLP-SOG)*			
May 15	24	7	.6	.9	79.7
GammaelIslamiya	25	14	1.1	1.9	81.6
ALF	26	3	.2	.4	82.0
ACO	27	11	.9	1.5	83.4
BSO	28	60	4.9	7.9	91.4
JDL	29	38	3.1	5.0	96.4
	30	*(Gush Emunim Undergound omitted on account of overlap with Group 8 TNT))*			
PDFLP	31	5	.4	.7	97.1
PSF	32	3	.2	.4	97.5
Moslem Brothd	33	10	.8	1.3	98.8
al-Jihad (Egypt)	34	6	.5	.8	99.6
alsaiqa	35	3	.2	.4	100.0
Group	36	*(PLA omitted on account of overlap with Group 11 PLO)*			
	--	482	39.0	Missing	
Total	1237	100.0	100.0	100.0	

Source: Chasdi, Richard J. 1995. "The Dynamics of Middle East Terrorism, 1968-1993: A Functional Typology of Terrorist Group-Types." Ph.D. dissertation. Purdue University.

Figure 5: Relative Frequency of Middle East Terrorism by Location, 1968-1993

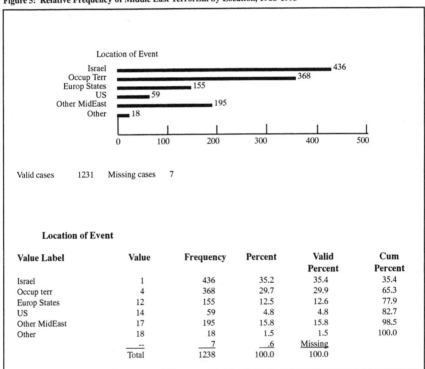

Valid cases   1231   Missing cases   7

Location of Event

Value Label	Value	Frequency	Percent	Valid Percent	Cum Percent
Israel	1	436	35.2	35.4	35.4
Occup terr	4	368	29.7	29.9	65.3
Europ States	12	155	12.5	12.6	77.9
US	14	59	4.8	4.8	82.7
Other MidEast	17	195	15.8	15.8	98.5
Other	18	18	1.5	1.5	100.0
	--	7	.6	Missing	
	Total	1238	100.0	100.0	

Source: Chasdi, Richard J. 1995. "The Dynamics of Middle East Terrorism, 1968-1993: A Functional Typology of Terrorist Group-Types." Ph.D. dissertation. Purdue University.

in over fifty deaths was only four. Those incidents constitute outlier observations, which means that while the sample distribution of terrorist incidents is bell shaped, those observations lie several standard deviations away from the mean for numbers of dead.[36] Nonetheless, a common thread powerfully ties together those "high intensity" terrorist acts. In all four of those extreme outlier observations, the location of the event was at a site outside of Israel and the Occupied Territories.[37]

In a similar vein, terrorist attacks resulted in relatively low numbers of injured persons when compared to the number of people injured in incidents of other forms of political violence.[38] For instance, only 383 incidents (32.5%) out of 1,180 resulted in injuries to between one and fifty persons. In fact, 776 (65.8%) incidents that happened between 1968 and 1993 did not cause any injuries (see Figure 7). Likewise, the number of terrorist incidents that caused injuries to between 51 and 100 persons was only 16 (1.4%). Further still, only five incidents caused injuries to over one hundred people. Clearly, those results mirror the findings of the distribution of death rates since these five incidents took place outside of Israel and the Occupied Territories.[39]

Middle East terrorist assaults also caused relatively low levels of property damage. There were 682 incidents out of 1,096 (62.2%) where no property damage resulted. In 298 acts (27.2%), only slight damage, defined as less than or about $15,000, was caused. Moderate damage, defined as from about $30,000 to $100,000 was inflicted in 63 incidents (5.7%). High levels of damage, defined as from about $100,000 to $1 million, was inflicted in 38 incidents (3.5%). Severe damage in excess of $1 million was caused in 15 incidents (1.4%) (see Figure 8).

A breakdown of terrorist incidents by target type reveals that an overwhelming number were directed against civilian targets. Nine hundred and sixty-nine incidents (80.5%) out of 1,203 involved civilian targets as compared with 234 incidents (19.5%) that involved government targets. Thirty-four incidents (2.7%) involved infrastructure or multiple target combinations (see Figure 9).

The foregoing analysis leads to several intriguing conclusions about the basic parameters of Middle East terrorism. First, terrorism in the Middle East, like terrorism in other parts of the world has a cyclical configuration. The frequency of terrorist attacks ebb and flow in regular patterns. Equally important, it is clear is that there has been a significant increase in Middle East terrorism between 1968 and 1993. Second, the data show that the most dynamic group-type in the region between 1968-1993 was the ethnocentric group-type. The ideo-ethnocentric charismatic group-type placed second, but groups comprising that category were only about half as busy as ethno-

Figure 6: Relative Frequency of Numbers of Dead in Middle East Terrorist Incidents, 1968-1993
(0=0; 1=1 thru 50; 2=51 thru 100)

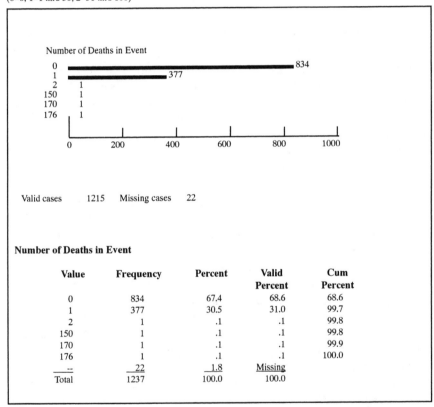

Number of Deaths in Event

Value	Frequency	Percent	Valid Percent	Cum Percent
0	834	67.4	68.6	68.6
1	377	30.5	31.0	99.7
2	1	.1	.1	99.8
150	1	.1	.1	99.8
170	1	.1	.1	99.9
176	1	.1	.1	100.0
--	22	1.8	Missing	
Total	1237	100.0	100.0	

Source: Chasdi, Richard J. 1995. "The Dynamics of Middle East Terrorism, 1968-1993: A Functional Typology of Terrorist Group-Types." Ph.D. dissertation. Purdue University.

Figure 7: Relative Frequency of Numbers of Injured in Middle East Terrorist Incidents, 1968-1993
(0=0; 1=1 thru 50; 2=51 thru 100)

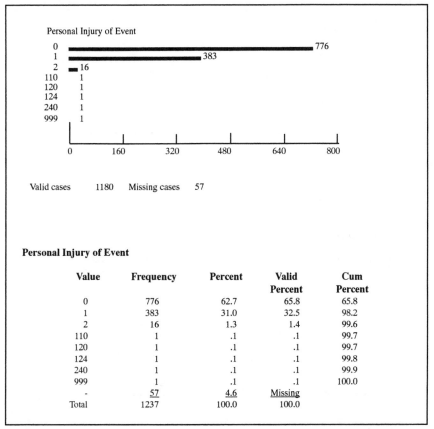

Personal Injury of Event

Value	Frequency	Percent	Valid Percent	Cum Percent
0	776	62.7	65.8	65.8
1	383	31.0	32.5	98.2
2	16	1.3	1.4	99.6
110	1	.1	.1	99.7
120	1	.1	.1	99.7
124	1	.1	.1	99.8
240	1	.1	.1	99.9
999	1	.1	.1	100.0
-	57	4.6	Missing	
Total	1237	100.0	100.0	

Source: Chasdi, Richard J. 1995. "The Dynamics of Middle East Terrorism, 1968-1993: A Functional Typology of Terrorist Group-Types." Ph.D. dissertation. Purdue University.

Figure 8: Levels of Property Damage Caused by Middle East Terrorist Attacks, 1968-1993

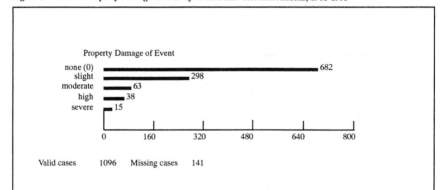

Property Damage of Event

Value Label		Frequency	Percent	Valid Percent	Cum Percent
none (0)		682	55.1	62.2	62.2
slight		298	24.1	27.2	89.4
moderate		63	5.1	5.7	95.2
high		38	3.1	3.5	98.6
severe		15	1.2	1.4	100.0
		141	11.4	Missing	
	Total	1237	100.0	100.0	

Source: Chasdi, Richard J. 1995. "The Dynamics of Middle East Terrorism, 1968-1993: A Functional Typology of Terrorist Group-Types." Ph.D. dissertation. Purdue University.

Figure 9: Relative Frequency of Middle East Terrorism Target Types, 1968-1993

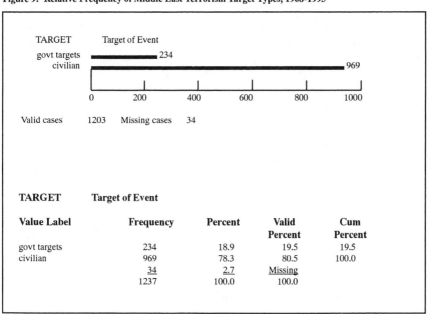

TARGET   Target of Event

Value Label	Frequency	Percent	Valid Percent	Cum Percent
govt targets	234	18.9	19.5	19.5
civilian	969	78.3	80.5	100.0
	34	2.7	Missing	
	1237	100.0	100.0	

Source: Chasdi, Richard J. 1995. "The Dynamics of Middle East Terrorism, 1968-1993: A Functional Typology of Terrorist Group-Types." Ph.D. dissertation. Purdue University.

centric groups. An identical pattern is revealed at the group level. At that
level, the most active group is the ethnocentric group al-Fatah, followed by
an ideo-ethnocentric charismatic group, the Popular Front for the Liberation
of Palestine (PFLP).

Third, with respect to location, the largest number of Middle East
terrorist attacks took place in Israel, followed by the Occupied Territories
which has been under Israeli control since the 1967 Six Day War. Equally
important is the finding that Europe has been plagued with almost as much
Middle East terrorism as other parts of the Middle East between 1968-1993.

Fourth, the analysis shows that most Middle East terrorist events cause
relatively few casualties and little property damage. While devastation rates
remain low consistently, incidents of terrorism that are outlier observations
happen outside of Israel and the Occupied Territories. That finding is
consistent with the idea that the quality of counter-terrorism measures affects
the overall impact of terrorism. Sadly, the bleakest foreboding of all is that
the widely shared conception of Middle East terrorists bent on attacking
civilians is true. While the degree of physical devastation remains low,
terrorists favor assaults on civilian targets by over a 4:1 margin (see
Figure 9).

Variable Analysis

Political Ideology and Target Selection

This section will examine the validity of the following hypotheses that
presuppose and derive from the work of several well known terrorism
specialists:[40]

Hypothesis One: Ideo-ethnocentric terrorist groups will attack government targets (i.e., courthouses, military administration facilities, military
recruitment centers, and non-combatant troops such as U.N. peacekeepers) more often than ethnocentric, theocentric and Jewish theocentric
terrorist groups

Hypothesis Two: Theocentric terrorist groups will attack civilian targets
more often than ethnocentric terrorist groups

Analysis of the influence of group ideology on target selection indicates
a statistical association between the political ideology of a terrorist group
and the type of target chosen. That suggests a systematic and substantive

relationship between those variables.[41] A breakdown of the data shows that ideo-ethnocentric charismatic groups had the highest rate of terrorist attacks directed at civilian targets with 77.8% or 84 out of 108 acts. Ethnocentric groups had the second highest percentage of attacks against civilian targets with 77.5% or 158 out of 204 acts (see Table 2). In turn, Jewish theocentric groups had the third highest percentage of attacks of this sort with 76.4% or 42 out of 55 acts.

At the other extreme, Jewish theocentric charismatic groups and ideo-ethnocentric groups had the lowest rate of civilian target attacks. For Jewish theocentric charismatic groups, 52.5% or 32 out of 61 acts involved civilian targets, as compared to a virtually identical rate of 52.6% or 10 out of 19 acts for ideo-ethnocentric groups. Ethnocentric charismatic groups had the second lowest percentage of attacks against civilian targets with 63.0% or 34 out of 54 acts.

In contrast, ideo-ethnocentric groups had the highest percentage of attacks aimed at government targets with 47.4% or nine out of 19 acts. Jewish theocentric charismatic groups had the second highest rate of attacks against government targets with 44.3% or 27 out of 61 acts. Ethnocentric charismatic groups had the third highest percentage of attacks of this kind with 37.0% or 20 out of 54 incidents.

Attention to target types that do not fall into "civilian" or "government" categories brings the outlier cases into sharp focus. Ideo-ethnocentric charismatic groups had the largest percentage of attacks against infrastructure with 5.6% or 6 out of 108 incidents. Ethnocentric groups attacked infrastructure only 2% of the time (four out of 204 acts) but that was the second highest percentage recorded. Middle East terrorist assaults that involved multiple targets were even more infrequent. Jewish theocentric charismatic groups had the highest rate of attacks where the primary target was a government facility and a civilian target was secondary. Attacks of that sort accounted for a mere 3.3% (2 acts out of 61) of events attributable to that group-type. Ethnocentric groups had the second highest rate of attacks of this kind with 1.5% or 3 out of 204 incidents.

Conversely, theocentric charismatic and theocentric groups had the highest percentage of attacks where the primary target was civilian and a government target was secondary. In both cases, that kind of attack accounted for a mere 1% of the total number of events for each group-type. Finally, ethnocentric groups were the only type to engage in attacks where the primary target was civilian and the secondary target was infrastructure. Attacks of that sort accounted for only .5% (one incident) of all incidents carried out by ethnocentric groups.

A considerable number of uncompleted and unclaimed terrorist assaults

TABLE 2
Relative Frequency of Terrorist Targets
by Group-Type, 1968-1993

TARGET   Target of Event by GTYPE   Type of Group

GTYPE Count Col Pct	Theo-Charis 1	Jew-Theo-Charis 2	Ideoethno-Charis 3	Jew-Theo 4	Uncompleted 5	Row Total
TARGET 1 govt targets	23 25.0	27 44.3	18 16.7	11 20.0	27 23.5	229 20.4
2 infrastructure	1 1.1		6 5.6	2 3.6	3 2.6	19 1.7
3 civilian	67 72.8	32 52.5	84 77.8	42 76.4	82 71.3	861 76.9
6 govt-civilian		2 3.3			2 1.7	7 .6
Column (Continued) Total	92 8.2	61 5.4	108 9.6	55 4.9	115 10.3	1120 100.0

GTYPE Count Col Pct	unclaimed 6	Theocen 7	Ethnocen 8	Ethno-Charis 9	Ideo-ethno 10	Row Total
TARGET 1 govt targets	29 9.3	27 26.7	38 18.6	20 37.0	9 47.4	229 20.4
2 infrastructure	3 1.0		4 2.0			19 1.7
3 civilian	279 89.7	73 72.3	158 77.5	34 63.0	10 52.6	861 76.9
6 govt-civilian			3 1.5			7 .6
Column (Continued) Total	311 27.8	101 9.0	204 18.2	54 4.8	19 1.7	1120 100.0

GTYPE Count Col Pct	Theo-Charis 1	Jew-Theo-Charis 2	Ideoethno-Charis 3	Jew-Theo 4	uncompleted 5	Row Total
TARGET 7 civilian-govt	1 1.1				1 .9	3 .3
9 civilian-infrast						1 .1
Column (Continued) Total	92 8.2	61 5.4	108 9.6	55 4.9	115 10.3	1120 100.0

GTYPE Count Col Pct	unclaimed 6	Theocen 7	Ethnocen 8	Ethno-Charis 9	Ideo-ethno 10	Row Total
TARGET 7 civilian-govt		1 1.0				3 .3
9 civilian-infrast			1 .5			1 .1
Column Total	311 27.8	101 9.0	204 18.2	54 4.8	19 1.7	1120 100.0

Number of Missing Observations: 117

Source: Chasdi, Richard J. 1995. "The Dynamics of Middle East Terrorism, 1968-1993: A Functional Typology of Terrorist Group-Types." Ph.D. dissertation, Purdue University.

involved civilian targets. In the case of uncompleted acts, 71.3% of incidents (82 out of 115 acts) involved civilian targets, while 23.5% (27 out of 115 acts) involved government targets. For unclaimed acts, the rate was even higher with 89.7% (279 out of 311 acts) of attacks aimed at civilian targets as compared to 9.3% (29 out of 311 acts) aimed at government targets. Clearly, that pattern is consistent with the demonstrated preference for civilian targets by the other group-types under consideration.

All of the foregoing leads to the basic question of which hypotheses are supported by the analysis. Hypothesis one is supported by the analysis. I found that ideo-ethnocentric terrorist groups attacked government targets 47.4% of the time, and ethnocentric, theocentric and Jewish theocentric groups only attacked government targets in 18.6%, 26.7% and 20.0% of attacks, respectively. In contrast, the findings do not support hypothesis two. Theocentric terrorist groups carried out 72.3% of attacks against civilian targets, but ethnocentric terrorist groups carried out 77.5% of attacks against civilian targets.

One standout finding of the analysis is that nearly 90% (279 out of 311 incidents) of unclaimed acts were directed against civilian targets. As we have seen, unclaimed acts accounted for 27.8% (311 out of 1,120 acts) of the total, making it the single, largest category of terrorist acts. It is possible to extrapolate from those findings and suggest that in the absence of accountability, the rate of terrorist group civilian target attacks will increase. Those data suggest that if the cause and underlying themes of a political struggle and the goals of both sides are sufficiently clear, it may be in the interest of a terrorist group to engage in some degree of anonymous activity (i.e., a "mixed bundle" of terrorist goods) provided there are other terrorist groups active in the political fray.[42]

Political Ideology and Numbers of Dead

The major aim of this analysis is to test the following hypothesis:[43]

Hypothesis Three: Theocentric terrorist groups will have a higher percentage of terrorist acts that cause deaths than acts committed by ethnocentric and ideo-ethnocentric terrorist groups

The significance testing indicates a statistical association between the political ideology of a terrorist group and numbers of deaths sustained in a terrorist attack.[44] Theocentric groups had the highest percentage of incidents in which one to fifty persons were killed with 57.3% or 55 out of 96 acts. Ethnocentric charismatic groups had the second highest rate of incidents that caused the deaths of between one and fifty people with 55.6% or 30 out of 54 incidents. By comparison, Jewish theocentric charismatic groups had the lowest rate: 4.9% or three out of 61 acts.[45] The latter also had the highest percentage of non-lethal incidents, with 95.1% or 58 out of 61 incidents. Jewish theocentric groups were responsible for the second highest total of non-lethal events with 88.7% or 47 out of 53 events.

One notable statistic is that over 87.7% of unclaimed incidents (271 out of 309 acts) caused no loss of life. Some 12.0% of all unclaimed acts (37 acts) caused the deaths of between one and fifty people. Those findings are consistent with the idea that many unclaimed acts are rather "unspectacular," involving explosive devices and other weapons capable of only low-level damage.[46]

Hypothesis three is supported by the results. I found that 57.3% of theocentric group attacks caused the deaths of between one and fifty people. In contrast, 35.2% of ethnocentric terrorist group attacks and 47.1% of ideo-ethnocentric terrorist group attacks caused between one and fifty fatalities. What also is significant is that Jewish theocentric and Jewish theocentric charismatic groups acted differently than other terrorist groups. Since an overwhelming amount of Jewish terrorism happened in Israel, the Occupied Territories, and the United States, and the relative frequency figures were so low, those findings probably reflect the fact that Jewish terrorist groups operated predominantly in "friendly" areas.[47]

We can interpret those findings further and suggest that leaders of those organizations refrained from overly bloody assaults in part because they saw their groups, to use Hoffman's phrase, as "political pressure groups" that could have some effect on the political process and public policy outcomes.[48] It is not unreasonable to extrapolate from this and surmise that Jewish theocentric terrorist groups in Israel also view low-level violence as necessary for effective participation in the political system.[49]

Rabbi Meir Kahane's comments about the role that violence plays within the context of the Jewish religious and historical experience and JDL activity in the U.S. during the early 1970's provides insight into this way of thinking. Kahane said, "The Jewish concept of violence is that it's a bad thing - but sometimes necessary. I can bring in a hundred quotes. And not just quotes but events in Jewish history. Innocent people should never be harmed. The Jewish concept is that no one pays for the sins of anyone else."[50] The emergent reality is that an exception to this is the Jewish extremists, such as those who live in Hebron, who often subject Palestinians to intimidation and the use of force. In fact, the threat, use, or promotion of force by Jewish extremists in the Occupied Territories is entirely consistent with my definition of terrorism.

TABLE 3
Relative Frequency of Numbers of Dead in Terrorist Incidents
by Group-Type, 1968-1993 (0=0; 1=1 thru 50)

DEATHS	Count Col Pct	GTYPE Theo- Charis 1	Jew-Theo -Charis 2	Ideoethno -Charis 3	Jew-Theo 4	uncomp- leted 5	Page 1 of 4 Row Total
0		61 68.5	58 95.1	66 62.3	47 88.7	116 98.3	821 74.5
1		26 29.2	3 4.9	40 37.7	6 11.3	2 1.7	277 25.1
62							1 .1
150							1 .1
(Continued)	Column Total	89 8.1	61 5.5	106 9.6	53 4.8	118 10.7	1102 100.0

DEATHS	Count Col Pct	GTYPE unclaimed 6	Theocen 7	Ethnocen 8	Ethno -Charis 9	Ideoethno 10	Page 2 of 4 Row Total
0		271 87.7	40 41.7	129 64.8	24 44.4	9 52.9	821 74.5
1		37 12.0	55 57.3	70 35.2	30 55.6	8 47.1	277 25.1
62		1 .3					1 .1
150			1 1.0				1 .1
(Continued)	Column Total	309 28.0	96 8.7	199 18.1	54 4.9	17 1.5	1102 100.0

DEATHS	Count Col Pct	GTYPE Theo- Charis 1	Jew-Theo -Charis 2	Ideoethno -Charis 3	Jew-Theo 4	uncomp- leted 5	Page 3 of 4 Row Total
170		1 1.1					1 .1
176		1 1.1					1 .1
(Continued)	Column Total	89 8.1	61 5.5	106 9.6	53 4.8	118 10.7	1102 100.0

DEATHS	Count Col Pct	GTYPE unclaimed 6	Theocen 7	Ethnocen 8	Ethno -Charis 9	Ideoethno 10	Page 4 of 4 Row Total
170							1 .1
176							1 .1
(Continued)	Column Total	309 28.0	96 8.7	199 18.1	54 4.9	17 1.5	1102 100.0

Number of Missing Observations: 135

Source: Chasdi, Richard J. 1995. "The Dynamics of Middle East Terrorism, 1968-1993: A Functional Typology of Terrorist Group-Types." Ph.D. dissertation, Purdue University.

Political Ideology and Numbers of Injuries

The purpose of this section is to evaluate the following hypothesis:[51]

Hypothesis Four: Theocentric terrorist groups will have a higher percentage of terrorist acts that cause injuries than acts committed by ethnocentric and ideo-ethnocentric groups

There is a statistical association between the political ideology of a terrorist group and numbers of injuries that are caused in terrorist attacks. That finding indicates that those variables are statistically correlated.[52] Ideo-ethnocentric charismatic groups and ethnocentric groups had the highest percentage of events in which one to fifty persons were hurt. In the case of the former, 50% or 51 out of 102 incidents caused one to fifty injuries. In the case of the later, 49.5% or 97 out of 196 acts resulted in injuries to between one and fifty people. Alternately, Jewish theocentric charismatic groups had the lowest rate of incidents in which one to fifty people were hurt with 6.8% or four out of 59 acts.[53]

Ideo-ethnocentric groups had the highest percentage of incidents in which between fifty-one to one hundred persons were injured with 11.8% or two out of 17 incidents. Ethnocentric charismatic groups had the second highest percentage of events in which fifty-one to one hundred people were injured with 5.8% or three out of 52 events. The extreme outlier cases for numbers of injured were discussed earlier in this chapter, but it is important to note here that only two theocentric incidents involved injuries to fifty-one or more people. It suffices to say that the breakdown by group-type presented here is consistent with the idea mentioned previously that terrorism in the Middle East produces relatively low numbers of dead and wounded.

At the other extreme, Jewish theocentric charismatic groups had the highest percentage of acts in which no injuries were reported with 93.2% or 55 out of 59 acts. Jewish theocentric groups were second with 78.8% or 41 out of 52 incidents. Likewise, nearly 67% of unclaimed acts (204 out of 306 acts) caused no injuries. Thus, only one-third (102 out of 306 acts) of unclaimed acts injured anyone at all.

It is clear that hypothesis four is not supported by the analysis. Ethnocentric terrorist groups caused injuries in 52.1% of attacks while theocentric and ideo-ethnocentric groups caused injuries in only 41.1% and 41.2% of attacks, respectively.[54] At the same time, the findings about unclaimed terrorist acts are tantalizing. Clearly, injury and death rates are consistently low for acts perpetrated by anonymous groups or "lone

TABLE 4
Relative Frequency of Numbers of Injured in Terrorist Incidents by Group-Type, 1968-1993 (0=0; 1=1 thru 50; 2=51 thru 100)

PJURY1	Count Col Pct	GTYPE Theo-Charis 1	Jew-Theo -Charis 2	Ideoethno -Charis 3	Jew-Theo 4	uncomp-leted 5	Page 1 of 4 Row Total
	0	36 50.7	55 93.2	46 45.1	41 78.8	118 99.2	679 63.5
	1	32 45.1	4 6.8	51 50.0	11 21.2	1 .8	369 34.5
	2	1 1.4		4 3.9			16 1.5
	110			1 1.0			1 .1
(Continued)	Column Total	71 6.6	59 5.5	102 9.5	52 4.9	119 11.1	1069 100.0

PJURY1	Count Col Pct	GTYPE unclaimed 6	Theocen 7	Ethnocen 8	Ethno -Charis 9	Ideoethno 10	Page 2 of 4 Row Total
	0	204 66.7	55 57.9	94 48.0	20 38.5	10 58.8	679 63.5
	1	102 33.3	38 40.0	97 49.5	28 53.8	5 29.4	369 34.5
	2		1 1.1	5 2.6	3 5.8	2 11.8	16 1.5
	110						1 .1
(Continued)	Column Total	306 28.6	95 8.9	196 18.3	52 4.9	17 1.6	1069 100.0

PJURY1	Count Col Pct	GTYPE Theo-Charis 1	Jew-Theo -Charis 2	Ideoethno -Charis 3	Jew-Theo 4	uncomp-leted 5	Page 3 of 4 Row Total
	120	1 1.4					1 .1
	124						1 .1
	240	1 1.4					1 .1
	999						1 .1
(Continued)	Column Total	71 6.6	59 5.5	102 9.5	52 4.9	119 11.1	1069 100.0

PJURY1	Count Col Pct	GTYPE unclaimed 6	Theocen 7	Ethnocen 8	Ethno -Charis 9	Ideoethno 10	Page 4 of 4 Row Total
	120						1 .1
	124				1 1.9		1 .1
	240						1 .1
	999		1 1.1				1 .1
(Continued)	Column Total	306 28.6	95 8.9	196 18.3	52 4.9	17 1.6	1069 100.0

Number of Missing Observations: 168

Source: Chasdi, Richard J. 1995. "The Dynamics of Middle East Terrorism, 1968-1993: A Functional Typology of Terrorist Group-Types." Ph.D. dissertation, Purdue University.

operatives" and Jewish fundamentalist groups, suggesting that anonymous acts and acts carried out by Jewish terrorist groups perform a similar function. It seems plausible that unclaimed terrorist acts may introduce substantial pressure into the political system in much the same way it was suggested that many Jewish fundamentalist terrorist acts did. After all, the raison d'être of unclaimed terrorist assaults is to remind the ruling elite of the need for substantive change.[55]

Political Ideology and Property Damage

The aim of this section is to test the theoretical proposition that there is a relationship between the political ideology of a terrorist group and property damage. The hypothesis below makes it possible to measure that relationship empirically:[56]

Hypothesis Five: Ideo-ethnocentric terrorist groups will commit acts that result in greater amounts of property damage than acts committed by ethnocentric and theocentric terrorist groups

Based on the statistical association observed, the analysis indicates there is a substantive relationship between those two variables.[57] Jewish theocentric charismatic groups had the highest percentage of incidents in which slight damage resulted, with 58.6% or 34 out of 58 acts. Ideo-ethnocentric charismatic groups were second with 40.4% or 40 out of 99 incidents. Overall, terrorist attacks which caused only slight damage accounted for 30.1% (297 out of 988 incidents) of the total number.

Ideo-ethnocentric groups had the highest percentage of incidents in which moderate damage was caused with 13.3% or two out of 15 acts. Theocentric charismatic groups were next, with 12.0% or 10 out of 83 incidents. By comparison, high and severe levels of property damage caused by Middle East terrorist assaults were very infrequent. Only 3.8% or 38 out of 988 acts caused high levels of property damage. Ideo-ethnocentric groups had the greatest percentage of incidents that caused high levels of property damage with 26.7% or four out of 15 incidents. Terrorist attacks that caused severe damage were extreme outlier cases that only made up 1.5% (15 out of 988 acts) of the total. Ideo-ethnocentric charismatic groups had the highest rate of attacks of this kind with 6.1% or six out of 99 acts.[58]

At the other extreme, theocentric charismatic groups carried out the largest percentage of incidents in which no property damage occurred with 63.9% or 53 out of 83 acts. Jewish theocentric groups had an almost identical rate with 60.8% or 31 out of 51 acts. Anonymous terrorist assaults

TABLE 5
Level of Property Damage Caused in Middle East Terrorist Incidents
by Group-Type, 1968-1993

		GTYPE Theo-Charis	Jew-Theo -Charis	Ideoethno -Charis	Jew-Theo	uncomp- leted	Page 1 of 4
	Count Col Pct						Row
PROPDAM		1	2	3	4	5	Total
none (0)	1	53 63.9	23 39.7	37 37.4	31 60.8	114 97.4	575 58.2
slight	2	14 16.9	34 58.6	40 40.4	19 37.3	3 2.6	297 30.1
moderate	3	10 12.0	1 1.7	9 9.1	1 2.0		63 6.4
high	4	4 4.8		7 7.1			38 3.8
(Continued)	Column Total	83 8.4	58 5.9	99 10.0	51 5.2	117 11.8	988 100.0

		GTYPE unclaimed	Theocen	Ethnocen	Ethno -Charis	Ideoethno	Page 2 of 4
	Count Col Pct						Row
PROPDAM		6	7	8	9	10	Total
none (0)	1	158 58.1	46 53.5	88 54.0	21 47.7	4 26.7	575 58.2
slight	2	88 32.4	29 33.7	48 29.4	17 38.6	5 33.3	297 30.1
moderate	3	20 7.4	4 4.7	14 8.6	2 4.5	2 13.3	63 6.4
high	4	4 1.5	4 4.7	11 6.7	4 9.1	4 26.7	38 3.8
(Continued)	Column Total	272 27.5	86 8.7	163 16.5	44 4.5	15 1.5	988 100.0

		GTYPE Theo-Charis	Jew-Theo -Charis	Ideoethno -Charis	Jew-Theo	uncomp- leted	Page 3 of 4
	Count Col Pct						Row
PROPDAM		1	2	3	4	5	Total
severe	5	2 2.4		6 6.1			15 1.5
(Continued)	Column Total	83 8.4	58 5.9	99 10.0	51 5.2	117 11.8	988 100.0

		GTYPE unclaimed	Theocen	Ethnocen	Ethno -Charis	Ideoethno	Page 4 of 4
	Count Col Pct						Row
PROPDAM		6	7	8	9	10	Total
severe	5	2 .7	3 3.5	2 1.2			15 1.5
(Continued)	Column Total	272 27.5	86 8.7	163 16.5	44 4.5	15 1.5	988 100.0

Number of Missing Observations: 249

Source: Chasdi, Richard J. 1995. "The Dynamics of Middle East Terrorism, 1968-1993: A Functional Typology of Terrorist Group-Types." Ph.D. dissertation, Purdue University.

were almost as likely not to inflict property damage. No property damage occurred in 58.1% of unclaimed acts (158 out of 272 acts). In the case of anonymous terrorist assaults, when property damage did happen, the damage was slight nearly one-third of the time.[59]

Those findings about ideo-ethnocentric terrorist groups are the expected results. Nearly three-quarters of the acts they committed caused some type of property damage; somewhat more than one quarter of those incidents caused high levels of damage. Ethnocentric charismatic groups came in a very distant second with 9.1% or four out of 44 acts. Moreover, that pattern is very similar for other property damage categories. Clearly, those findings are consistent with the underlying theme that Marxist-Leninist terrorist groups in the Middle East devote special attention to property destruction.

Group Size and Target Selection

One proposition that has been asserted is a relationship exists between terrorist group size and target selection.[60] The hypothesis offered below expounds that relationship in a way that can be measured:

Hypothesis Six: Small Middle Eastern terrorist groups will have a higher percentage of civilian target attacks than large Middle Eastern terrorist groups

Significance test results indicate the likelihood that those two variables are independent of one another is small. At the same time the findings indicate that the modest, positive relationship that is observed is a statistically significant association at the .10 level of confidence.[61]

Turning to the data distribution, small groups of between fifty-one and one hundred activists had the highest rate of attacks against civilian targets with 84.7% or 61 out of 72 incidents. Very large groups of between some twenty-five hundred and eleven thousand or more activists had the second highest rate of attacks against civilian targets with 77.8% or 175 out of 225 acts. Moderate groups of about one hundred to five hundred activists had the greatest number of attacks directed against government targets with slightly more than one third. Very small groups of between twenty and fifty activists ranked second with one-fourth of all attacks aimed at government targets.

Attacks against infrastructure were very unusual. The highest rate recorded was for very small groups with 4.2% or one out of 24 incidents. Large groups of between some five hundred to twenty-five hundred had the second largest percentage of attacks against infrastructure with 2.6% or six out of 230 incidents. Attacks against multiple targets were even more

TABLE 6
Relative Frequency of Target Type by Terrorist Group Size, 1968-1993
(1 = very small; 2 = small; 3 = moderate; 4 = large; 5 = very large)

TARGET   Target of Event   by   Size   Size of Group

TARGET		SIZE 1	2	3	4	5	Page 1 of 2 Row Total
govt targets	1	6 25.0	11 15.3	46 33.8	49 21.3	41 18.2	153 22.3
infrastructure	2	1 4.2		2 1.5	6 2.6	5 2.2	14 2.0
civilian	3	17 70.8	61 84.7	85 62.5	174 75.7	175 77.8	512 74.5
govt-civilian	6			2 1.5		3 1.3	5 .7
(Continued)	Column Total	24 3.5	72 10.5	136 19.8	230 33.5	225 32.8	687 100.0

Count / Col Pct

TARGET   Target of Event   by   Size   Size of Group

TARGET		SIZE 1	2	3	4	5	Page 2 of 2 Row Total
civilian-govt	7			1 .7	1 .4		2 .3
civilian-infrast	9					1 .4	1 .1
(Continued)	Column Total	24 3.5	72 10.5	136 19.8	230 33.5	225 32.8	687 100.0

Count / Col Pct

Number of Missing Observations: 550

Source: Chasdi, Richard J. 1995. "The Dynamics of Middle East Terrorism, 1968-1993: A Functional Typology of Terrorist Group-Types." Ph.D. dissertation, Purdue University.

infrequent. In the case where a government facility was the primary target and the secondary target was civilian, moderate size groups ranked first with 1.5% or two out of 136 incidents. In the opposite case, moderate size and large groups carried out one attack each. The only attack against a multiple target in which the primary target was civilian and the secondary target was infrastructure was carried out by a very large terrorist group.

Those findings are consistent with hypothesis six. Small terrorist groups had the highest rate of attacks against civilian targets with 84.7% or 61 out of 72 acts. In contrast, a little more than three-quarters of the terrorist incidents carried out by large groups were aimed at civilian targets. Notwithstanding that, the variation level of those results is revealing. The fact that only 20% distinguishes the range is indicative of a modest, positive relationship between the variables. What also stands out here is there is no linear relationship between the size of a terrorist group and target type, as Oots' findings on death rates suggest.[62] Instead, the relationship between those variables is curvilinear, with a marked drop in attacks that involve civilian targets for moderate size groups.

Group Age and Target Selection

Another theoretical proposition suggests there is a relationship between the age of a terrorist group and the type of target selected. The following hypothesis captures the essence of that proposition:[63]

Hypothesis Seven: Older Middle Eastern terrorist groups will have a higher percentage of civilian target attacks than younger Middle Eastern terrorist groups

The testing results signify there is a statistical association between those two variables. Those findings show that it is extremely unlikely those variables are unrelated. In addition, the results also show that the weak, positive relationship observed is a statistically significant association.[64]

Older terrorist groups between the age of twenty-one and thirty-five years ranked first in attacks against civilian targets with 88.0% or 110 out of 125 incidents. Middle age terrorist groups between the age of eleven and twenty years ranked second with three-quarters of all attacks aimed at civilian targets (174 out of 232 acts). Young terrorist organizations ten years of age or less had the lowest percentage of attacks with 69.4% or 220 out of 317 acts. That ranking order is reversed for government targets of terrorist assaults. Young terrorist organizations ranked first in attacks against government targets with 26.2% or 83 out of 137 acts. Middle age terrorist groups had the second highest rate of attacks with 21.6% or 83 out of 317 acts. Older terrorist groups placed a distant third with 12.0% or 15 out of 125 acts.

Those findings are consistent with the relationship proposed in hypothesis seven. To recapitulate, 88.0% of older terrorist group attacks were directed at civilian targets as compared to 69.4% for young terrorist groups. Those results are striking because they are consistent with the notion that as leaders of Middle East terrorist groups become more experienced, they understand increasingly that the essence of effective terrorism revolves around the central idea of attacking civilian targets. That "maturity cycle," to use Lasswell's phrase, is one of several possible explanatory factors that needs further testing.[65]

Another finding is that as terrorist groups become older, the rate of attacks on infrastructure, already quite low, declined even further. Young terrorist groups ranked first in assaults against infrastructure with 2.8% or nine out of 317 acts, while middle age groups ranked second with 1.7% or four out of 232 acts. By contrast, older terrorist groups did not commit any terrorist assaults against infrastructure targets. Analysis of the relationship between group age and multiple targeting reinforces further the idea that target schemes change with the passage of time. Young terrorist groups had the most attacks against multiple targets with a mere 1.6% (five out of 317 acts). In four out of five events, the primary target was a government facility and the secondary target was civilian. Only four other multiple target attacks were recorded and those were for middle age terrorist groups.

Location and Target Selection

The theoretical proposition that a relationship exists between the location of an event and target type is explored:[66]

Hypothesis Eight: Terrorist attacks in Israel will have the highest percentage of attacks aimed at civilian targets while terrorist attacks in the Occupied Territories will have the second highest percentage of attacks aimed at civilian targets

Location is the fourth independent variable that is statistically associated with target type. The analysis suggests a substantive and systematic relationship between those variables.[67] The analysis reveals that the Occupied Territories ranked first in attacks against civilian targets with 91.6% or 336 out of 367 acts. Israel ranked a close second with 89.8% or 389 out of 433 acts. European states came in a distant third with 68.4%

TABLE 7
Relative Frequency of Target Type by Terrorist Group Age, 1968-1993
(1 = 1 thru 10 years; 2 = 11 thru 20 years; 3 = 21 thru 35 years)

TARGET	Target of Event	by	Age	Age of Group	
	AGE				Page 1 of 2
	Count				
	Col Pct				Row
TARGET	1	2	3		Total
1 govt targets	83 26.2	50 21.6	15 12.0		148 22.0
2 infrastructure	9 2.8	4 1.7			13 1.9
3 civilian	220 69.4	174 75.0	110 88.0		504 74.8
6 govt-civilian	4 1.3	2 .9			6 .9
Column (Continued) Total	317 47.0	232 34.4	125 18.5		674 100.0

TARGET	Target of Event	by	Age	Age of Group	
	SIZE				Page 2 of 2
	Count				
	Col Pct				Row
TARGET	1	2	3		Total
7 civilian-govt	1 .3	1 .4			2 .3
9 civilian-infrast		1 .4			1 .1
Column (Continued) Total	317 47.0	232 34.4	125 18.5		674 100.0

Number of Missing Observations: 563

Source: Chasdi, Richard J. 1995. "The Dynamics of Middle East Terrorism, 1968-1993: A Functional Typology of Terrorist Group-Types." Ph.D. dissertation, Purdue University.

(106 out of 155 acts). That ranking order is reversed for government targets of terrorist assaults. The smallest percentage of attacks against government targets was in the Occupied Territories with 7.9% or 29 out of 367 acts. Israel came in second with 8.3% or 36 out of 433 acts. European states placed third with 29.0% or 45 out of 155 events (see Table 8).

With respect to other target types, infrastructure was attacked in 3.1% of all acts in the Middle East outside of Israel and the Occupied Territories (six out of 195 acts). Israel ranked second with 1.6% (seven out of 433 acts) and European states ranked third with 1.3% (two out of 155 acts). Terrorist assaults that involved multiple targets were extreme outlier observations. What stands out however is that the United States ranked first in attacks that involved multiple targets with 6.8% (four out of 59 acts).

Those findings are inconsistent with hypothesis eight. I found that the highest rate of attacks against civilian targets took place in the Occupied Territories with 91.6%, while 89.8% of attacks in Israel were aimed at civilian targets. Nonetheless, the difference between those values is small. Presumably, those findings reflect some small difference in anti-terrorist security measures and/or effectiveness, or indicate that the attack rates are basically the same in both locations.

Political Events and Target Selection

One fundamental question that has been relatively neglected by researchers is whether or not a connection exists between Middle East terrorism and political events that take place in the region or are otherwise connected to it. In other words, does terrorism in the Middle East happen largely in response to political activity or is terrorism comprised mostly of "independent" events?

The idea that terrorism may be largely a reactive rather than a proactive endeavor is based on Brecher and James' model of political violence in the Middle East.[68] The following hypothesis captures the substance of that model:

Hypothesis Nine: Most terrorist activity will be linked to political events in the region such as wars, visits by major political figures, diplomatic initiatives, the commemoration of religious and secular events and counter-terrorism activity

The analysis indicates there is a statistical association between the intervening variable (political events) and the type of target selected. More specifically, we can interpret those findings to mean that when terrorism is

TABLE 8
Relative Frequency of Target Type by Location,
1968-1993

TARGET   Target of Event   by   LOC   Location of Event

LOC					Page 1 of 4
Count	Israel	Occup	Europ	US	Other
Col Pct		Terr	States		Mid East	Row
TARGET	1	4	12	14	17	Total
1 govt targets	36 8.3	29 7.9	45 29.0	32 54.2	82 42.1	231 18.8
2 infrastructure	7 1.6	2 .5	2 1.3		6 3.1	19 1.5
3 civilian	389 89.8	336 91.6	106 68.4	22 37.3	104 53.3	966 78.7
6 govt-civilian	1 .2		2 1.3	4 6.8		7 .6
Column (Continued) Total	433 35.3	367 29.9	155 12.6	59 4.8	195 15.9	1227 100.0

TARGET   Target of Event   by   LOC   Location of Event

LOC		Page 2 of 4
Count	Other	Row
TARGET Col Pct	18	Total
1 govt targets	7 38.9	231 18.8
2 infrastructure	2 11.1	19 1.5
3 civilian	9 50.0	966 78.7
6 govt-civilian		7 .6
Column (Continued) Total	18 1.5	1227 100.0

TARGET   Target of Event   by   LOC   Location of Event

LOC					Page 3 of 4
Count	Israel	Occup	Europ	US	Other
Col Pct		Terr	States		East	Row
TARGET	1	4	12	14	17	Total
7 civilian-govt				1 1.7	2 1.0	3 .2
9 civilian-infrast					1 .5	1 .1
Column (Continued) Total	433 35.3	367 29.9	155 12.6	59 4.8	195 15.9	1227 100.0

TARGET   Target of Event   by   LOC   Location of Event

LOC		Page 4 of 4
Count	Other	Row
TARGET Col Pct	18	Total
7 civilian-govt		3 .2
9 civilian-infrast		1 .1
Column (Continued) Total	18 1.5	1227 100.0

Number of Missing Observations: 10

Source: Chasdi, Richard J. 1995. "The Dynamics of Middle East Terrorism, 1968-1993: A Functional Typology of Terrorist Group-Types." Ph.D. dissertation, Purdue University.

linked to political events, there is a statistical association between the type of political event happening and the target type that is chosen.[69]

However, a complete breakdown of those data makes it clear that most terrorist incidents were unrelated to political events. Incidents that had no relationship to political events comprised the largest proportion of the total: 71.1% or 859 out of 1208 incidents. Of the 859 acts that were unrelated to political events, over three-quarters of them (79.6% or 684 acts) were directed at civilian targets (see Table 9).

The remaining categories of "political events" are comprised of outlier observations. The largest of those categories is made-up of terrorist events that took place in response to major political events. Terrorist acts in response to major political events such as diplomatic initiatives, amounted to 6.8% (82) of the total number. While attacks in response to major political events formed the bulk of the outlier cases, they were not characterized by an especially sharp focus against the general population. It is observed that only around three-quarters of those attacks (62 out of 82 acts) involved civilian targets. Those findings may reflect the largely "symbolic" nature of those terrorist attacks, which were launched in protest against particular political initiatives.

Terrorist activity undertaken in response to government policy at the national level, such as Israeli support for the Lebanese militia in southern Lebanon, formed the second largest group of outlier observations. While over half of those attacks (57.6% or 38 acts) involved civilian targets, 39.4% (26 out of 66 acts) involved government targets. That figure represents the highest number of "reactive" terrorist assaults against government targets. Attacks in commemoration of landmark events such as the anniversary of the Sabra/Shatilla massacre comprised the third largest outlier category with 3.4% of the total number of incidents. Equally important, terrorist attacks in commemoration of landmark events had the second highest rate of attack against civilians with 92.7% or 38 out of 41 incidents.

By comparison, terrorist actions in reaction to war and government counter-terrorist assassinations, were very rare occurrences. Terrorist attacks undertaken in reaction to war only comprised .2% of 1,208 acts and always involved civilian targets (2 out of 2 acts). Terrorist incidents committed in reaction to counter-terrorist assassinations amounted to only .7% of the total. Those attacks had the highest percentage of assaults against infrastructure with 12.5% (1 out of 8 acts). In turn, terrorist incidents carried out in commemoration of religious holidays had the second highest percentage of attacks against infrastructure with 4.5%, but that was only one incident. Likewise, terrorist attacks undertaken to commemorate secular holidays had

TABLE 9
Relative Frequency of Target Type by Political Event, 1968-1993

TARGET   Target of Event by POLEVNT   Type of Political Event

POLEVNT	no rel	reac maj pol eve	reac shell	reac air	reac govt assass	Row Total
Count Col Pct	0	1	2	3	4	
TARGET 1 govt targets	152 17.7	20 24.4	1 25.0	4 13.3	1 12.5	228 18.9
2 infrastructure	15 1.7				1 12.5	19 1.6
3 civilian	684 79.6	62 75.6	3 75.0	26 86.7	6 75.0	950 78.6
6 govt-civilian	4 .5					7 .6
Column (Continued) Total	859 71.1	82 6.8	4 .3	30 2.5	8 .7	1208 100.0

SPSS/PC+

TARGET   Target of Event by POLEVNT   Type of Political Event

POLEVNT	reac kid	reac war	comm land events	comm rel holi	comm sec holi	Row Total
Count Col Pct	5	6	7	8	9	
TARGET 1 govt targets	1 50.0		3 7.3	2 9.1	2 11.8	228 18.9
2 infrastructure				1 4.5		19 1.6
3 civilian	1 50.0	2 100.0	38 92.7	19 86.4	14 82.4	950 78.6
6 govt-civilian					1 5.9	7 .6
Column (Continued) Total	2 .2	2 .2	41 3.4	22 1.8	17 1.4	1208 100.0

TARGET   Target of Event by POLEVNT   Type of Political Event

POLEVNT	reac terror	reac grnd attk	reac govt pol	reac min pol eve	Row Total
Count Col Pct	10	12	13	14	
TARGET 1 govt targets	8 22.2		26 39.4	8 33.3	228 18.9
2 infrastructure		1 6.7		1 4.2	19 1.6
3 civilian	28 77.8	14 93.3	38 57.6	15 62.5	950 78.6
6 govt-civilian			2 3.0		7 .6
Column (Continued) Total	36 3.0	15 1.2	66 5.5	24 2.0	1208 100.0

SPSS/PC+

Source: Chasdi, Richard J. 1995. "The Dynamics of Middle East Terrorism, 1968-1993: A Functional Typology of Terrorist Group-Types." Ph.D. dissertation, Purdue University.

TABLE 9 continued
Relative Frequency of Target Type by Political Event, 1968-1993

TARGET Target of Event by POLEVNT   Type of Political Event
POLEVNT

Count Col Pct	no rel 0	reac maj pol eve 1	reac shell 2	reac air 3	reac govt assass 4	Row Total
TARGET 7 civilian-govt	3 .3					3 .2
9 civilian-infrast	1 .1					1 .1
Column (Continued) Total	859 71.1	82 6.8	4 .3	30 2.5	8 .7	1208 100.0

TARGET Target of Event by POLEVNT   Type of Political Event
POLEVNT

Count Col Pct	reac kid 5	reac war 6	comm land events 7	comm rel holi 8	comm sec holi 9	Row Total
TARGET 7 civilian-govt						3 .2
9 civilian-infrast						1 .1
Column (Continued) Total	2 .2	2 .2	41 3.4	22 1.8	17 1.4	1208 100.0

SPSS/PC+

TARGET Target of Event by POLEVNT   Type of Political Event
POLEVNT

Count Col Pct TARGET	reac terror 10	reac grnd attk 12	reac govt pol 13	reac min pol eve 14	Row Total
7 civilian-govt					3 .2
9 civilian-infrast					1 .1
Column Total	36 3.0	15 1.2	66 5.5	24 2.0	1208 100.0

Number of Missing Observations: 29

Source: Chasdi, Richard J. 1995. "The Dynamics of Middle East Terrorism, 1968-1993: A Functional Typology of Terrorist Group-Types." Ph.D. dissertation, Purdue University.

the highest percentage of attacks against multiple targets with 5.9%, but again, this involved only a single event.

Clearly, the results of the analysis are inconsistent with hypothesis nine and as a result, that hypothesis is rejected. At the same time, the analysis suggests that proactive activities carried out by government agencies may elicit terrorist responses that resonate with similar thematic emphases. For example, "symbolic" political initiatives seemed to be matched by "symbolic" terrorist activity. Similarly, the analysis shows that government policy outputs evoked the highest number of "reactive" terrorist attacks aimed at government targets.

The analysis also suggests that events that exert a powerful pull on visceral emotions, such as the commemoration of landmark events, prompted terrorist attacks that focused greater attention on civilian targets. Likewise, violent government activity that affected large numbers of people directly, perhaps even profoundly, elicited terrorist attacks that matched the fundamentally invasive and thereby "intimate" nature of those government activities with equivalent intensity against civilians. For example, 86.7% of attacks in reaction to air-strikes involved civilian targets, while 93.3% and 100% of attacks in reaction to ground attacks and war respectively, involved civilian targets.

Conclusions

General Trends

Crosstabulation analysis provides valuable insight into understanding Middle East terrorism by revealing its broader characteristics and variations according to group-type. At the most basic level, the analysis reveals that while there has been a general increase in Middle East terrorism in absolute terms since 1968, the frequency of Middle East terrorism ebbs and flows in a cyclical configuration.

Another rudimentary finding concerns where Middle East terrorism takes place. While an overwhelming number of terrorist incidents happened in Israel and the Occupied Territories, European nations were afflicted with nearly as much Middle East terrorism as Middle East locations outside of Israel and the Occupied Territories.

The analysis shows that ethnocentric groups were the most dynamic type of group between 1968-1993. Ethnocentric groups carried out 204 acts of terrorism during that period. Ideo-ethnocentric charismatic groups were the second most active type of group, carrying out 108 acts. By far, the largest number of acts were committed by anonymous terrorist organizations or "lone operatives." Unknown groups or "lone operatives" launched over 300 acts between 1968-1993. When the analysis is focused at the group level, similar trends in the data are discernable. For example, al-Fatah carried out the highest number of terrorist acts (118) followed by 94 acts credited to the Popular Front for the Liberation of Palestine (PFLP).

The widely shared belief that terrorists focus primary attention against civilians in pursuit of political goals is supported by the results. When all locations are included in the analysis, Middle East terrorists favored assaults against civilian targets by over a 4:1 margin. When the locations Israel and the Occupied Territories are examined separately, that ratio increased to approximately 10:1 (see Figure 9, Table 8, and Methodological Appendix). Irrespective of location, however, the results indicate that in addition to a focus on civilian targets, terrorist assaults linked to the Middle East remained relatively straightforward operations that usually involved one target. Incidents involving multiple targets were extremely rare occurrences that comprised only some 1% of all terrorist incidents (see Table 2).

What degree of damage does Middle East terrorism cause? The analysis shows that the costs of Middle East terrorism, if measured in purely physical terms, have been low. The sample mean for numbers of dead is 1.454 and the sample mean for numbers of injured is 4.639.[70] Comparable low levels of property damage from Middle East terrorist assaults were recorded. More than half of all incidents caused no property damage, and less than 4% resulted in high levels of property damage.

The Role of Political Ideology

How do these data support the theoretical framework described at the start? The continuum for non-structuralist and structuralist terrorist group-types is presented and overlaid with data on non-charismatic group-types and target-type with good results (see Figure 10).

Political ideology is found to be influential in terms of what type of target was chosen. The analysis determines that ideo-ethnocentric terrorist groups attacked government targets (i.e., courthouses, military administration facilities, military recruitment centers and non-combatant troops such as U.N. peacekeepers) more often than ethnocentric and theocentric groups, as well as Jewish theocentric terrorist groups. This finding strongly supports the notion that "structuralist" Middle East terrorist groups carry out terrorist attacks that place more emphasis on government targets.

At the same time, the analysis reveals that ethnocentric terrorist groups attacked civilian targets more frequently than theocentric groups. At the

Figure 10: Continuum of 'Structuralist' and 'Non-Structuralist' Middle East Terrorist Group-Types for Non-charismatic Group Types and Target (Jewish Fundamentalist Terrorist Group Types Excluded)

"structuralist"		"non-structuralist"
Ideo-ethnocentric	Theocentric	Ethnocentric
Civilian Targets		
52.6%	72.3%	77.5%
Government Targets		
47.4%	26.7%	18.6%

Source: Chasdi, Richard J. 1995. "The Dynamics of Middle East Terrorism, 1968-1993: A Functional Typology of Terrorist Group-Types." Ph.D. dissertation. Purdue University.

start, I believed that Islamic fundamentalist terrorist groups and nationalist-irredentist groups were both "non-structuralist" in nature.[71] These findings, however, seem to suggest that theocentric groups, while less "structuralist" than "Marxist-Leninist" groups, are more "structuralist" than ethnocentric groups. At a theoretical level, that approach seems justifiable since Islamic fundamentalism not only focuses heavily on an individual's declared loyalties and beliefs, but is "structuralist" in the sense that it perceives the world as essentially divided up between an Islamic East and hordes of "unbelievers" under the control of a Christian West.[72]

The analysis of terrorism "attribute" variables is less supportive of the theory that drives this work. Having said that, location as an explanatory variable may not only explain why Jewish terrorism remains consistently low in terms of intensity, but seems to explain, inter-alia, why death rates for ethnocentric groups, clearly a "deviant finding," seem to be muted.

In the case of ethnocentric groups, the death rate is comparatively low. One possible explanation for that finding is that a full 42.9% of ethnocentric attacks took place in Israel, while only 13.9% of theocentric attacks happened in Israel. Ethnocentric group-type death rates are likely influenced by that distribution. Ethnocentric group-type death rates may be low because of two factors that work alone or in tandem. At a functional level, Israeli counter-terrorism measures may make terrorist assaults with very high death rates difficult to carry out. At a political level, ethnocentric groups are the type of terrorist group most interested in a political settlement with Israel. If ethnocentric assaults crossed a threshold of "acceptable" numbers of deaths, they would have elicited the looming catastrophe of decisive Israeli retaliation that would have more than offset any political gains made.[73]

The Relationships Between Terrorist Group Size, Group Age and Targets

Precious little can be said about what generates the curvilinear relationship between terrorist group size and terrorist group target that appears in the findings. Clearly, one or a combination of explanatory variables could be at work with respect to why moderate size terrorist groups focus on civilian targets less often and government targets more often than smaller or larger Middle East terrorist groups. What seems significant here is that it would probably be a mistake to reject the notion of a relationship between the variables terrorist group size and target type. To be sure, a Kendall's tau-b statistic value of .0641 certainly suggests a relationship that is not terribly strong, but since the critical value is 1.53 at 4 degrees of freedom at the .10 level of confidence, and the T value generated is 1.738, it would be imprudent to reject the likelihood of a relationship since there is over a ninety percent chance that would be incorrect.

Turning to the relationship between terrorist target type and terrorist group age, the findings suggest a moderate positive relationship between the two variables. A Kendall's tau-b statistic of .12176 is generated, along with a T value of 3.453, that is beyond the critical value of 2.92 at 2 degrees of freedom at the .05 level of confidence. Clearly, those values show that at the .05 level, the null hypothesis of no relationship between the variables can be rejected. To be sure, all that can be said about this positive relationship between the variables terrorist group age and target type is that the findings are consistent with the notion that as leaders of Middle East terrorist groups become more seasoned, they are more apt to carry out terrorist assaults against civilian targets. By the same token, there are other propositions available and the data do not differentiate between them. For example, one factor at work may be that terrorist assaults against government targets may increase the chance of capture or death for terrorists, as compared to terrorist assaults against civilians that hold precious little in the way of risk for terrorists. Indeed, what we are observing might presuppose and derive from a combination of those two factors or others at work. Suffice it to say, those findings merit further investigation in the future.

Location

Seen from another angle, the crosstabulation results also indicate that location of the terrorist assault heavily influences the target selection process. It is found that terrorist attacks in the Occupied Territories had the highest percentage of attacks against civilian targets, while attacks in Israel had the second highest rate. The European states placed a distant third. While those first and second place rankings are not the expected findings, the results are consistent with the idea that the frequency of attacks involving civilians in Israel and the Occupied Territories is greater than in other locations. Moreover, while those findings are inconsistent with hypothesis eight, the difference in attack frequency rates between locations in very small. As mentioned previously, those findings either reflect some small difference in anti-terrorism measures or their implementation, or suggest that attack rates are basically the same in both locations.

Charismatic Leadership: Impact on Islamic Fundamentalist, Marxist-Leninist, and Nationalist-Irredentist Terrorist Groups

One of the underlying themes of this study is that charismatic leaders of Arab/Islamic fundamentalist terrorist groups influence terrorist group behavior. While the data support that idea in some cases, many of the results do not conform with predictions made earlier in this study. The following is a summary of the findings about charismatic leadership for Islamic fundamentalist, Marxist-Leninist, and nationalist-irredentist terrorist groups.

The data suggest the presence of a charismatic leader at the helm of Islamic fundamentalist terrorist groups makes little difference in terms of target selection and intensity of attack. For example, while theocentric charismatic groups attacked civilian targets in 72.8% of all attacks, theocentric groups did so in 72.3% of attacks. With respect to intensity of attacks, the observed data show that while a lower percentage of theocentric charismatic group attacks *killed* between one and fifty persons, a higher percentage of theocentric charismatic attacks *injured* between one and fifty persons. What seems significant here is the connection between numbers of deaths in terrorist assaults and *location* as an explanatory variable. A full 36% of theocentric charismatic attacks took place in Israel and the data show that only 29.2% of theocentric charismatic attacks killed between one and fifty persons. By contrast, only 13.9% of theocentric attacks took place in Israel and 57.3% of theocentric attacks killed between one and fifty

Figure 11: Continuum of 'Structuralist' and 'Non-Structuralist' Middle East Terrorist Group-Types and
Target (Jewish Fundamentalist Terrorist Group Types Excluded)

"structuralist"				"non-structuralist"	
Ideo-ethnocentric	Ethnocentric Charismatic	Theocentric	Theocentric Charismatic	Ethnocentric	Ideo-ethnocentric Charismatic
Civilian Targets					
52.6%	63.0%	72.3%	72.8%	77.5%	77.8%
Government Targets					
47.4%	37.0%	26.7%	25.0%	18.6%	16.7%

Source: Chasdi, Richard J. 1995. "The Dynamics of Middle East Terrorism, 1968-1993: A Functional Typology of
Terrorist Group-Types." Ph.D. dissertation. Purdue University.

persons.[74]

The analysis fails to reveal any pattern in terms of property damage
levels caused by Islamic fundamentalist terrorist assaults. For example,
while theocentric and theocentric charismatic groups had the same percentage of attacks that caused *high amounts* of property damage, theocentric
groups had a much higher percentage of attacks that caused *slight damage,*
whereas theocentric charismatic groups had a much higher percentage that
caused *moderate damage.* Interestingly enough, the results suggest location
is not an explanatory variable for lower amounts of property damage. For
example, with over one-third of theocentric charismatic attacks in Israel, a
full 12% of theocentric charismatic attacks caused moderate property
damage. That 12% figure is nearly three times greater than the 4.7%
amount for theocentric groups, which attacked targets in Israel only 13.9%
of the time.[75]

In the case of Marxist-Leninist terrorist groups, the data generally
support the proposition that groups led by a charismatic leader commit
terrorist acts that more closely resemble incidents carried out by other types
of groups calling for a Pan-Arab or Pan-Islamic Middle East. The strongest
evidence of a link between an increase in violence against the general
population and the presence of a charismatic leader is found in the analysis
of *target choice.* A breakdown of observed data reveals that while ideo-
ethnocentric group attacks involved civilian targets in nearly 53% of all
incidents, close to 78% of ideo-ethnocentric charismatic group attacks were
directed at civilian targets.

Analysis of the intensity of terrorist incidents carried out by ideo-ethnocentric and ideo-ethnocentric charismatic groups seems to be, *prime facie,* less supportive of that relationship. For example, the data show that a greater percentage of ideo-ethnocentric group attacks *killed* between one and fifty persons than ideo-ethnocentric charismatic attacks. Meanwhile, ideo-ethnocentric charismatic groups had a much higher percentage of attacks that *wounded* between one and fifty persons than did ideo-ethnocentric groups. However, analysis of location and group type suggests location as an explanatory variable. While nearly two-thirds of all ideo-ethnocentric charismatic group attacks took place in Israel and the Occupied Territories, there were no attacks by ideo-ethnocentric groups in those locales. In fact, analysis shows that nearly 58% of all ideo-ethnocentric attacks were carried out in other Middle East countries like Syria and Lebanon. The remaining 42% of ideo-ethnocentric assaults took place in Europe.[76]

In the case of nationalist-irredentist terrorist groups, the data suggest the presence of a charismatic leader has an influence on target type and intensity, although that influence is different for each. It is observed that ethnocentric terrorist groups carry out *civilian target attacks* (77.5%) more frequently than ethnocentric charismatic groups (63.0%). For ethnocentric charismatic groups, the roughly "60-40" split between civilian and government targets mirrors the Abu Nidal Organization's seemingly more balanced targeting of civilian and government targets.[77]

With respect to intensity, however, it is observed that nearly 56% of ethnocentric charismatic group attacks *killed* between one and fifty persons as compared to 35.2% for ethnocentric groups. Likewise, nearly 54% of ethnocentric charismatic attacks caused *injuries* to between one and fifty persons as compared to slightly less than 50% for ethnocentric groups. Once again, location seems to be the explanatory variable for the different findings about target choice and terrorist assault intensity. Very few ethnocentric charismatic attacks took place in Israel (7.4% or 4 out of 54 acts), while 42.9% of ethnocentric attacks happened in Israel.[78]

The Behavioral Patterns of Jewish Fundamentalist Terrorist Groups

One of the cornerstones of the theory that drives this study is that Jewish fundamentalist terrorist groups ought to attack targets with less intensity than their Islamic counterparts. The results of the analysis about the characteristics of "Jewish terror" strongly support that idea.[79] Specifically, the data show that Jewish theocentric charismatic groups had the highest percentage of non-lethal incidents, while Jewish theocentric groups had the second highest amount. The analysis also reveals that Jewish theocentric charismatic groups had the highest percentage of injury-free attacks while Jewish theocentric groups came in second place. Finally, it is observed that neither Jewish theocentric charismatic nor Jewish theocentric groups committed acts that caused high amounts of property damage. In fact, only around two percent of all acts for both group-types resulted in even moderate amounts of damage. To be sure, some 93% of Jewish theocentric charismatic attacks happened in the "friendly" areas of Israel, The Occupied Territories, and the United States. Indeed, a full 100% of Jewish theocentric attacks happened in Israel and The Occupied Territories alone.[80]

The data suggest that the reason for this self-styled restraint by Jewish fundamentalist terrorist groups is twofold. At one level, it seems obvious that the restraint shown served to prevent the lurking prospect of a full-scale military crackdown by Israel's General Security Service. At another level, those findings suggest that leaders of those organizations refrained from undertaking devastating assaults on a consistent basis because they viewed their groups, to use Hoffman's expression, as "political pressure groups" that could influence the Israeli and/or American political systems.[81] Furthermore, those findings suggest systemic or structural factors (i.e., whether or not a terrorist group is "indigenous" or "exogenous" to the political system under attack) have significant effects on terrorist event characteristics.[82]

The Influence of Political Events

Middle East terrorism is found to be a largely proactive rather than a reactive undertaking. The analysis reveals that some 70.0% of all terrorist activity between 1968-1993 was unrelated to political events. When terrorism was linked to political events, there was a statistical association between target type and political event type. Furthermore, the analysis suggests that terrorist actions taken in response to particular political events share similar underlying themes with them. That finding has powerful implications for counter-terrorism policy. If there is evidence that indicates particular types of political events elicit attacks that place predictable emphasis on certain kinds of targets, more effective counter-terrorism policy can be crafted and implemented.

Terrorism by Anonymous Groups or "Lone Operatives"

Terrorist attacks by anonymous groups or "lone operatives" are found to be the most common type of attack between 1968-1993. In addition, nearly 90% of all unclaimed attacks involved civilian targets. For terrorist assaults against civilian targets, that percentage figure is the highest measure recorded for any category.

While the vast majority of unclaimed terrorist acts were aimed at the general population, those acts caused little damage. The percentage of anonymous terrorist assaults that caused at least one death or injury was comparatively low. In addition, nearly one-third of all anonymous attacks resulted in a slight amount of property damage.

What seems significant here is the findings suggest that effective counter-terrorism measures are largely dependent on whether or not a terrorist group is identifiable. It follows that a "mixed bundle" of anonymous and claimed acts of terrorism that are low intensity in nature may be an effective strategy for terrorist leaders if the underlying themes and goals of the political struggle are sufficiently clear and other terrorist groups are active in the political fray.[83] At a more theoretical level, the findings suggest that an important function of anonymous terrorist activity is to remind the ruling elite of the need for structural political change or accommodation.

Reflections

The crosstabulation analysis makes it clear that the targeting practices of Middle East terrorist groups are based on much more than chance and opportunity. In fact, that analysis reveals discernable and at times dramatic patterns of terrorist group targeting behavior when Middle East terrorist groups are broken down according to three defining characteristics: ideology, goals, and recruitment patterns.[84] Inasmuch as those results begin to shed light on which types of terrorist groups commit particular types of assaults, the set of interconnections between political events and the actions of various types of terrorist groups, and what the risks of Middle East terrorism are, this research lends itself to predictions about the future.

Plainly, while it is beyond the scope of this article to provide a "laundry list" of policy prescriptions for counter-terrorism planners, some insight about "target hardening" can be extrapolated from the data. First, while making efforts to generate or sustain security around potential civilian targets of terrorism is an ineluctable conclusion, the findings also suggest close attention should be devoted to potential targets on anniversaries and celebrations, and potential government targets when national policy directives are carried out.

Second, the data indicate special attention ought to be devoted to potential government targets with respect to Jewish fundamentalist, and Arab nationalist-irredentist groups with charismatic leaders, and Marxist-Leninist nationalist-irredentist groups without them. All of the aforementioned suggests that counter-terrorism planners might identify and sort out qualitative differences in policy directives, thereby in effect helping to prepare counter-terrorism contingency plans for types of intensity levels in terrorist assaults that seem bound up with specific kinds of policy directives. Equally important, linkages should be made between delineated "policy types" and terrorist groups affected, to promote better risk assessment. Bearing in mind that some terrorist assaults happen on anniversaries or to celebrate events, it follows that such a classification scheme might isolate and identify particular time periods where implementation of specific "policy types" is fraught with peril because of possible "joint effects" that presuppose and derive from political events and policy directives.

Third, trends in the data suggest that counter-terrorism planners should *anticipate* an overwhelming number of Middle East terrorism assaults that involve one target. What seems significant here however, is that counter-terrorism planners should *prepare* for the possibility of a shift in strategy, namely to terrorist assaults that involve multiple targets and perhaps, multiple target-type combinations. In essence, counter-terrorism planners need to introduce even more flexibility into the counter-terrorism system by means of additional resource acquisition, and enhanced organizational capacity both within and between government agencies, that may presuppose and derive from even more coordinated terrorist event and response "simulations."[85]

Fourth, since the data suggest a very high number of anonymous terrorist assaults, policymaking officials might consider ways to reduce that proportion. Because those anonymous assaults may be associated with a political setting in which the political goals of the state and several terrorist groups, perceived to be "clear," are all too frequently couched in zero-sum terms, then at one level, the question becomes how to "blur" the political goals of particular terrorist organization "constituency groups" under consideration that have articulated political demands and aspirations.[86] One approach may be to use what David Baldwin calls "positive sanctions," aimed at terrorist group constituencies, to make it more difficult for them to agree on the range of tactical choices to endorse for terrorist groups.[87] "Positive sanctions" that establish a set of interconnections between a state (e.g., Israel, the United States) and "constituency groups" might include resources for urban renewal, education, housing, and medical supplies for Gaza and to be sure, other locales now under the aegis of a continuously evolving Palestinian nation.[88]

At another level, it may be in the Israeli government's interest, and in the national security interest of Israel, to continue "the peace process" if only for the sake of keeping low the number and type of terrorist groups active in the political fray.[89] Compounding the challenge even more, it may be advantageous, in particular situations or with specific terrorist groups, to engage in some type of dialogue (e.g., prisoner exchange, the scope of prisoner health or visitation rights under consideration) if only to help reduce the likelihood of a solid "hardline" consensus among terrorist tacticians about terrorist group tactics.

In conclusion, inasmuch as this study ties together work on terrorism and places its own findings within the context of a theoretical framework, this study serves as a first step within the realm of terrorism studies toward what Zinnes calls the "cumulative integration" of scholarly work.[90] To be sure, those findings demonstrate it is possible to move over and beyond the "coffee table logic" of fragmented rhetorical arguments that shape much of what is discussed about terrorism in the Middle East. Hopefully, the basic structure of this research can assist others in their work, and thus contribute to efforts to learn more about a form of political violence that remains largely untouched by empirical investigation.

METHODOLOGICAL APPENDIX

Relative Frequency of Terrorist Attack Locations by Group-Type, 1968-1993

			SPSS/PC+				
LOC	**Location of Event by GTYPE**			**Type of Group**			
		GTYPE					
	Count Col Pct	Theo- Charis 1	Jew-Theo Charis 2	Ideoethno- Charis 3	Jew-Theo 4	Uncompleted 5	Row Total
LOC	1	32	15	39	29	72	432
Israel		36.0	25.0	36.1	53.7	60.5	38.6
	4	7	12	29	25	9	259
Occ terr		7.9	20.0	26.9	46.3	7.6	23.2
	12	7	3	22		13	155
Europ States		7.9	5.0	20.4		10.9	13.9
	14	1	29	4		9	59
US		1.1	48.3	3.7		7.6	5.3
	Column	89	60	108	54	119	1118
(Continued)	Total	8.0	5.4	9.7	4.8	10.6	100.0

LOC	**Location of Event by GTYPE**			**Type of Group**			
		GTYPE					
	Count Col Pct	Unclaimed 6	Theocen 7	Ethnocen 8	Ethno- Charis 9	Ideo- ethno 10	Row Total
LOC	1	140	14	87	4		432
Israel		45.0	13.9	42.9	7.4		38.6
	4	123	22	28	4		259
Occ terr		39.5	21.8	13.8	7.4		23.2
	12	32	3	42	25	8	155
Europ States		10.3	3.0	20.7	46.3	42.1	13.9
	14	2	3	9	2		59
US		.6	3.0	4.4	3.7		5.3
	Column	311	101	203	54	19	1118
(Continued)	Total	27.8	9.0	18.2	4.8	1.7	100.0

Source: Chasdi, Richard J. 1995. "The Dynamics of Middle East Terrorism, 1968-1993: A Functional Typology of Terrorist Group-Types." Ph.D. dissertation, Purdue University.

METHODOLOGICAL APPENDIX (Continued)
Relative Frequency of Terrorist Attack Locations by Group-Type, 1968-1993

SPSS/PC+

LOC   Location of Event by GTYPE   Type of Group

Count Col Pct	GTYPE Theo-Charis 1	Jew-Theo Charis 2	Ideoethno-Charis 3	Jew-Theo 4	Uncompleted 5	Row Total
LOC 17 Other MidEast	40 / 44.9	1 / 1.7	13 / 12.0		14 / 11.8	195 / 17.4
18 Other	2 / 2.2		1 / .9		2 / 1.7	18 / 1.6
(Continued) Column Total	89 / 8.0	60 / 5.4	108 / 9.7	54 / 4.8	119 / 10.6	1118 / 100.0

LOC   Location of Event by GTYPE   Type of Group

Count Col Pct	GTYPE Unclaimed 6	Theocen 7	Ethnocen 8	Ethno-Charis 9	Ideo-ethno 10	Row Total
LOC 17 Other MidEast	13 / 4.2	59 / 58.4	26 / 12.8	18 / 33.3	11 / 57.9	195 / 17.4
18 Other	1 / .3		11 / 5.4	1 / 1.9		18 / 1.6
(Continued) Column Total	311 / 27.8	101 / 9.0	203 / 18.2	54 / 4.8	19 / 1.7	1118 / 100.0

Number of missing Observations: 119

MIDDLE EAST TERRORIST GROUP BY TERRORIST GROUP TYPE

Theocentric Charismatic	Theocentric	Ethnocentric	Ethnocentric Charismatic	Ideo-Ethnocentric Charismatic
(Khomeini-Khomeini Inspired) • Hezbollah • Hezbollah/Palestine • Turk Islamic Jihad	• Al-Jihad (Egypt) • Gama'el Islamiya • Amal • Hamas (Izzedine al Quassam) • Moslem Brotherhood	• PLO • PLA • Fatah • May 15 Arab Organization • al-saiqa • Arab Liberation Front (ALF) • Abu Musa Faction • Popular Struggle Front (PSF) • Black September Organization (BSO)	• PLF-Muhammed Abu al-Abbas • ANO-Sabri al-Banna (Abu Nidal)	• PFLP-Dr. George Habash • PFLP-SOG - Wadi Haddad • DFLP-Naif Hawatamah • PDFLP • PFLP-GC-Ahmed Jibril
	Ideoethnocentric • Arab Communist Organization (ACO) • Lebanese Armed Revolutionary Faction (LARF)		**Jewish Theocentric Charismatic** *(Kahane-Kahane Inspired)* • Kach • Kahane Cahi • Jewish Defense League	**Jewish Theocentric** • TNT • Lifte Gang • the Sicarii • Keshet • The Hasmoneans

Source: Chasdi, Richard J. 1995. "The Dynamics of Middle East Terrorism, 1968-1993: A Functional Typology of Terrorist Group-Types." Ph.D. dissertation, Purdue University.

METHODOLOGICAL APPENDIX II
Relative Frequency of Target Type by Group-Name, 1968-1993

SPSS/PC+

TARGET   Location of Event by GNAME   Name of Group

Count Col Pct	GNAME Hezbollah	Kach	Kahane Chai	PFLP	DFLP	Row Total
	1	2	3	4	5	
TARGET 1 govt targets	19 21.6	4 14.8		14 15.2	1 4.2	172 23.0
2 infrastructure	1 1.1			6 6.5		14 1.9
3 civilian	67 76.1	23 85.2	2 100.0	72 78.3	23 95.8	551 73.8
6 govt-civilian						6 .8
Column (Continued) Total	88 11.8	27 3.6	2 .3	92 12.3	24 3.2	747 100.0

Count Col Pct	GNAME Keshet	Sicarri	TNT	The Hasmoneans	Lifta Gang	Row Total
	6	7	8	9	10	
TARGET 1 govt targets		5 29.4	1 7.7			172 23.0
2 infrastructure	1 20.0					14 1.9
3 civilian	4 80.0	12 70.6	12 92.3	1 100.0	1 100.0	551 73.8
6 govt-civilian						6 .8
Column (Continued) Total	5 .7	17 2.3	13 1.7	1 .1	1 .1	747 100.0

Count Col Pct	GNAME Hezbollah	Kach	Kahane Chai	PFLP	DFLP	Row Total
	1	2	3	4	5	
TARGET 7 civilian-govt	1 1.1					3 .4
9 civilian-infrast						1 .1
Column (Continued) Total	88 11.8	27 3.6	2 .3	92 12.3	24 3.2	747 100.0

Count Col Pct	GNAME Keshet	Sicarri	TNT	The Hasmoneans	Lifta Gang	Row Total
	6	7	8	9	10	
TARGET 7 civilian-govt						3 .4
9 civilian-infrast						1 .1
Column (Continued) Total	5 .7	17 2.3	13 1.7	1 .1	1 .1	747 100.0

Source: Chasdi, Richard J. 1995. "The Dynamics of Middle East Terrorism, 1968-1993: A Functional Typology of Terrorist Group-Types." Ph.D. dissertation, Purdue University.

METHODOLOGICAL APPENDIX II (Continued)
Relative Frequency of Target Type by Group-Name, 1968-1993

SPSS/PC+

TARGET   Location of Event by GNAME   Name of Group

Count Col Pct	GNAME PLO 11	ANO 12	PLF 13	Abu Mussa 14	Turk Isl Jihad 15	Row Total
TARGET 1 govt targets	4 8.5	21 35.0		1 20.0	2 50.0	172 23.0
2 infrastructure			1 12.5			14 1.9
3 civilian	43 91.5	38 63.3	7 87.5	4 80.0	2 50.0	551 73.8
6 govt-civilian						6 .8
(Continued) Column Total	47 6.3	60 8.0	8 1.1	5 .7	4 .5	747 100.0

Count Col Pct	GNAME Hezbollah/ Pales 16	Hamas 17	Fatah 18	Shiite Amal 19	LARF 20	Row Total
TARGET 1 govt targets		6 16.7	13 11.4	1 14.3	5 62.5	172 23.0
2 infrastructure			4 3.5			14 1.9
3 civilian	3 100.0	30 83.3	96 84.2	6 85.7	3 37.5	551 73.8
6 govt-civilian			1 .9			6 .8
(Continued) Column Total	3 .4	36 4.8	114 15.3	7 .9	8 1.1	747 100.0

Count Col Pct	GNAME PLO 11	ANO 12	PLF 13	Abu Mussa 14	Turk Isl Jihad 15	Row Total
TARGET 7 civilian-govt		1 1.7				3 .4
9 civilian-infrast						1 .1
(Continued) Column Total	47 6.3	60 8.0	8 1.1	5 .7	4 .5	747 100.0

Count Col Pct	GNAME Hezbollah/ Pales 16	Hamas 17	Fatah 18	Shiite Amal 19	LARF 20	Row Total
TARGET 7 civilian-govt						3 .4
9 civilian-infrast						1 .1
(Continued) Column Total	3 .4	36 4.8	114 15.3	7 .9	8 1.1	747 100.0

Source: Chasdi, Richard J. 1995. "The Dynamics of Middle East Terrorism, 1968-1993: A Functional Typology of Terrorist Group-Types." Ph.D. dissertation, Purdue University.

METHODOLOGICAL APPENDIX II (Continued)
Relative Frequency of Target Type by Group-Name, 1968-1993

SPSS/PC+

TARGET   Location of Event by GNAME   Name of Group

Count Col Pct	GNAME PFLP-GC 21	PFLP-SOG 22	May 15 24	Gammael Islamiya 25	ALF 26	Row Total
TARGET 1 govt targets	4 25.0		1 14.3	4 28.6		172 23.0
2 infrastructure						14 1.9
3 civilian	12 75.0	2 100.0	6 85.7	8 57.1	3 100.0	551 73.8
6 govt-civilian				1 7.1		6 .8
(Continued) Column Total	16 2.1	2 .3	7 .9	14 1.9	3 .4	747 100.0

Count Col Pct	GNAME ACO 27	BSO 28	JDL 29	PDFLP 31	Row Total
TARGET 1 govt targets	4 36.4	24 40.0	27 73.0		172 23.0
2 infrastructure		1 1.7			14 1.9
3 civilian	7 63.6	32 53.3	8 21.6	5 100.0	551 73.8
6 govt-civilian		2 3.3	2 5.4		6 .8
(Continued) Column Total	11 1.5	60 8.0	37 5.0	5 .7	747 100.0

Count Col Pct	GNAME PFLP-GC 21	PFLP-SOG 22	May 15 24	Gammael Islamiya 25	ALF 26	Row Total
TARGET 7 civilian-govt				1 7.1		3 .4
9 civilian-infrast						1 .1
(Continued) Column Total	16 2.1	2 .3	7 .9	14 1.9	3 .4	747 100.0

Count Col Pct	GNAME ACO 27	BSO 28	JDL 29	PDFLP 31	Row Total
TARGET 7 civilian-govt					3 .4
9 civilian-infrast		1 1.7			1 .1
(Continued) Column Total	11 1.5	60 8.0	37 5.0	5 .7	747 100.0

Source: Chasdi, Richard J. 1995. "The Dynamics of Middle East Terrorism, 1968-1993: A Functional Typology of Terrorist Group-Types." Ph.D. dissertation, Purdue University.

Chapter Five

METHODOLOGICAL APPENDIX II (Continued)
Relative Frequency of Target Type by Group-Name, 1968-1993

SPSS/PC+

TARGET   Location of Event by GNAME   Name of Group

	GNAME				
Count Col Pct TARGET	PSF 32	Moslem Brothd 33	al-Jihad (Egypt) 34	alsaiqa 35	Row Total
1 govt targets		4 40.0	4 66.7	1 33.3	172 23.0
2 infrastructure					14 1.9
3 civilian	3 100.0	6 60.0	2 33.3	2 66.7	551 73.8
6 govt-civilian					6 .8
Column (Continued) Total	3 .4	10 1.3	6 .8	3 .4	747 100.0

	GNAME				
Count Col Pct TARGET	PSF 32	Moslem Brothd 33	al-Jihad (Egypt) 34	alsaiqa 35	Row Total
7 civilian-govt					3 .4
9 civilian-infrast					1 .1
Column (Continued) Total	3 .4	10 1.3	6 .8	3 .4	747 100.0

Source: Chasdi, Richard J. 1995. "The Dynamics of Middle East Terrorism, 1968-1993: A Functional Typology of Terrorist Group-Types." Ph.D. dissertation, Purdue University.

Notes

Reprinted with the kind permission of *The Journal of Conflict Studies*, except for work on terrorist group age, group size, and group-type typology (*The Journal of Conflict Studies*, XVII, No. 2).

1. Nef reports that, "unfortunate as it may seem from a moral viewpoint, terrorism turns out to be quite a 'rational' technique, if by rational we assume an instrumental relationship between ends and means" (Nef 1978, 19-20). Hutchinson is another writer who accepts the rationality assumption in decision-making for terrorist group leaders. We are told, "Paradoxically terrorism, which must appear irrational and unpredictable, in order to be effective, is an eminently rational strategy, calculated in terms of predictable costs and benefits" (Nef 1978, 20; Chasdi 1995, 1,2, 92, 95, 119).

2. For example, a strong case can be made that Islamic fundamentalist terrorists attacked commuter buses in Israel and killed over 60 Israelis during four successive attacks precisely because terrorist group decision-makers reasoned that such carnage would severely disrupt if not destroy the "peace process" (Schmemann 1996, pp. A-1, A-6; Ibrahim 1996, A-5; Pearson and Rochester 1998, 445-465; 659-652).

3. Long 1990, 18-19, 211; Taheri 1987, 89; Parsons 1964, 361.

4. Schmid and Jongman 1988, 44.

5. TVI Report 1990, 2.

6. See Abu Khalil 1991, 394-395, 399. Although it may be hard to believe, the organizational structure of many religious, nationalist and Marxist-Leninist terrorist groups seems to be remarkably similar. For example, AbuKhalil tells us the structural shape of Hizbollah is in reality an Islamic version of traditional Leninist structuralist standards of organization. For AbuKhalil, "Hizbollah is not an Islamic stipulation. It is an Islamic adaptation to the era of Leninist revolutionary organizations." For instance, AbuKhalil reports that the Shura Council, which is Hizbollah's most powerful and exclusive leadership organ, closely mirrors the Soviet Politburo in functional terms.

7. See *Webster's New Collegiate Dictionary* 1977, 205. Parenthetically, it should be noted that "common values," as used in this definition of a clan, are inclusive of religious values. For example, the Lebanese Armed Revolutionary Faction (LARF) is a Marxist-Leninist terrorist organization that "... consists mostly of Lebanese Christians from the villages of Qubayyat and Andaqat in northern Lebanon" (United States Department of Defense 1988, 19 hereafter USDOD; Long 1990, 42).

8. Norton 1988, 16-17.

9. Ibid., 15, 17.

10. *Jerusalem Post* 1984b, 5; Sprinzak 1988, 200, 194, 214; Rosenberg 1984a, 1, 2; Rosenberg 1984b, 1, 17; Rosenberg 1984c, 1, 2; Rosenberg 1984d, 1, 10; *Jerusalem Post* 1983c, 1, 2; *Jerusalem Post* 1983b 1, 2; Richardson and Rosenberg 1984, 1,8; Wilkinson 1977, 204-205.

11. TVI Report 1989a, 2.

12. TVI Report 1989b, 10.

13. TVI Report 1989c, 13.

14. Starr and Most 1985, 32-52.

15. Starr and Most 1985, 33-52; Chasdi 1995, 3-5, 100-105, 344-350. The structural outline of this functional terrorist group-type typology derives from Starr and Most's quantitative analysis of third world conflicts, and was developed with the invaluable assistance of Professor Michael S. Stohl (Starr and Most 1985, 33-52).

The coding scheme is as follows:

A = Ideology: 1 = Marxist-Leninist; 2 = religious; 3 = Palestinian nationalist

B = Recruitment: 1 = clan; 2 = followers of a charismatic leader; 3 = Palestinian refugees*

C = Goals: 1 = Islamic state in Palestine and/or other areas of the Middle East; 2 = secular Palestinian state; 3 = Marxist-Leninist state in Palestine and/or other areas of the Middle East; 4 = religious Jewish state in Israel

*Although some overlap happens, groups are categorized according to discernible trends based on available data and/or information that can be extrapolated from newspaper accounts.

The following is a list of the possible thirty-six combinations of terrorist group-types:

$A^1 B^1 C^1$ 1, 1, 1, - a Marxist-Leninist terrorist group recruiting from a clan, with the goal of an Islamic state in Palestine and/or other areas of the Middle East

$A^1 B^1 C^2$ 1, 1, 2, - a Marxist-Leninist terrorist group recruiting from a clan, with the goal of a secular Palestinian state

$A^1 B^1 C^3$ 1, 1, 3, - a Marxist-Leninist terrorist group recruiting from a clan, with the goal of a Marxist-Leninist state in Palestine and/or other areas of the Middle East ("Marxist-Leninist" terrorist groups like the Lebanese Armed Revolutionary Faction [LARF] and the Arab Communist Organization [ACO])

$A^1 B^1 C^4$ 1, 1, 4, - a Marxist-Leninist terrorist group recruiting from a clan, with the goal of a religious Jewish state in Israel

$A^1 B^2 C^1$ 1, 2, 1, - a Marxist-Leninist terrorist group recruiting from followers of a charismatic leader with the goal of an Islamic state in Palestine and/or other areas of the Middle East

$A^1 B^2 C^2$ 1, 2, 2, - a Marxist-Leninist terrorist group recruiting from followers of a charismatic leader with the goal of a secular Palestinian state

$A^1 B^2 C^3$ 1, 2, 3, - a Marxist-Leninist terrorist group recruiting from followers of a charismatic leader with the goal of a Marxist-Leninist state in Palestine and/or other areas of the Middle East ("Marxist-Leninist" terrorist groups led by a charismatic leader like the Popular Front for the Liberation of Palestine [PFLP] led by Dr. George Habash, and the Democratic Front for the Liberation of Palestine [DFLP] led by Naif Hawatamah)

$A^1 B^2 C^4$ 1, 2, 4, - a Marxist-Leninist terrorist group recruiting from followers of a charismatic leader with the goal of a religious Jewish state in Israel

$A^1 B^3 C^1$ 1, 3, 1, - a Marxist-Leninist terrorist group recruiting from Palestinian refugees with the goal of an Islamic state in Palestine and/or other areas of the Middle East

$A^1 B^3 C^2$ 1, 3, 2, - a Marxist-Leninist terrorist group recruiting from Palestinian refugees with the goal of a secular Palestinian state

$A^1 B^3 C^3$ 1, 3, 3, - a Marxist-Leninist terrorist group recruiting from Palestinian refugees with the goal of a Marxist-Leninist state in Palestine and/or other areas of the Middle East

$A^1 B^3 C^4$ 1, 3, 4, - a Marxist-Leninist terrorist group recruiting from Palestinian refugees with the goal of a religious Jewish state in Israel

$A^2 B^1 C^1$ 2, 1, 1, - a religious terrorist group, recruiting from a clan, with the goal of an Islamic state in Palestine and/or other areas of the Middle East (Islamic fundamentalist terrorist groups like Hamas, Amal, and al-Jihad [Egypt])

$A^2 B^1 C^2$ 2, 1, 2, - a religious terrorist group, recruiting from a clan with the goal of a secular Palestinian state

$A^2 B^1 C^3$ 2, 1, 3, - a religious terrorist group recruiting from a clan with the goal of a Marxist-Leninist state in Palestine and/or other areas of the Middle East

$A^2 B^1 C^4$ 2, 1, 4, - a religious terrorist group recruiting from a clan with the goal of a religious Jewish state in Israel (Jewish fundamentalist terrorist groups like "Terror Against Terror" [TNT], the Hasmoneans, the Lifta Gang, the Sicarri, and Keshet)

$A^2 B^2 C^1$ 2, 2, 1, - a religious terrorist group recruiting from followers of a charismatic leader with the goal of an Islamic state in Palestine or other areas of the Middle East (Islamic fundamentalist terrorist groups led by a charismatic leader like Hezbollah, Hezbollah/Palestine, and Turkish Islamic Jihad that were led or inspired by Ayatollah Ruhollah Khomeini and his clerics)

$A^2 B^2 C^2$ 2, 2, 2, - a religious terrorist group recruiting from followers of a charismatic leader with the goal of a secular Palestinian state

$A^2 B^2 C^3$ 2, 2, 3, - a religious terrorist group recruiting from followers of a charismatic leader with the goal of a Marxist-Leninist state in Palestine and/or other areas of the Middle East

$A^2 B^2 C^4$ 2, 2, 4, - a religious terrorist group recruiting from followers of a charismatic leader with the goal of a religious Jewish state in Israel (Jewish fundamentalist terrorist groups led by a charismatic leader like The Jewish Defense League [JDL], Kach, and Kahane Chai)

$A^2 B^3 C^1$ 2, 3, 1, - a religious terrorist group recruiting from Palestinian refugees with the goal of an Islamic state in Palestine and/or other areas of the Middle East

$A^2 B^3 C^2$ 2, 3, 2, - a religious terrorist group recruiting from Palestinian refugees with the goal of a secular Palestinian state

$A^2 B^3 C^3$ 2, 3, 3, - a religious terrorist group recruiting from Palestinian refugees with the goal of a Marxist-Leninist state in Palestine and/or other areas of the Middle East

$A^2 B^3 C^4$ 2, 3, 4, - a religious terrorist group recruiting from Palestinian refugees with the goal of a religious Jewish state in Israel

$A^3 B^1 C^1$ 3, 1, 1, - a Palestinian nationalist terrorist group recruiting from a clan with the goals of an Islamic state in Palestine and/or other areas of the Middle East

$A^3 B^1 C^2$ 3, 1, 2, - a Palestinian nationalist terrorist group recruiting from a clan with the goal of a secular Palestinian state

$A^3 B^1 C^3$ 3, 1, 3, - a Palestinian nationalist terrorist group recruiting from a clan with the goal of a Marxist-Leninist state in Palestine and/or other areas of the Middle East

$A^3 B^1 C^4$ 3, 1, 4, - a Palestinian nationalist terrorist group recruiting from a clan with the goal of a religious Jewish state in Israel

$A^3 B^2 C^1$ 3, 2, 1, - a Palestinian nationalist terrorist group recruiting from followers of a charismatic leader with the goal of an Islamic state in Palestine and/or other areas of the Middle East

$A^3 B^2 C^2$ 3, 2, 2, - a Palestinian nationalist terrorist group recruiting from followers of a charismatic leader with the goal of a secular Palestinian state (nationalist-irredentist terrorist groups led by a charismatic leader like The Abu Nidal Organization [ANO] led by Sabri al-Banna; the Popular Front for the Liberation of Palestine-General Command [PFLP-GC] led by Ahmed Jabril; the Palestine Liberation Front [PLF] led by Muhammed Abu al-Abbas)

$A^3 B^2 C^3$ 3, 2, 3, - a Palestinian nationalist terrorist group recruiting from followers of a charismatic leader with the goal of a Marxist-Leninist state in Palestine and/or other areas of the Middle East

$A^3 B^2 C^4$ 3, 2, 4, - a Palestinian nationalist terrorist group recruiting from followers of a charismatic leader with the goal of a religious Jewish state in Israel

$A^3 B^3 C^1$ 3, 3, 1, - a Palestinian nationalist terrorist group recruiting from Palestinian refugees with the goal of an Islamic state in Palestine and/or other areas of the Middle East

$A^3 B^3 C^2$ 3, 3, 2, - a Palestinian nationalist terrorist group recruiting from Palestinian refugees with the goal of a secular Palestinian state (nationalist-irredentist terrorist groups like al-Fatah, the Arab Liberation Front [ALF] and the Palestine Liberation Organization [PLO])

$A^3 B^3 C^3$ 3, 3, 3, - a Palestinian nationalist terrorist group recruiting from

Palestinian refugees with the goal of a Marxist-Leninist state in Palestine and/or other areas of the Middle East

A^3 B^3 C^4 3, 3, 4, - a Palestinian nationalist terrorist group recruiting from Palestinian refugees with the goal of a religious Jewish state in Israel

16. This classification scheme draws primarily from Flemming's typology of terrorist groups that operate in Western Europe. Flemming creates three categories of terrorist groups. The first category is "Euroclass," which is comprised of terrorist groups that engage in anti-imperialist struggles. The second category is "Europrimordial," comprised of terrorist groups that wage war against the ruling elite for autonomy. The third category is Palestinian nationalist, which is made up of Palestinian terrorist groups that wage war against Israel and the West. See Flemming 1992, 95. Other works, including Russell, Banker and Miller's article also influenced the development of this classification scheme. See Russell, Banker and Miller 1979, 3-42.

17. Examples of such typologies abound, including Wilkinson 1979, 1974, Iviansky 1977, and Rubenstein 1987 in the case of the former, and Pluchinsky 1981 in the case of the latter. See Chapter Two for a comprehensive discussion about those typologies.

18. I use Wallerstein's phrase "world systems" to describe that conceptualization (Wallerstein, 1974). This construct was developed with the invaluable assistance of Michael S. Stohl and Patricia T. Morris. Marxist-Leninist terrorist groups are considered structuralist, while Islamic fundamentalist terrorist groups and nationalist-irredentist terrorist groups are considered to be more "non-structuralist" (Chasdi 1995, 104, 314).

19. Plainly, the Arab Middle East has a long-standing tradition of making distinctions between groups based on religious affiliation (Norton 1988, 13-14). It is that practice which generates and sustains a prevailing social ideology that highlights the importance of religion and group identification. It seems plausible that charismatic leaders of terrorist groups with political ideologies that are antithetical to the prevailing social ideology (Islam) might encourage their groups to act in ways more like other Arab/Islamic terrorist groups in order to develop and nurture a set of political interconnections.

20. Hoffman 1984, 10-15; Goodman 1971, 116, 118-119, 122; Lasswell 1978, 258; Pfaltzgraf 1986, 292; Lustick 1988, 67-71; Sprinzak 1988, 194-216; Merkel 1986, 25; Wilkinson 1986, 204-205.

21. Beres 1987; Beres 1988a, 293, 299 n14; Beres 1988b, 335; Beres 1990, 130, 132, 133; Blakesley 1992, 35-37; Blakesley and Lagodny 1991; Detter Delupis 1987, 75, 242, 242 n76; Gal-Or 1985; Intoccia 1985, 136-139; Joyner 1988, 37; Schmid 1983, 119-158; Wardlaw 1988, 235; Fried 1985, 98, 99-100, 107-108; Brierly 1963; Falvey 1986; Murphy 1978; Bassiouni 1978; Bassiouni 1986; Chasdi 1994, 66; Pearson and Rochester 1998, 448.

22. Mickolus 1980. In a broader sense, I used the works of Mickolus, Sandler, and Murdock as a reference and guide for acquiring reports from the *Jerusalem Post* (Mickolus, Sandler, and Murdock 1989a, 1989b).

23. Chasdi 1995, 123-126.

24. *The Arab News* 1993, 4; *The Arab News* 1994, 4.

25. Weimann and Winn 1994, 71.

26. Chasdi 1995, 126-127.

27. For example, see Kellet, Beanlands and Deacon 1991, 40.

28. Getzler 1983, 1, 2; Shapiro 1983, 3; *The Jerusalem Post* 1987a, 1; Struminski 1987, 1; Blitzer 1987a, 1; Blitzer 1987b, 1; *The Jerusalem Post* 1987b, 1.

29. Norusis 1991, 269-270, 275-276, 229-230, 322, 325; White 1990, 350-354, 156; Wonnacott and Wonnacott 1990, 43, 262, 293-295, 549-560; Elifson, Runyon and Haber 1982, 432-435, 161.

30. Livingstone and Halevy 1990, 18; Alexander and Sinai 1989, 130, 131.

31. Norusis, 1991, 270.

32. Norusis 1991, 85-87, 270, 132-133.

33. Mickolus 1980, xviii; Flemming 1992, 133 n2; Enders, Parise and Sandler 1992, 305-306; Johnson 1978, 270; Jenkins 1988, 252.

34. A substantial number of terrorist assaults in the United States were reported to have been committed by the Jewish Defense League (JDL). A coder reliability test was performed on seventeen terrorism entries for the more subjective data categories such as "target," "property damage," "political event" and "location" (Shimko 1995, 56-57). Out of a possible 100%, the coder reliability score was 96.1%, which means that the Purdue University graduate students who assisted me coded in ways very similar to how I coded (Chasdi 1995, 130, 142, 343).

35. Long 1990, 1; Flemming 1992, 164, 180, 194-195, 203-204; Gurr 1988, 45-46; Mickolus 1980, xxii-xiii.

36. The sample mean is 1.454 and the standard deviation is 9.342. A terrorist incident that killed fifty or more people would lie over five standard deviations away from the mean. Accordingly, those terrorist assaults are termed extreme outlier cases (Chasdi 1995, 375).

37. *The Jerusalem Post* 1983d, 1-2; *The Jerusalem Post* 1981c; Bernstein 1981, 1, 2; *The Jerusalem Post* 1986b, 3; *The Jerusalem Post* 1989a, 1; *The Jerusalem Post* 1989c, 12.

38. Horowitz 1985; von der Mehden 1973.

39. The sample mean is 4.639 and the standard deviation is 31.774. A terrorist incident that injured over one hundred persons would lie over three standard deviations away from the mean (Chasdi 1995, 376); Hoffman, Morris and Billing 1985, 1, 2; Oked 1985, 2; Makovsky 1992, 1; Makovsky and Izenberg 1992, 1, 3; Tsur 1993, 3; *The Jerusalem Post* 1993a, 3; *The Jerusalem*

Post 1981a, 1; *The Jerusalem Post* 1981b, 2.

40. Crenshaw 1983, 29; Bassiouni 1978, 523-524; Aston 1980, 59-92; Smart 1987, 5; Mickolus 1976, 1317; Flemming 1992, 70, 115-118. In the narrower sense, those hypotheses draw from Flemming's framework of analysis.

41. The Pearson chi square statistic is 29.06 with 7 degrees of freedom and a p value of .00014 [Minimum Expected Frequency: 4.884; Cells with Expected Frequency < 5 1 OF 16 (6.3%); Number of Missing Observations: 564] (Chasdi 1995, 162). While analysis of the table residuals and group-type relative frequencies suggest a breakdown of the data into eight Middle East terrorist group-types may contribute to the statistical association observed, that analysis is done to retain useful information, and for theoretical reasons based on empirical observations about terrorist groups in the political landscape.

42. Duvall and Stohl 1983, 207-211; Stohl 1988, 161-163.

43. My thinking about the targeting practices of Islamic fundamentalist terrorist groups was influenced primarily by Martin 1987, 55-71; Rapoport 1987, 72-88; Taheri 1987; Dawisha 1986; Pisano 1988; Long 1990.

44. The Pearson chi square statistic is 71.24 with 7 degrees of freedom and a p value of less than .0001 [Minimum Expected Frequency 6.021; Number of Missing Observations 565] (Chasdi 1995, 168).

45. Chasdi 1995, 168-170.

46. Chasdi 1995, 377-387.

47. From the observed data the analysis shows that 93.3% of Jewish theocentric charismatic attacks happened in Israel, the Occupied Territories and the United States. In the case of Jewish theocentric groups, 100% of all incidents happened in Israel and the Occupied Territories (Methodological Appendix). To be sure, Flemming (1992, 77-78) makes a similar argument about the influence that constituency groups have on the intensity of terrorist assaults in Western Europe.

48. Hoffman 1984, 11; Shultz 1978, 10; Lasswell 1978, 258; Pfaltzgraff 1986, 292.

49. Goodman 1971, 32, 33, 115-116, 118-119, 121-122.

50. Ibid., 116-118.

51. n43.

52. The Pearson chi square statistic is 55.94 with 7 degrees of freedom and a p value of less than .0001 [Minimum Expected Frequency: 6.404; Number of Missing Observations 614] (Chasdi 1995, 174).

53. Chasdi 1995, 174-176.

54. For theocentric groups 40.0% + 1.1% = 41.1% and for ideo-ethno-centric groups 29.4% + 11.8% = 41.2%.

55. Zariski 1989, 264; Johnson 1982, 164.

56. Flemming's ideas about the targeting practices of "Euroclass" terrorist groups in Western Europe influenced my way of thinking about similar types of terrorist groups in the Middle East (Flemming 1992, 146, 149, 157, 161).

57. The Pearson chi square statistic is 26.44 with 7 degrees of freedom and a p value of .00042 [Minimum Expected Frequency: 3.642; Cells With Expected Frequency < 5 1 OF 16 (6.3%); Number of Missing Observations: 728] (Chasdi 1995, 183).

58. Chasdi 1995, 185-186.

59. Those findings are consistent with the analysis of unclaimed acts found in Chasdi 1995, 377-387.

60. That theoretical proposition is based on the writings of Crenshaw (1983, 26 n12); Russell, Banker and Miller (1979, 34); Smart (1987, 10); Oots (1984, 63, 65, 88-105).

61. The Pearson chi square statistic is 15.50 with 4 degrees of freedom and a p value of .00376 [Minimum Expected Frequency: 5.292; Number of Missing Observations: 572], Chasdi 1995, 188, 229-230; Kendall's tau-b value: .06041; ASE1: .03468; T-value: 1.73819; Chasdi 1995, 188.

62. Oots 1984, 89, 104-105.

63. That theoretical proposition is based on the writings of Flemming (1992, 231); Long (1990, 24); Karber and Mengel (1983, 23-39).

64. The Pearson chi square statistic is 11.977 with 2 degrees of freedom and a p value of .00251 [Minimum Expected Frequency: 28.374; Number of Missing Observations: 585]; Kendall's tau-b value: .12176; ASE1: .03477; T-value: 3.45372; Chasdi 1995, 192.

65. I am using Lasswell's terminology to describe the growth of the power of political entities which presumably applies to sub-national as well as national actors. See Lasswell 1935, 37, 107, 110, 252, 253; Lasswell 1978, 261-263; Long 1990, 24; Crozier 1960, 127; Flemming 1992, 231.

66. Merari et al. 1985; Waugh 1982, 53, 56; Shultz 1978, 10; O'Neill 1978, 34,40, 25; Osmond 1979, 115-118, 57-58, 101-102, 90-93, 142- 143; Flemming 1992, 91.

67. The Pearson chi square statistic is 207.78 with 5 degrees of freedom and a p value of less than .0001 [Minimum Expected Frequency: 3.088; Cells with Expected Frequency <5 1 OF 12 (8.3%); Number of Missing Observations: 40] (Chasdi 1995, 196).

68. Brecher and James 1987, 4-23.

69. The Pearson chi square statistic is 24.43 with 10 degrees of freedom and a p value of .00652 [Minimum Expected Frequency: .466; Cells with Expected Frequency <5 7 OF 22 (31.8%); Number of Missing Observations: 911].

70. Chasdi 1995, 375, 376.

71. n18.

72. Taheri 1987, 121, 20, 21.

73. Ibid.

74. Ibid.; Chasdi 1995, 169-170.
75. Ibid.; Chasdi 1995, 185-186.
76. Ibid.; Chasdi 1995, 392.
77. See Methodological Appendix II.
78. Methodological Appendix I.
79. Goodman 1971.
80. Methodological Appendix I.
81. Hoffman 1984, 11.
82. Merari 1978, 331-346; Waugh 1982, 53, 56, 60, 63, 80; Pluchinsky 1981, 40, 48, 52, 60, 71.
83. See n40.
84. Chasdi 1995, 97-98.
85. McEwen and Sloan 1980; National Governors Association 1979; Trent 1979, 46; Farrell 1986, 53, 54; Kupperman and Friedlander 1979, 57; Evans 1982, 241-253; Jenkins 1981, 176; Hocking 1986, 303.
86. Flemming 1992, 77-78; Harris 1989, 75-100; Gurr 1988, 1989a, 1989b; Rubenstein, 1989, 308-309; Graham 1989, 336-338; Dollard et al., 1939; Lasswell 1935, 32, 37, 100-101, 107, 110-111, 237, 252, 253.
87. Baldwin 1971; Baldwin 1985; Beres 1992, interview, Purdue University; Wardlaw 1982, 66.
88. Cohen 1973, 13.
89. Methodological Appendix I.
90. Zinnes 1976a, 1976b.

Chapter Six

Conclusions

Qualitative Analysis

All of the aforementioned really leads to the basic question of what has been learned from this treatment about Middle East terrorism. The framework for discussion involves: a summary of qualitative reflections about how Middle East terrorist group formation and evolution dovetails with the Reiss and Roth "risk factor matrix"; a summary about discernible trends in the empirical data about the behavior of different types of Middle East terrorist groups; and a description of findings in terms of applications to counter-terrorism stratagems in the larger world of action.

To be sure, there is precious little in the way of work that sheds light on the formative processes of terrorist groups that begins to tackle such issues as why terrorist groups form in the first place, why certain persons gravitate toward and fall into the orbit of political terrorism, and why terrorist groups oftentimes "splinter," thereby in effect invoking "offshoot" terrorist groups that in many cases grow and thrive in effective and sustained ways. I have tried to make the case throughout this study that the idea of a "terrorist personality," that really presupposes and derives from the shopworn notion that terrorists are "madmen" or "psychotic," is not only flawed, but bears little fruit in terms of helping to understand the complex set of processes related to political context that is intrinsic to what political terrorism is all about. Closer to the mark, I think, is work that focuses special attention on the dynamics of political context, inclusive of the process of change sparked by political-social events that has effects on existing political and social infrastructure that serve as seedbeds for communities.

Qualitative analysis on Middle East terrorist group formation and evolution suggests there is what Reiss and Roth call an "interplay" between various explanatory variables discussed above, across different levels of analysis, that coincide in ways that make terrorist group formation, be it within the context of initial formation or "group splitting," more likely to happen.[1] Picture, for example, a relatively stable political-social system, replete with low-level strains and tensions between groups perhaps due to competing claims or profound and lasting ethnic or religious fissures, that is rent apart by long-haul ("predisposing"), middle-range ("situational") and short-run ("activating" or "triggering") change in the political setting. In terms of long-range factors, demographic change, perhaps due to immigration and land purchase, leads to gradual "pressurization" of the political-social system with the passage of time. To be specific, those long-haul or "predisposing" factors were at work in Palestine probably starting from the 1880's, when increasing Jewish immigration and land purchase within the context of the fledgling Zionist movement began to introduce pressure.

The notion that those long term ("predisposing") factors can presuppose and derive from long-standing and time-honored fissures along religious and ethnic lines, resonates in terms of the dynamics between Shi'as and Sunnis in Lebanon, that revolve around central themes of political and economic discrimination for many Shi'as particularly in southern Lebanon.[2] Both Amal, under the aegis of Sayyid Musa al-Sadr, and Hezbollah, under the aegis of Ayatollah Sayyid Muhammed Hussayn Fadlallah, have been able to tap into the energy generated and sustained by the "macrosocial" and "microsocial" alignment of religious minority status, coupled with economic and political discrimination.[3] At the same time, long term disproportion of wealth between "the haves and the have-nots" in Egypt seems to be an important cornerstone in terms of tracing an arc to the origins of many more contemporary revivalist or fundamentalist terrorist groups in Egypt.

Compounding the "pressure" even more, are the strains and tensions generated and sustained by middle-range ("situational") factors. In this application of Reiss and Roth's work "situational" factors have middle-range effects and coincide with the effects of the long term factors described above. For example, one may think about the British proposal for "quasi-government" through "devolution" for both Arab and Jewish Palestinians as a "situational" factor that had profound and lasting effects for both groups with the passage of time.

It is commonplace to note that Jewish Palestinian leaders took advantage of that opportunity, while Arab Palestinian leaders looked askance at the proposal. It seems plausible that the emergent reality of Jewish "proto-government," which gave Palestinian Jews a clear cut advantage in terms of organization over their Palestinian Arab counterparts, contributed to the frustration and anxiety that was an explanatory factor for terrorist assaults to come. In other political settings discussed in this book, middle-range ("situational") factors seem to have played an important role with respect to the genesis of new "splinter" or "offshoot" terrorist groups. For example, Cobban tells us that the formation of the PLO in 1964, which interestingly enough can trace an arc to the short-run "activating" factor of the Israel National Water Carrier project in the Negev (the Israeli desert), spawned efforts on the part of Habash and Haddad to craft a new terrorist group, the National Front for the Liberation of Palestine (NFLP), an antecedent to the Popular Front For the Liberation of Palestine (PFLP).[4]

To be sure, the volcanic-like eruptions of short-run "activating" factors dovetail nicely with the long-range and middle-range factors that stem from the Reiss and Roth analysis and that were previously mentioned. One short-run "activating factor" responsible for "Marxist-Leninist" terrorist group formation was The Six Day War in 1967 that besmirched Nasser's role as the guidepost of the struggle against Western imperialism.[5] The profound and lasting residual effects of Nasser's military defeat served as a catalyst for the merger of the NFLP with other small groups into the generally recognizable PFLP. Plainly, the findings depict how the death of a "charismatic leader" like Dr. Waddi Haddad or Rabbi Meir Kahane is a type of short-run "activating" factor that generates and sustains terrorist group "splitting" and terrorist group "offshoots." The foregoing discussion provides only a few examples of how political events can help give structural shape to terrorist group formation and splitting. To be sure, the tantalizing question of whether or not knowledge about terrorist group "splitting" can be used by counter-terrorism planners to manipulate the "splitting" process in pursuit of geopolitical considerations and political gain will be considered below.

In the broader sense, an underlying issue to mull over concerns the role that explanatory factors have at what Reiss and Roth call the "individual" level of analysis with respect to terrorist group formation. In the narrower sense, it is possible to chronicle how this work's qualitative analysis sheds light on why particular persons gravitate toward political terrorism as a vehicle of political expression and personal empowerment. From the start, it is critical to recognize that very few persons actually become terrorist activists, in contrast to the cacophony of voices that make up a "constituency group." Clearly, one ineluctable question that deserves increased attention is what makes for the difference?

The qualitative analysis of terrorist group leaders seems to suggest that factors at the "individual level" like cognitive processing difficulties (e.g., misreadings of history, spurious interconnections between political events) or rage management issues, or perhaps a combination of both, serve to amplify existing political and social conditions like war or communal conflict short of full-blown war and the traumas associated with those conditions. To be sure, the full-blown or near full-blown alignment of explanatory factors at the "individual" level with those at the "social" level of analysis evokes depression, rage, and similar feelings that makes those pre-existing social conditions unbearable and intolerable. For example, in the case of Abu Nidal, both Melman and Seale suggest that Sabri al-Banna's seething rage, which may have helped to generate and sustain especially vicious ANO terrorist assaults, presupposes and derives from a psyche fraught with an inflexibility that made it difficult to differentiate between events to be interpreted as personal assaults and catastrophic loss due to conditions such as war or exploitation.[6]

Clearly, in less dramatic ways perhaps, it seems plausible that many persons who gravitate toward the use of terrorist assaults, may have an alignment of factors, be they "psychosocial" or "biological" to use Reiss and Roth's labels, that also amplify existing social, economic and political conditions. It follows that the foregoing alignment or "mixture" of explanatory factors at the "individual" level of analysis, even among those with an enormous capacity for carrying out terrorist assaults, varies from one person to another. Unequivocally, more work needs to be done to isolate and identify the effects of explanatory variables both among and between different levels of analysis.

The analysis suggests there are meaningful differences between Middle East terrorist groups led by charismatic leaders and Middle East terrorist groups that are not. From the vantage of recruitment, this study has covered how, in the case of charismatic leaders like Habash, Haddad, Hawatamah, Fadlallah, Khomeini, and Kahane, the structural shape of the struggle is imprinted indelibly by the leader's singular vision of the struggle. That is very different, for example, from Yasser Arafat's eschewing of a formal ideology for al-Fatah, and his penchant for reliance on clarion calls to armed struggle as a substitute.[7]

What seems significant here is that followers of a charismatic leader are often distinct groups, defined in religious terms that oftentimes seem to obscure an economic dimension to the political fray. For example, Norton describes how Shi'as are a religious minority group in Lebanon that are afflicted with economic discrimination.[8] In Egypt, both Auda and Gaffney suggest that many persons who fall into the orbit of more contemporary Islamic revivalist terrorist organizations are persons shackled on the fringes of society.[9] In a similar vein, Livingstone and Halevy suggest that PFLP's underlying recruitment efforts played a Marxist-Leninist interpretation of events against the looming backdrop of oil-rich Gulf states, oil-rich Saudi Arabia, and the Western imperialist powers.[10] In summation, it is probably no exaggeration to say that followers fall into "camps" based on individual appraisals of "the struggle" and an array of what Reiss and Roth call "individual factors" at work.

Quantitative Analysis

What follows is a comprehensive summary of the major trends in the data, with the aim of tying together pieces of information that shed light on what Middle East terrorism is all about. To recapitulate, the structural basis of that quantitative analysis revolves around three defining characteristics that distinguish among terrorist group-types: ideology, goals and recruitment patterns. Based on those characteristics, a typology of Middle East terrorism is developed that can categorize terrorist groups in a way that makes it possible to generate and test hypotheses about terrorist group behavior.

Those hypotheses revolve around the influence of five independent and intervening variables: political ideology, group size, group age, location, and political events. At the most basic level, the typology is functional because the data from the hypothesis testing reveal regular patterns of behavior that lends themselves to predictions about the future. Notwithstanding that, intrinsic to the concept of typology functionality is the capacity to respond to the inevitability of change. This typology meets that criterion as well because it provides a blueprint for the classification of Middle East terrorism group-types that may emerge over time.

The following discussion will summarize some of the general trends in the data about terrorism and showcase some trends in the behavior of specific types of Middle East terrorist groups. A first pass at the data reveals that Middle East terrorism is characterized by cyclical activity. The "peak years" of activity between 1978 and 1993 were the years 1978, 1985, 1989 and 1993. To be sure, that finding is consistent with the findings of other studies on terrorist assault event patterns.[11] In the broader sense, there has been a pronounced increase in the frequency of Middle East terrorism. Clearly, the threat of Middle East terrorism has grown larger with the passage of time

A breakdown of the data reveals that the single most predominant number of terrorist acts were committed by anonymous groups or "lone operatives." It is possible that anonymous terrorist assaults suffice in a condition where issue areas and groups in fierce competition are clearly articulated and well known. An analysis by group-type shows that national-ist-irredentist terrorist groups were the most prolific terrorist groups in operation. The number of nationalist-irredentist terrorist group incidents easily outpaced the second place amount posted by Marxist-Leninist terrorist groups led by a charismatic leader, by nearly a 2:1 margin. Alternately, Marxist-Leninist terrorist groups without a charismatic leader were the least active of all types of Middle East terrorist groups. Not surprisingly, that pattern remains constant when individual terrorist groups are evaluated. Al-Fatah was the most prolific group, while the Popular Front for the Liberation of Palestine (PFLP) followed in second place.

An analysis of the location of terrorist activity reveals that an over-whelmingly large amount of Middle East terrorism took place in Israel and the Occupied Territories. What also seems significant with respect to location is that Europe was afflicted with almost as much Middle East terrorism as other parts of the Middle East. With respect to targeting, several discernible trends in Middle East terrorism are revealed. For one thing, the idea that terrorism causes relatively low levels of devastation in comparison to other forms of political violence is borne out. An important finding is that terrorist assaults that killed or wounded fifty or more people were very rare occurrences. Moreover, those terrorist assaults only took place outside of Israel and the Occupied Territories.

At a theoretical level, those findings provide evidence that the full-blown effect of terrorism does not rely on large scale devastation but rather on the profound and lasting psychological damage that results. The findings also highlight the importance of the influence of location on terrorist outcomes. To be more specific, they suggest that characteristics of locations, perhaps including the types of counter-terrorist measures in place, have a consider-able impact on the nature of terrorist acts. Another finding that dovetails nicely with the foregoing discussion is that terrorists overwhelmingly favor attacks against civilians rather than against government institutions. The analysis shows that in general, terrorists prefer civilian targets by over a 4:1 margin. When the analysis focuses exclusive attention on Israel and the Occupied Territories, that ratio increases to about 10:1.

Turning to the underlying theory of the work, the continuum for "structuralist" and "non-structuralist" terrorist group-types is a good fit with data on non-charismatic terrorist group-types and target type. Political ideology is found to be influential in terms of whether civilian targets or government targets were chosen. The notion that Marxist-Leninist terrorist groups place emphasis on government targets is borne out by the data analysis. Those findings are consistent with the notion that "structuralist groups," namely terrorist groups that wage war against what Wallerstein calls a "world system" like capitalism or imperialism, place more emphasis on government targets.[12]

Further, the results indicate that while Islamic fundamentalist terrorist groups see some value in terrorist assaults against government targets, nearly three-quarters of terrorist assaults were carried out against civilian targets. Those findings are consistent with the notion that Islamic revivalist terrorist groups have "structuralist" and "non-structuralist" strands of thinking about the struggle that reflects emphasis on individual piety and loyalty, coupled with the notion of an unbreachable schism between the Muslim East and the Christian West. Finally, the results indicate that nationalist-irredentist terrorist groups commit terrorist assaults against civilian targets over three-quarters of the time. Those findings are consistent with the idea that "the struggle" is perceived more in terms of individuals or groups of individuals that inhabit land they do not rightfully own.

The findings indicate that the presence or absence of a charismatic leader at the helm of Islamic fundamentalist groups makes little difference with respect to the type of target chosen and intensity of attack. In the case of Marxist-Leninist terrorist groups, the data generally support the notion that Marxist-Leninist terrorist groups led by a charismatic leader commit terrorist assaults that more closely resemble the terrorist assaults carried out by types of terrorist groups more in sync with the "prevailing social ideology" of Islam. In the case of nationalist-irredentist terrorist groups, the data suggest the presence of a charismatic leader may contribute to an increase in attack intensity and an increase in assaults against government targets. What seems significant here is that particular finding may be a reflection of the type of terrorist assaults carried out by Sabri al-Banna's Abu Nidal Organization (ANO). The results show that Jewish fundamentalist terrorist groups led by a charismatic leader had the highest percentage of non-lethal and injury-free terrorist attacks. Those findings are consistent with the idea that leaders of those terrorist groups view them, to use Hoffman's expression, as "political pressure groups" or as vehicles to influence the political system.[13]

Implications For Counter-Terrorism Planners

Turning to the matter of counter-terrorism strategy, the underlying issue here is how to present the findings to counter-terrorism planners in ways that can inject a high dosage of flexibility and utility into counter-terrorism analysis. In the broader sense, one way of thinking about integrating qualitative and quantitative findings is to draw from Reiss and Roth's discussion and depiction of "interventions" to offset the prospect of violent outcomes.[14] The authors suggest that an approach toward intervention must closely parallel the multi-level analysis that helps to describe why violent outcomes happen. In other words, as the authors suggest, a multi-level understanding of the sources of violent outcomes in the domestic sphere, necessitates a multi-level "counter-terrorism" interventions scheme.[15] It follows that a multi-level counter-terrorism taxonomy is crafted that, among other things, underscores the importance of the multi-faceted approach counter-terrorism planners must use in efforts to constrain terrorism.

In that taxonomy, three types of counter-terrorism "interventions" are posited in rows, ranging from tactical crisis management interventions to positive strategic interventions to negative strategic interventions.[16] In turn, those intervention types are broken down into time periods of "long-haul," "middle-run," and "short-run" factors. In the taxonomy itself, descriptive policy alternatives are posited, offering some examples of policy alternatives. From the start, it should be clear these are not meant to be mutually exclusive categories, but rather a pedagogical tool to demonstrate a flexible multi-level response to the lurking catastrophe of terrorism.[17]

The following is a brief discussion about how some of those taxonomy descriptive characteristics presuppose and derive from the quantitative and qualitative findings of this study. First, one quantitative result found here is that the single most predominant number of Middle East terrorist assaults were carried out by anonymous terrorist groups or "lone operatives."

One interpretation offered to explain that finding revolves around the central idea that a clear-cut political setting, in which goals and terrorist group demands and aspirations are clearly understood and articulated, may contribute to a higher number of anonymous terrorist assaults. If further empirical investigation determines that interpretation is correct, or at least accounts for part of what is observed here, one policy option might be to invoke a counter-terrorism application of what Baldwin calls "positive sanctions" to soften and fragment terrorist constituency groups, thereby in effect "blurring" the political landscape.[18]

The underlying reason that approach vis à vis constituent groups may be effective is precisely because constituent group members, in my judgment, seem to fall along a spectrum of sorts, ranging from those unequivocally committed to the struggle in ideological terms, to those who may be described as "hanger-on" types, perhaps with a mixed bundle of ideological and economic motivations.[19] To be sure, this condition is observed with

FIGURE 12
Counter-Terrorism Intervention Taxonomy

	Long Haul	Middle Run	Short Term
tactical crisis management	• third party interconnections	• constituent group contact	• acts of prisoner exchange
	• protracted contact with groups	• prisoner's family contact	• acts of communications with terrorist groups
positive strategic interactions	• promotion of participatory democracy	• support for infrastructure of constituency groups (e.g. schools, non-lethal technologies, hospitals)	• acts of medicine transportation and disbursement
	• economic support for refugee camps and other economic backwater areas		• acts of assistance for humanitarian reasons (e.g. earthquakes, floods)
negative strategic interactions	• appraisal of threat region by region	• INTERPOL	• counter terrorism assassination
	• support various chieftains in ways that support group splitting (e.g. funneling monies)	• coordination with allies in military terms	• other counterterrorism measures
		• effective counterterrorism legislation	• disinformation campaigns

respect to the Gush Emunim movement in the Occupied Territories, where there is a combination of "settler-types," ranging from hard-core ideologues to those persons motivated by more pedestrian economic factors, such as the prospect of acquiring housing at less expensive rates.[20]

If Harris is correct, and constituent groups generate and sustain considerable influence on terrorist group tactics, then those less committed in ideological terms may be fraught with doubt for ethical or economic reasons about certain tactics and voice those concerns in ways that have profound and lasting effects on terrorist group unity and tactics. Equally important from the vantage of policy, that leverage point could be used to introduce flexibility into the counter-terrorism system where planners might encourage terrorist group splitting if the geopolitical considerations of nation-state leaders warrant those types of counter-terrorist measures.

An application of Baldwin's notion of "positive sanctions" for counter-terrorism measures would include effective and sustained contacts and dialogue with parts of constituency groups, perhaps through inducements, financial or otherwise or some form of co-optation. Indeed, there might be some contact or dialogue with terrorist groups themselves by means of prisoner exchanges, the manipulation of prisoner condition issues like prison sentence restructuring, living conditions or visitation rights, all with the aim of sowing differences in perception about "the enemy" among terrorists both in and out of jail, and constituent supporters. It follows that variants of "positive sanctions" applications would include monies for constituency group infrastructure and the overall improvement of economic backwater conditions. The idea of promoting participatory democracy as a concomitant really revolves around the notion that more free-wheeling discussion about policy options among constituency group members underscores the rather one dimensional approach of violent struggle, and may thereby in effect showcase the shortcomings and rigidities of blunt force as the tactic of choice.

One underlying issue is under what conditions counter-terrorism planners might want to manipulate political context, thereby in effect helping to encourage or discourage terrorist group solidarity or splitting. It is clearly beyond the scope of this study to make any carefully reasoned and precise evaluation of that, but some generally recognizable observations might provide some insights that might serve as the basis for further empirical investigation.

From the vantage of the qualitative analysis, there seems to be some relationship between extreme political conditions fraught with peril for political actors and terrorist group splitting. For example, the book has discussed how several authors underscore the interconnections between the "activating factor" of President Nasser's enormous defeat during the Six Day War of 1967 and the emergent reality of Palestinian resistance "splinter groups." In the case of Hamas, itself an "offshoot" of the Muslim Brotherhood in the Occupied Territories, rather extreme economic deprivation and unmet political demands and aspirations that might be thought of as "situational factors" were detonated by the "activating factor" of a car crash that started the Intifadeh ("uprising") in December 1987. In a similar vein, both Auda and Gaffney trace the emergent reality of the Jihad Organization, an "offshoot group" of the Muslim Brotherhood in Egypt, to an array of economic afflictions that plagued segments of Egyptian society in the 1970's and 1980's.[21]

Those conclusions are a good fit with Karber and Mengel's proposition that there is an inverse relationship between terrorist group splintering and the capacity of the parent group to act in effective and sustained ways. For Karber and Mengel, "The extent of success achieved by this movement is, in the main, the measure for the likelihood of a splinter element evolving into a terrorist group. The greater the degree of success, the less likely members will be inclined to resort to violence."[22]

Taken at first blush, one possible way to promote terrorist group cohesion is to orchestrate a set of "activating factors" against symbolic targets designed to pull at the heartstrings of emotion to solidify the group. Other possible ways might include orchestrating the release of high ranking terrorist group leaders from prison to inject a new flexibility into fractious intra-group dynamics. In fact, Cobban suggests that idea when she recounts how Dr. Habash's absence from the PFLP political fray hurt the cause of PFLP unity. Cobban reports, "In November 1968, Habash managed to escape from his Syrian jail and immediately tried to reassert the supremacy of the ANM traditionalists inside the PFLP. A new PFLP conference was scheduled for February 1969, but amidst an escalating campaign of intimidation against Hawatma's followers, just before the conference was due to open the Hawatma group decided to secede."[23]

A first pass at the qualitative descriptions covered suggests there may be a relationship between more temperate political conditions among political actors and terrorist group solidarity. Recall that Azar, Jureidini, and McLaurin suggest that the political context of intractable conflict is a kind of servo-mechanism that keeps political events from being too belligerent or too cooperative.[24] What seems illustrative of both of the foregoing is President Anwar Sadat's assassination in 1981 that stemmed from the "cooperative event" of the Camp David Accords of 1978. Again, in my judgment, those conclusions square with Karber and Mengel's assertion that, "Conversely, as frustration builds because of the lack of success or because of actual repression, the more probable a terrorist group will result."[25]

At an empirical level, the findings of this work suggest that many Middle East terrorism assaults that are interconnected with political events are carried out in response to major government policy such as diplomatic initiatives. If further empirical work indicates that relationship between major government initiatives and terrorist assaults reflects some degree of terrorist group cohesion, counter-terrorism planners might want to encourage terrorist group splitting through financial support to chieftains in fierce competition with one another, selective assassination, and other counter-terrorism measures. The process of terrorist group splitting may reduce the risk to civilian targets precisely because of findings that suggest smaller and younger terrorist groups do not favor civilian targets as much as larger and older terrorist groups.

In the broader sense, this "proactive approach" to counter-terrorism stratagems that presupposes and derives from a "realist approach" to international politics is a political matter that, in my judgment, may have some difficulty resonating with an electorate versed in the American liberal tradition. What seems significant here is that terrorism, to paraphrase Secretary of State Madeleine Albright, may be the wave of the future in terms of how nationalist sentiments and other similar feelings are expressed in the post-Cold War world, and faced with that threat, counter-terrorism analysts and the policymakers who guide them need to respond in effective and sustained ways. In summation, this is a fledgling conception and, to be sure, work on the basic propositions associated with an approach to political context shifting by means of manipulation deserves increased devotion by scholars.

In closing, it is important to chronicle what insights this work offers for the study of terrorism and terrorist group behavior in other parts of the contemporary world. In the broader sense, a close reading of qualitative descriptions about various Middle East terrorist groups suggests that change in political context has profound and lasting implications for terrorist group formation and evolution. Against that backdrop, the quantitative analysis makes it clear that the targeting practices of Middle East terrorist groups are based on much more than chance and opportunity.

At first blush, those findings suggest there should be efforts to isolate and identify pivotal phases of terrorist group development and trace an arc to political events that correspond to structural change in terrorist group development and structural shifts in strategy or tactics. Once that is accomplished, the functional typology crafted in this work allows the researcher to classify and categorize terrorist groups according to group-type, and generate hypotheses about terrorist group behavior that will shed light on the parameters of terrorism in various regions of the world. In fact, testing to see if the defining characteristics and classification schemes used here produce similar results when terrorist group-types in other parts of the world are examined serves as the first step in what Zinnes calls the "cumulative integration" of scholarly work.[26]

At the same time, meaningful research should serve as a cornerstone for more advanced study about terrorism and counter-terrorism measures. Seen from that angle, a logical first step for researchers may be to try to operationalize a set of hypotheses that presuppose and derive from the foregoing qualitative discussion about continuously evolving political landscapes that make interconnections between types of political context change and the sources, origins, and development of terrorist groups. In this respect, a logical next step for researchers may be to use "path analysis" through the construction of a reciprocal model that measures the "joint determination" of key variables that explain terrorism.

Compounding the challenge even more, empirical investigation in the realm of counter-terrorism stratagems deserves the increased devotion of terrorism specialists. To be specific, more empirical work needs to be done to determine whether or not interconnections exist between the commission of various types of terrorist assaults and degrees of terrorist group solidarity or splitting. Empirical investigations of that type may serve as fundamental cornerstones in efforts to craft a more functional counter-terrorism intervention taxonomy.

In so far as this study provides some insight into the formative conditions and processes associated with Middle East terrorist group formation and development, and has unraveled discernable trends in Middle East terrorist group behavior, it has proven to be a valuable approach with far-reaching applications. By the same token, it is my hope this book will provide students, researchers, policymakers, law enforcement officials and others concerned about terrorism with new and probing ways of thinking about how to address gaps in knowledge, thereby in effect helping to move the study of terrorism forward in meaningful ways.

Notes

1. Reiss and Roth 1993, 297.
2. Norton 1987.
3. Norton 1987; Kramer 1997.
4. Cobban 1984, 142; Yaari 1970.
5. Gresh 1983, 26-30; Nassar 1991, 19, 91.
6. Melman 1986; Seale 1992.
7. Nassar 1991, 80-82; Gresh 1983, 18.

8. Norton 1987; Norton 1988.

9. Auda 1994, 401; Gaffney 1997, 263-264.

10. Livingstone and Halevy 1990, 143.

11. Mickolus 1980, xviii; Enders, Parise and Sandler 1992, 305-306; Flemming 1992, 133 n2; Karber and Mengel 1983, 33.

12. Wallerstein 1974.

13. Hoffman 1984.

14. Reiss and Roth 1993, 312.

15. Ibid., 310-319.

16. That notion presupposes and derives from Baldwin's conceptualization of "positive sanctions" (Baldwin 1971; Baldwin 1985).

17. Reiss and Roth 1993; Nye 1993.

18. Baldwin 1971; Baldwin 1985.

19. Harris 1989.

20. Sprinzak 1991.

21. Auda 1994; Gaffney 1997.

22. Karber and Mengel 1983, 25.

23. Cobban 1984, 145.

24. Azar, Jureidini, and McLaurin 1978, 43, 51-53.

25. Karber and Mengel 1983, 25.

26. Zinnes 1976a, 1976b.

Bibliography

Abu-Amr, Ziad. 1997. "Shaykh Ahmad Yasin and the Origins of Hamas." In *Spokesmen of the Despised: Fundamentalist Leaders of the Middle East,* ed. R. Scott Appleby, 225-255. Chicago: The University of Chicago Press.

AbuKhalil, As'ad. 1991. "Ideology and Practice of Hizballah in Lebanon: Islamization of Leninist Organizational Principles." *Middle Eastern Studies* 27(3): 390-403.

———. 1994. "Lebanon." In *Political Parties of the Middle East and North Africa,* ed. Frank Tachau. Westport, CT: Greenwood Press.

Ahmad, Feroz. 1982. "Unionist Relations with the Greek, Armenian and Jewish Communities of the Ottoman Empire, 1908-1914." In *The Central Lands.* Vol. *1 of Christians and Jews in the Ottoman Empire: The Functioning of a Plural Society,* eds. Benjamin Braude and Bernard Lewis. New York: Holmes & Meier.

Aldrich, John H. and Forrest D. Nelson. 1984. *Linear Probability, Logit and Probit Models.* Newburg Park, CA: Sage Publications.

Alexander, Yonah. 1983. "Terrorism and High-Technology Weapons." In *Perspectives on Terrorism,* eds. Lawrence Zelic Freedman and Yonah Alexander. Wilmington, DE: Scholary Resources.

Alexander, Yonah and John Gleason, eds. 1981. *Behavioral and Quantitative Perspectives on Terrorism.* New York: Pergamon Press.

Alexander, Yonah and Joshua Sinai. 1989. *Terrorism: The PLO Connection.* New York: Taylor & Francis.

Allen, Richard. 1974. *Imperialism and Nationalism in the Fertile Crescent: Sources and Prospects of the Arab-Israeli Conflict.* London: Oxford

University Press.

Allport, Gordon W. 1954. *The Nature of Prejudice*. Cambridge, MA: Addison-Wesley Publishing.

Amon, Moshe. 1982. "The Unraveling of the Myth of Progress." In *The Morality of Terrorism: Religious and Secular Justifications*, eds. David C. Rapoport and Yonah Alexander. New York: Pergamon Press.

Anderson, Ray R., Robert F. Siebert, and Jon G. Wagner. 1998. *Politics and Change in the Middle East: Sources of Conflict and Accommodation*, 5th Ed. Upper Saddle River, NJ: Prentice Hall.

Arab News: Saudi Arabia's First English Language Daily. 1993. "8 Austrian tourists hurt in Cairo bus attack." 28 December.

————. 1994. "Egypt thwarts attack plans." 1 January.

————. 1994. "60 Egyptians held in anti-violence crackdown." 20 January.

————. 1994. "38 Arrested in south Egypt crackdown." 24 January.

————. 1994. "Two policemen killed in Egypt attack." 29 January.

Art, Robert J. 1974. "Bureaucratic Politics: A Critique." *Policy Sciences* (4).

Aston, Clive C. 1980. "Restrictions Encountered in Responding to Terrorist Seiges: An Analysis." In *Responding to the Terrorist Threat: Security and Crisis Management*, eds. Richard H. Shultz and Stephen Sloan. New York: Pergamon Press.

Auda, Gehad. 1994. "The 'Normalization' of the Islamic Movement in Egypt from the 1970's to the early 1990's." In *Accounting for Fundamentalisms: The Dynamic Character of Movements*, eds. Martin E. Marty and R. Scott Appleby, 374-412. Chicago: The University of Chicago Press.

Ayalon, Ami. 1989. "Regime Opposition and Terrorism in Egypt." In *Terror As a State and Revolutionary Strategy*, ed. Barry Rubin. Lanham, MD: University Press of America.

Azar, Edward E., Paul Jureidini, and Ronald McLaurin. 1978. "Protracted Social Conflict Theory and Practice in the Middle East." *Journal of Palestine Studies* 8(1): 41-60.

Baali, Fuad and Ali Wardi. 1981. *Ibn Khaldun and Islamic Thought-Styles: A Social Perspective*. Boston: G. K. Hall.

Bahn, Sushella, Ramanand Malaviya, Chand Mohan, Sudhir Mattoo, and C. Rayalakshmi. 1989. *Terrorism: An Annotated Bibliography*. New Delhi: Concept Publishing Company.

Baldwin, David. 1971. "The Power of Positive Sanctions." *World Politics* 24(1).

————. 1985. *Economic Statecraft*. Princeton, NJ: Princeton University Press.

Bardakjian, Kevork B. 1982. "The Rise of the Armenian Patriarchate of Constantinople." In *The Central Lands. Vol. 1 of Christians and Jews in the Ottoman Empire: The Functioning of a Plural Society*, eds. Benjamin Braude and Bernard Lewis. New York: Holmes & Meier.

Barsoumian, Hagop. 1982. "The Dual Role of the *Amira* Class within the Ottoman Government and the Armenian *Millet* (1750-1850)." In *The Central Lands. Vol. 1 of Christians and Jews in the Ottoman Empire: The Functioning of a Plural Society*, eds. Benjamin Braude and Bernard Lewis. New York: Holmes & Meier.

Bassiouni, M. Cherif. 1978. "Criminological Policy." In *Legal Aspects of International Terrorism*, eds. Alona E. Evans and John F. Murphy. Lexington, MA: Lexington Books.

———. 1986. *Crimes. Vol. 1 of International Criminal Law*. New York: Transnational Publishers.

Bell, Bowyer J. 1975. *Transnational Terror*. Washington, DC: American Enterprise Institute for Public Policy Research.

Benac, Nancy. 1998. "Clinton orders strikes on Afghan, Sudanese Terrorist Sites." *The Associated Press*. APTV-08-20-98 1614 EDT 20 August.

Beres, Louis Rene. 1987. *America Outside the World: The Collapse of U.S. Foreign Policy*. Lexington, MA: D.C. Heath and Company.

———. 1988. "Terrorism and International Law." *Florida International Law Journal* 3(3): 291-306.

———. 1988. "Genocide, Law and Power Politics." *Whittier Law Review* 10(2): 329-351.

Beres, Louis Rene. 1990. "Confronting Nuclear Terrorism." *The Hastings International and Comparative Law Review* 14(1): 129-154.

Bernstein, David. 1981. "Syria poised to renew war on Brotherhood." *Jerusalem Post*, 30 November.

Blakesley, Christopher L. 1992. *Terrorism, Drugs, International Law and the Protection of Human Liberty: A Comparative Study of International Law, Its Nature, Rule and Impact in Matters of Terrorism, Drug Trafficking, War and Extradition*. New York: Transnational Publishers.

Blakesley, Christopher L. and Otto Lagodny. 1991. "Finding Harmony Amidst Disagreement Over Extradition, Jurisdiction, The Role of Human Rights, and Issues of Extraterritoriality Under International Criminal Law." *Vanderbilt Journal of Transnational Law* 24(1): 1-73.

Blitzer, Wolf. 1987. "U.S. weighing military strike to free hostages." *Jerusalem Post*, 26 January.

———. 1987. "Two more kidnapped in Beirut." *Jerusalem Post*, 27 January.

———. 1989. "'New York Times': Fatah hires killers to assassinate 'collaborators'." *Jerusalem Post*, 25 October.

Bosworth, C. E. "The Concept of *Dhimma* in Early Islam." In *The Central Lands. Vol. 1 of Christians and Jews in the Ottoman Empire: The Functioning of a Plural Society*, eds. Benjamin Braude and Bernard Lewis. New York: Holmes & Meier.

Bozeman, Adda B. 1971. *The Future of Law in a Multicultural World*. Princeton, NJ: Princeton University Press.

Braude, Benjamin. 1982. "Foundation Myths of the *Millet* System." In *The Central Lands. Vol. 1 of Christians and Jews in the Ottoman Empire: The Functioning of a Plural Society*, eds. Benjamin Braude and Bernard Lewis. New York: Holmes & Meier.

Braude, Benjamin and Bernard Lewis, eds. 1982. *The Central Lands. Vol. 1 of Christians and Jews in the Ottoman Empire: The Functioning of a Plural Society*. New York: Holmes & Meier.

———. 1982. *The Arabic-Speaking Lands. Vol. 2 of Christians and Jews in the Ottoman Empire: The Functioning of a Plural Society*. New York: Holmes & Meier.

Brecher, Michael and Patrick James. 1987. "Crisis Management in the Arab-Israeli Conflict." In *Conflict Management in the Middle East*, eds. Gabriel Ben-Dor and David B. Dewitt. Lexington, MA: D.C. Heath and Company.

Bremer, L. Paul III. 1987. "Practical Measures for Dealing with Terrorism." *Bureau of Public Affairs*. Washington, DC: United States Department of State. Current Policy No. 913, 1-4.

———. 1987. "Counterterrorism: Strategy and Tactics." *Bureau of Public Affairs*. Washington, DC: United States Department of State. Current Policy No. 1023, 1-4.

———. 1988. "Terrorism: Myths and Reality." *Bureau of Public Affairs*. Washington, DC: United States Department of State. Current Policy No. 1047, 1-4.

———. 1989. "Continuing the Fight Against Terrorism." *Terrorism* 12(2): 81-87.

Brierly, J. L. 1963. *The Law of Nations: An Introduction to the International Law of Peace Sixth Edition*. Oxford: Oxford University Press.

Brilliant, Joshua. 1982. "New Jewish terror groups?" *Jerusalem Post*, 12 July.

———. 1982. "GSS probing possible links between Sicarii and Kach." *Jerusalem Post*, 2 August.

Broad, William J. 1998. "How Japan Germ Terror Altered World." *New York Times*, 26 May.

Brown, Richard Maxwell. 1989. "Historical Patterns of Violence." In *Pro-

test, Rebellion, Reform. Vol. 2 of Violence in America, ed. Ted Robert Gurr. Newbury Park, CA: Sage Publications.

Brown, Seyom. 1994. *The Faces of Power, Second Edition*. New York: Columbia University Press.

Buckelew, Alvin H. 1985. "Fighting Terrorism: Does the United States need a new response structure?" *Security Management*, June: 36-42.

Burns, John F. 1989. "Afghans Disclose Deaths of 11,000." *New York Times*, 9 November, A-15.

Burton, Anthony M. 1975. *Urban Terrorism: Theory, Practice & Response*. New York: The Free Press.

Campbell, Donald T. and Julian C. Stanley. 1963. *Experimental and Quasi-Experimental Designs for Research*. Boston: Houghton Mifflin.

Carr, Maurice. 1958. "The Revolution of Despair." *Jerusalem Post*, 18 July.

———. 1962. "Salan Proud of Heading O.A.S.: Claims Government Responsible for Algerian Bloodshed." *Jerusalem Post*, 18 May.

Celmer, Marc A. 1987. *Terrorism, US Strategy and Reagan Policies*. Westport, CT: Greenwood Press.

Charters, David A. 1994. "Conclusions: Security and Liberty in Balance - Countering Terrorism in the Democratic Context." In *The Deadly Sin of Terrorism: Its Effect on Democracy and Civil Liberty in Six Countries*, ed. David A. Charters. Westport, CT: Greenwood Press.

Chasdi, Richard J. 1994. "Terrorism: Stratagems for Remediation from an International Law Perspective." *Shofar: An Interdisciplinary Journal of Jewish Studies* 12(4): 59-86.

———. 1995. "The Dynamics of Middle East Terrorism, 1968-1993: A Functional Typology of Terrorist Group-types." Ph.D. dissertation. Purdue University.

———. 1997. "Middle East Terrorism 1968-1993: An Empirical Analysis of Terrorist Group-Type Behavior." *The Journal of Conflict Studies*, Vol XVII, No. 2: 73-114.

Clarity, James F. 1998. "The Day After In Ulster Town: Now 'It's Back'." *New York Times*. 17 August.

Clogg, Richard. 1982. "The Greek *Millet* in the Ottoman Empire." In *The Central Lands Vol. 1 of Christians and Jews in the Ottoman Empire: The Functioning of a Plural Society*, eds. Benjamin Braude and Bernard Lewis. New York: Holmes & Meier.

Cobban, Helena. 1984. *The Palestinian Liberation Organization: People, Power and Politics*. Cambridge, England: Cambridge University Press.

Cohen, Amnon. 1982. "On the Realities of the Millet System: Jerusalem in the Sixteenth Century." In *The Central Lands Vol. 1 of Christians and*

Jews in the Ottoman Empire: The Functioning of a Plural Society, eds. Benjamin Braude and Bernard Lewis. New York: Holmes & Meier.

Cohen, Benjamin J. 1973. *A Question of Imperialism: The Political Economy of Dominance and Dependence*. New York: Basic Books.

Conde Nast Traveller: Truth in Travel. 1992. "The new face of Terrorism," May, 156-178.

Cook, Thomas D. and Donald T. Campbell. 1979. *Quasi-Experimentation Design & Analysis Issues for Field Settings*. Boston: Houghton Mifflin.

Corbett, Michael. 1993. *Research Methods in Political Science An Introduction Using Microcase*. Bellevue, WA: Microcase Corporation.

Corrado, Raymond R. 1981. "A Critique of the Mental Disorder Perspective of Political Terrorism." *International Journal of Law and Psychiatry* 4: 293-309.

Coser, Lewis A. 1956. *The Functions of Social Conflict*. New York: The Free Press.

Court, Andy. 1988. "Capital takes bomb in stride." *Jerusalem Post*, 28 December.

Crawford, James. 1979. *The Creation of States in International Law*. Oxford: Clarendon Press.

Crenshaw-Hutchinson, Martha. 1972. "The Concept of Revolutionary Terrorism." *The Journal of Conflict Resolution* 16(3): 383-396.

———. 1978. *Revolutionary Terrorism: The FLN in Algeria 1954-1967*. Stanford, CA: Hoover Institution Press.

Crenshaw, Martha, ed. 1983 *Terrorism, Legitimacy and Power: The Consequences of Political Violence*. Middleton, CT: Wesleyan University Press.

Crozier, Brian. 1960. *The Rebels: A Study of Post-War Insurrections*. Boston: Beacon Press.

Cubert, Harold M. 1998. *The PFLP's Changing Role in the Middle East*. Portland, OR: Frank Cass.

Danilenko, G.M. 1992. *Law Making in the International Community*. Boston: Martinus Nijhoff Publishers.

Davison, Roderic H. 1982. "The Millets as Agents of Change in the Nineteenth-Century Ottoman Empire." In *The Central Lands. Vol. 1 of Christians and Jews in the Ottoman Empire: The Functioning of a Plural Society*, eds. Benjamin Braude and Bernard Lewis. New York: Holmes & Meier.

Dawisha, Adeed. 1986. *The Arab Radicals*. New York: Council on Foreign Relations.

Demant, Peter. 1994. *Jewish Fundamentalism in Israel: Implications for the Mideast Conflict*. Israel Palestine Center for Research and Information

(IPCRI), Vol. 3, No. 3, August.

DeMaris, Alfred. 1992. *Logit Modeling: Practical Applications*. Newbury Park, CA: Sage Publications.

Department of Justice Terrorist Research and Analytical Center. 1983. *The FBI Analysis of Terrorist Incidents in the United States 1983*. Washington, DC: Federal Bureau of Investigation.

———. 1985. "Terrorism at Home and Abroad: The US Government View." In *The Politics of Terrorism, Third Edition, Revised and Expanded*, ed. Michael Stohl, 295-372. New York: Marcel Dekker.

———. 1986. *FBI Analysis of Terrorist Incidents in the United States 1986*. Washington, DC: Federal Bureau of Investigation.

Detter De Lupis, Ingrid. 1987. *The Law of War*. Cambridge, England: Cambridge University Press.

de Vattel, Emmerich. 1964. *The Law of Nations or the Principles of Natural Law: Applied to the Conduct and to the Affairs of Nations and Sovereigns*, ed. James Brown Scott. New York: Oceana Publications.

Diamond, Larry, Linz, Juan J., and Lipset, Seymour Martin. 1990. *Politics in Developing Countries: Comparing Experiences with Democracy*. Boulder, CO: Lynne Rienner Publishers.

DiLaura, Arnold E. 1987. "Preventing Terrorism: An Analysis of National Strategy." *SAIS Review* 7: 27-38.

Directorate of Intelligence. 1992. *Palestinian Organizations LDA 92-12531*. Washington, DC: Central Intelligence Agency.

Dollard, John, Leonard W. Doob, Neal E. Miller, O. H. Mowrer and Robert R. Sears. 1939. *Frustration and Aggression*. New Haven: Yale University Press.

Don-Yehiya, Eliezer. 1994. "The Book and the Sword: The Nationalist Yeshivot and Political Radicalism in Israel." In *Accounting for Fundamentalism: The Dynamic Character of Movements*, eds. Martin E. Marty and R. Scott Appleby, 264-302. Chicago: The University of Chicago Press.

Dror, Yehezkel. 1983. "Terrorism as a Challenge to the Democratic Capacity to Govern." In *Terrorism, Legitimacy and Power: The Consequences of Political Violence*, ed. Martha Crenshaw. Middleton, CT: Wesleyan University Press.

Dutter, Lee F. 1987. "Ethno-Political Activity and the Psychology of Terrorism." *Terrorism* 10(3): 145-164.

Duvall, Raymond D. and Michael Stohl. 1983. "Governance by Terror." In *The Politics of Terrorism, Second Edition, Revised and Expanded*, ed. Michael Stohl, 179-219. New York: Marcel Dekker.

Earle, Edward Mead, ed. 1944. *Makers of Modern Strategy: Military*

Thought from Machiavelli to Hitler. Princeton: Princeton University Press.

Eisner, Michael. 1993. "Jerusalem: An Analysis of Legal Claims and Political Realities." *Wisconsin International Law Journal* 12(2).

Elifson, Kirk W., Richard P. Runyon and Audrey Haber. 1982. *Fundamentals of Social Statistics*. New York: Random House.

Elliott, John D. 1977. "Transitions of Contemporary Terrorism." *Military Review* 57(5): 3-15.

Enders, Walter, Gerald Parise and Todd Sandler. 1992. "A Time Series Analysis of Transnational Terrorism: Trends and Cycles." *Defense Economics* 3: 305-320.

European Treaty Statute. 1968. Protocol (No. IV) to the European Convention for the Protection of Human Rights and Freedoms, 2 May. Europ. TS No. 46.

–––. 1978. European Convention on the Suppression of Terrorism, 4 August. Europ. TS No. 90.

Evans, Ernest. 1982. "Toward a More Effective U.S. Policy on Terrorism." In *Political Terrorism and Energy: The Threat and Response*, eds. Yonah Alexander and Charles K. Ebinger. New York: Praeger.

Falk, Richard. 1983. "Rethinking Counter-Terrorism." *Scandinavian Journal of Development Alternatives* 6(2/3): 19-36.

–––. 1988. *Revolutionaries and Functionaries: The Dual Face of Terrorism*. New York: E. P. Dutton.

Falkenrath, Richard A., Robert D. Newman, and Bradley A. Thayer. 1998. *America's Achilles Heel: Nuclear, Biological, and Chemical Terrorism and Covert Attack*. Cambridge, MA: The MIT Press.

Falvey, Anne. 1986. "Legislative Responses to International Terrorism: International and National Efforts to Deter and Punish Terrorists." *Boston College International and Comparative Law Review* 9(2): 323-359.

Farrell, William R. 1986. "Organized to Combat Terrorism." In *Fighting Back: Winning the War against Terrorism*, eds. Neil C. Livingstone and Terrell E. Arnold. Lexington, MA: D. C. Heath and Company.

Fattah, Ezzat A. 1981. "Terrorist Activities and Terrorist Targets: A Tentative Typology." In *Behavioral and Quantitative Perspectives on Terrorism*, eds. Yonah Alexander and John M. Gleason. New York: Pergamon.

Fenwick, Charles G. 1924. *International Law*. New York: The Century Company.

Findley, Carter V. 1982. "The Acid Test of Ottomanism: The Acceptance of Non-Muslims in the Late Ottoman Bureaucracy." In *The Central*

Lands. Vol. 1 of Christians and Jews in the Ottoman Empire: The Functioning of a Plural Society, eds. Benjamin Braude and Bernard Lewis. New York: Holmes & Meier.

Fischbach, Michael R. 1994. "The Palestinians." In *Political Parties of the Middle East and Africa*, ed. Frank Tachau. Westport, CT: Greenwood Press.

Fishkoff, Sue. 1993. "Moslem Terror Plot Foiled in New York." *Jerusalem Post*, 25 June.

Flemming, Peter A., Michael Stohl, and Alex P. Schmid. 1988. "The Theoretical Utility of Typologies of Terrorism: Lessons and Opportunities." In *The Politics of Terrorism: Third Edition, Revised and Expanded*, ed. Michael Stohl. New York: Marcel Dekker.

Flemming, Peter A. 1992. "Patterns of Transnational Terrorism in Western Europe, 1968-1987: A Quantitative Perspective." Ph.D. dissertation. Purdue University.

Fodor's Travel Publications. 1993. *Fodor's Israel*. New York: Fodor's Travel Publications.

Foreign Broadcast Information Service. 1998. "West Bank: Yasin Discusses Hamas 'Opposition' to PA." FBIS-NES-98-144. 24 May, publish date 05-24-98. Article Id. Drnes 05241998000109.

———. 1998. "Kakh Leaders Profiled: Party's Death Predicted." FBIS-NES-20-217. 7 November, publish date 8 November 1990.

Freudenheim, Yehoshua. 1967. *Government in Israel*. New York: Oceana Publications.

Fried, John H. E. 1985. "The Nuclear Collision Course: Can International Law Be of Help?" *Denver Journal of International Law and Policy* 14(1): 97-119.

Friedland, Nehemia. 1992. "Becoming a Terrorist: Social and Individual Antecedents." In *Terrorism: Roots, Impact, Responses*, ed. Lawrence Howard, 81-93. New York: Praeger.

Friedler, Ya'acov. 1984. "Threats breathe new life into controversial 'Messiah'." *Jerusalem Post*, 31 January.

Friedman, Robert I. 1987. "Terror on Sacred Ground: The Battle for the Temple Mount." *Mother Jones*, August/September, 37-44.

———. 1988. "How Shamir Used J.D.L. Terrorism: The Kahane Connection." *The Nation (247)*, 31 October.

———. 1990. *The False Prophet: Rabbi Meir Kahane: From FBI Informant to Knesset Member*. Brooklyn, NY: Lawrence Hill Books.

———. 1992. *Zealots for Zion: Inside Israel's West Bank Movement*. New York: Random House.

Friedman, Thomas L. 1993. "The Missiles' Message: Yes, Washington

Wants to Punish Hussein, But It Wants All State Terrorists to Beware."
   New York Times, 28 June.
Gaffney, Patrick D. 1997. "Fundamentalist Preaching and Islamic Militancy
   in Upper Egypt." In *Speaking for the Despised: Fundamentalist Leaders
   of the Middle East,* ed. R. Scott Appleby, 257-293. Chicago: University
   of Chicago Press.
Gage, Nicholas. 1977. "Palestinians Storm Embassy in Athens." *New York
   Times*, 19 November.
Gal-Or, Noemi. 1985. *International Cooperation to Suppress Terrorism.*
   New York: St. Martins.
Gentili, Alberico. 1964. *De Iure Belli Libri Tres,* ed. James Brown Scott.
   New York: Oceana Publications.
Getzler, Dvorah. 1983. "Grenade kills protester." *Jerusalem Post,*
   11 February.
Geyer, Georgie Anne. 1995. "Palestinian Islamics reject and threaten the
   peace process." *Chicago Tribune,* 3 February.
Ghalwash, Mae. 1993. "20 more die in Egypt unrest." *Arab News,* 21
   December.
Gibb, Cecil A. 1947. "The Principles and Traits of Leadership." *The
   Journal of Abnormal and Social Psychology* 42(3): 267-284.
Goldaber, Irving. 1979. "A Typology of Hostage-Takers." *The Police Chief*
   46(6): 21-23.
Goodman, Walter. 1971. "Rabbi Kahane says: 'I'd love to see the J.D.L.
   fold up. But-'.", *New York Times Magazine,* 21 November.
Gordon, Milton M. 1964. *Assimilation in American Life: The Role of Race,
   Religion and National Origins.* New York: Oxford University Press.
Graham, Hugh Davis. 1989. "Violence, Social Theory, and the Historians:
   The Debate over Consensus and Culture in America." In *Protest,
   Rebellion, Reform. Vol. 2 of Violence in America,* ed. Ted Robert Gurr.
   Newbury Park, CA: Sage Publications.
Gresh, Alain. 1983. *The PLO: The Struggle Within: Towards an Indepen-
   dent Palestinian State.* London: Zed Books Ltd.
Grotius, Hugo. 1964. *De Iure Pradae Commentarius,* ed. James Brown
   Scott. New York: Oceana Publication.
Gurr, Ted Robert. 1988. "Some Characteristics of Political Terrorism in the
   1960's." In *The Politics of Terrorism Third Edition, Revised and
   Expanded,* ed. Michael Stohl. New York: Marcel Dekker.
———. 1989. "Political Terrorism: Historical Antecedents and Contemporary Trends." In *Protest, Rebellion, Reform. Vol. 2 of Violence in
   America,* ed. Ted Robert Gurr. Newbury Park, CA: Sage Publications.
———. 1989. "The History of Protest, Rebellion and Reform in America:

An Overview." In *Protest, Rebellion, Reform. Vol. 2 of Violence in America*, ed. Ted Robert Gurr. Newbury Park, CA: Sage Publications.

Gurr, Ted Robert, and Barbara Harff. 1994. *Ethnic Conflict in World Politics*. Boulder, CO: Westview Press.

Haberman, Clyde. 1994. "Israel Votes Ban on Jewish Groups Linked to Kahane." *New York Times*, 14 March.

Hacker, Frederick J. 1976. *Crusaders, Criminals, Crazies: Terror and Terrorism in Our Time*. New York: Norton.

Hacker, Joseph R. 1982. "Ottoman Policy towards the Jews and Jewish Attitudes toward the Ottomans during the Fifteenth Century." In *The Central Lands. Vol. 1 of Christians and Jews in the Ottoman Empire: The Functioning of a Plural Society*, eds. Benjamin Braude and Bernard Lewis. New York: Holmes & Meier.

Hanauer, Lawrence S. 1995. "The Path to Redemption: Fundamentalist Judaism, Territory and Jewish Settler Violence in the West Bank." *Studies in Conflict and Terrorism* 18(4), 245-270.

Hannikainen, Lauri. 1988. *Peremptory Norms (Jus Cogens) in International Law: Historical Development, Criteria, Present Status*. Helsinki: Lakimiesliiton Kustannus Finnish Lawyers' Publishing Company.

Harkabi, Yehoshafat. 1974. *Palestinians and Israel*. New York: John Wiley & Sons.

Harris, Ben M. 1964. "Leadership Prediction As Related to Measures of Personal Characteristics." *Personnel Administration* 27(4): 31-34.

Harris, Rosemary. 1989. "Anthropological Views on 'Violence' in Northern Ireland." In *Ireland's Terrorist Trauma*, eds. Yonah Alexander and Alan O'Day. New York: St. Martin's Press.

Hewitt, Christopher. 1988. "The Cost of Terrorism: A Cross-National Study of Six Countries." *Terrorism* 11(3): 164-180.

Hocking, Jenny. 1986. "Terrorism and counter-terrorism: institutionalizing political order." *The Australian Quarterly* 58(3): 297-307.

Hoffman, Avi, Benny Morris and Lisa Palmieri Billing. 1985. "Airport Massacres blamed on Abu Nidal terror squad." *Jerusalem Post*, 29 December.

Hoffman, Bruce. 1984. "The Jewish Defense League." *Terrorism, Violence Insurgency Journal* 5(1): 10-15.

———. 1998. *Inside Terrorism*. London: Victor Gollancz.

Hogg, Ian V. 1990. *Jane's Infantry Weapons Sixteenth Edition 1990-1991*. Surrey, UK: Jane's Information Group.

Holsti, Kalevi, Jaakko. 1985. *The Dividing Discipline: Hegemony and Diversity in International Theory*. Boston: Allen & Unwin.

Holton, Gerald. 1977. "Reflections on Modern Terrorism." *The Jerusalem*

Journal of International Relations 3(1): 96-104.

Holy Bible Revised Standard Version Reference Edition. 1952.

Homer, Frederic D. 1983. "Terror in the United States: Three Perspectives." In *The Politics of Terrorism Second Edition, Revised and Expanded*, ed. Michael Stohl. New York: Marcel Dekker.

Horowitz, Dan and Moshe Lissak. 1978. *Origins of the Israeli Polity: Palestine under the Mandate.* Chicago: University of Chicago Press.

Horowitz, Donald L. 1985. *Ethnic Groups in Conflict.* Berkeley: University of California Press.

Howe, Marvine. 1977. "Protests and Skepticism Dominate Arab's Reaction." *New York Times*, 20 November.

Hubbard, David G. 1975. "A Glimmer of Hope: A Psychiatric Perspective." In *International Terrorism and Political Crimes*, ed. M. Cherif Bassiouni. Springfield, IL: Charles C. Thomas.

———. 1983. "The Psychodynamics of Terrorism." In *International Violence*, eds. Tunde Adeniran and Yonah Alexander. New York: Praeger Publishers.

Huntington, Samuel P. 1968. *Political Order and Changing Societies.* New Haven: Yale University Press.

Hutman, Bill. 1993. "Haredim blamed for torching Kollek's car." *Jerusalem Post*, 1 January.

———. 1993. "Haredi threat to Rabin's life." *Jerusalem Post*, 6 January.

———. 1994. "Journalist critical of Kahane attacked by Kahane-Hai members." *Jerusalem Post*, 11 January.

Hutman, Bill and Jon Immanuel. 1993. "Terrorist subdued after wounding 6 people." *Jerusalem Post*, 23 March.

Ibrahim, Youssef. 1996. "Hamas Chief Says He Can't Curb Terrorists." *The New York Times*, 9 March.

Immanuel, Jon. 1992. "Fatah gang linked to Jenin killings." *Jerusalem Post*, 27 January.

———. 1992. "Jewish terror group claims Freij attack." *Jerusalem Post*, 24 January.

Inalcik, Halil. 1982. "Ottoman Archival Materials on *Millets*." In *The Central Lands. Vol. 1 of Christians and Jews in the Ottoman Empire: The Functioning of a Plural Society*, eds. Benjamin Braude and Bernard Lewis. New York: Holmes & Meier.

Inbar, Efraim. 1991. "Israel's Small War: The Military Response to the *Intifada.*" *Armed Forces & Society* (18)1 Fall.

International Labor Conference. 1989. International Labor Organization Convention (No. 169) Concerning Indigenous and Tribal Peoples in Independent Countries, 27 June. Draft Report of the Committee on

Convention No. 107, Appendix I, C.C. 107/D. 303 (June 1989).

Intoccia, Gregory F. 1985. "International Legal and Policy Implications of an American Counter-Terrorist Strategy." *Denver Journal of International Law and Policy* 14(1): 121-146.

Isradi, Raphael, ed. 1983. *PLO in Lebanon: Selected Documents*. London: Weidenfeld and Nicolson.

Issawi, Charles. 1982. "The Transformation of the Economic Position of the *Millets* in the Nineteenth Century." In *The Central Lands. Vol. 1 of Christians and Jews in the Ottoman Empire: The Functioning of a Plural Society*, eds. Benjamin Braude and Bernard Lewis. New York: Holmes & Meier.

Iviansky, Ze'ev. 1977. "Individual Terror: Concept and Typology." *Journal of Contemporary History* 12(1): 43-63.

Izenberg, Dan. 1989. "Arab gunned down near Old City's Jaffa Gate." *Jerusalem Post*, 11 April.

Jaber, Hala. 1997. *Hezbollah: Born With A Vengeance*. New York: Columbia University Press.

Jenkins, Brian. 1981. "A U.S. Strategy for Combatting Terrorism." *Conflict* 3(2/3): 167-176.

Jenkins, Brian M. 1988. "Future Trends in International Terrorism." In *Current Perspectives on International Terrorism*, eds. Robert O. Slater and Michael Stohl, 246-266. Basingstoke, Hampshire: MacMillan Press.

Jenkins, Philip. 1988. "Under Two Flags: Provocation and Deception in European Terrorism." *Terrorism* 11(4): 275-287.

Jenkins, William O. 1947. "A Review of Leadership Studies with Particular Reference to Military Problems." *Psychological Bulletin* 44(1): 54-79.

Jerusalem Post. 1961. "21 Dead in Oran, Algiers After De Gaulle Address." 3 December.

———. 1962. "Salan Sentenced to Life Imprisonment." 24 May.

———. 1967. "Saboteurs blast Negev railway line." 8 June.

———. 1970. "El Al crew foils hijackers but 3 other planes seized." 7 September.

———. 1970. "BOAC airliner at desert strip." 10 September.

———. 1970. "UN Security Council Meets as British Plane Hijacked." 10 September.

———. 1970. "Terrorists blow up 3 airliners, Say They'll Free All But 40 Hostages." 13 September.

———. 1970. "Freed Hostages Tell of Chaos in Amman, Terror In Desert." 13 September.

———. 1974. "New terror group acts in Syria." 16 August.

———. 1974. "Blast at USIA in Damascus." 16 September.

————. 1975. "Egypt, Jordan embassies in Syria bombed." 5 January.

————. 1975. "Explosion in Tyre." 12 February.

————. 1975. "Leftist Arabs bomb US firm in Lebanon." 13 February.

————. 1975. "Syrian death sentence for five leftists." 30 July.

————. 1975. "12 Lebanese soldiers held as Communists." 31 July.

————. 1976. "American envoy, aide slain in Moslem quarter of Beirut." 17 June.

————. 1977. "Arabs Bitter." 20 November.

————. 1977. "Violent protest erupts throughout Arab world." 20 November.

————. 1978. "Ten accused of plot to overthrow government." 11 August.

————. 1979. "Natorei Karta admits planting false bomb." 15 October.

————. 1981. "Death toll at 39 in huge blast at US Embassy in Beirut." 19 April.

————. 1981. "Arab terrorists admit bombing tourist office." 29 July.

————. 1981. "Moslem fanatics held for Damascus blast." 3 December.

————. 1982. "US military attache shot dead in Paris." 19 January.

————. 1983. "Yeshiva students queried about attack on Arab's flat." 2 June.

————. 1983. "Hebron council sacked following Jew's murder." 8 July.

————. 1983. "3 killed in attack on Hebron college, West Bank Arabs call general strike." 27 July.

————. 1983. "US stunned by Beirut disaster." 24 October.

————. 1984. "Lifta suspect sent to mental hospital." 15 June.

————. 1984. "The Accused: Brief biographies of the suspects in the alleged Jewish terror underground, publication of whose identities was banned until yesterday's court decision." 19 June.

————. 1984. "Beirut Shi'ites bomb Libyan Embassy." 12 July.

————. 1984. "Woman's sharp eyes avert bomb disaster." 16 November.

————. 1984. "Suspected killer of Israeli diplomat held in Rome." 23 December.

————. 1985. "Beirut gunmen free Cypriot plane." 8 February.

————. 1985. "Jewish travel agency bombed in London." 7 June.

————. 1986. "Arab bombers vow: More Paris attacks." 21 September.

————. 1986. "Survivor gives details of Iraqi airliner hijack." 28 December.

————. 1987. "Second German abducted in Beirut." 22 January.

————. 1987. "Fears grow Waite now kidnap victim." 1 February.

————. 1988. "The Algerian Equation." 11 March.

————. 1989. "Keshet bomb detonated in Jerusalem after warning." 12 February.

———. 1989. "Jewish Intifada." 31 July.

———. 1989. "Islamic Jihad claims responsibility for French plane blast over Africa." 21 September.

———. 1989. "Hizbullah reportedly operating terror network in West Africa." 28 November.

———. 1990. "Fundamentalist bomb plot foiled in Egypt." 7 May.

———. 1990. "French friend Jacques Soustelle dies at age 78." 8 August.

———. 1991. "Turkish Islamic Jihad claims responsibility for Ankara attacks on American, Egyptian." 29 October.

———. 1992. "Mother of seven found murdered near Jenin." 14 April.

———. 1992. "Grenade kills one in Old City: Kahane Hai takes responsibility for attack in Moslem Quarter." 17 November.

———. 1993. "Police suspect terrorists behind bombing of World Trade Center." 28 February.

———. 1993. "Villager found murdered in Samaria." 23 July.

Johnson, Chalmers. 1978. "Perspectives on Terrorism." In *The Terrorism Reader: A Historical Anthology*, ed. Walter Laqueur. New York: New American Library.

———. 1982. *Revolutionary Change Second Edition*. Stanford, CA: Stanford University Press.

Johnson, Paul. 1987. *A History of the Jews*. London: Weidenfeld and Nicolson.

Joyner, Christopher C. 1988. "In Search for an Anti-Terrorism Policy: Lessons from the Reagan Era." *Terrorism* 11(1): 29-42.

Juckes, Jim J. 1995. *Opposition in South Africa: The Leadership of Z.K. Matthews, Nelson Mandela, and Stephen Biko*. Westport, CT: Praeger.

Kaplan, Abraham, 1978. "The Psychodynamics of Terrorism." *Terrorism: An International Journal* 1 (3/4): 237-254.

Kaplan, Kenneth and Michal Sela. 1989. "Security probe into American's 'kidnapping'." *Jerusalem Post*, 25 June.

Karber, Phillip A. and R. William Mengel. 1983. "Political and Economic Forces Affecting Terrorism" In *Managing Terrorism: Strategies for the Corporate Executive,* eds. Patrick J. Montana and George S. Roukis. Westport, CT: Quorum Books.

Karpat, Kemal H. 1982. "Millets and Nationality: The Roots of the Incongruity of Nation and State in the Post Ottoman Era." In *The Arabic-Speaking Lands. Vol. 2 of Christians and Jews in the Ottoman Empire: The Functioning of a Plural Society*, eds. Benjamin Braude and Bernard Lewis. New York: Holmes & Meier.

Katz, Samuel. 1968. *Days of Fire*. Garden City, NY: Doubleday & Company.

Kedourie, Elie. 1992. *Politics in the Middle East*. Oxford: Oxford University Press.

Keinon, Herb. 1993. "Kahane Hai calls arrests 'provocation'." *Jerusalem Post*, 14 July.

Kellet, Anthony, Bruce Beanlands, and James Deacon. 1991. *Terrorism in Canada 1960-1989 No. 1990-16*. Solicitor General Canada Ministry Secretariat.

Khalaf, Samir. 1982. "Communal Conflict in Nineteenth-Century Lebanon." In *The Arabic-Speaking Lands. Vol. 2 of Christians and Jews in the Ottoman Empire: The Functioning of a Plural Society*, eds. Benjamin Braude and Bernard Lewis. New York: Holmes & Meier.

Khouri, Fred J. 1976. *The Arab-Israeli Dilemma Second Edition*. Syracuse: Syracuse University Press.

Kifner, John. 1990. "Kahane Suspect Is a Muslim with a Series of Addresses." *New York Times*, 7 November.

———. 1990. "Kahane Suspect Said to Have Arms Cache." *New York Times*, 11 December.

Klan Watch Intelligence Report. 1996. "Terrorists in the Name of God and Race: Phineas Priests use Religious Arguments to Justify Their Violent Crimes." August #83, 1, 3.

———. 1996. "Three Suspected Phineas Priests Charged in Spokane Bombings: Idaho Militants Linked to Prominent Identity Minister and Publication." November #24, 1, 4.

Kramer, Martin. 1997. "The Oracle of Hizbullah: Sayyid Muhammad Husayn Fadlallah." In *Spokesmen of the Despised: Fundamentalist Leaders of the Middle East*, ed. R. Scott Appleby, 83-181. Chicago: The University of Chicago Press.

Kuhn, Thomas S. 1970. *The Structure of Scientific Revolutions*. Chicago: University of Chicago Press.

Kupperman, Robert H. and Robert A. Friedlander. 1979. "Terrorism and Social Control: Challenge and Response." *Ohio Northern University Law Review* 6(1): 52-59.

Lahoud, Lamia. 1992. "Inside the Black Panthers' den in the mountains of Jenin." *Jerusalem Post*, 3 July.

Lakos, Amos. 1991. *Terrorism, 1980-1990: A Bibliography*. Boulder, CO: Westview Press.

Laqueur, Walter. 1987. "Reflections on Terrorism." In *The Terrorism Reader: A Historical Anthology*, eds. Walter Laqueur and Yonah Alexander. New York: New American Library.

Laqueur, Walter and Yonah Alexander, eds. 1987. *The Terrorism Reader: A Historical Anthology*. New York: New American Library.

Lasswell, Harold D. 1935. *World Politics and Personal Insecurity*. New York: Whittlesey House, McGraw Hill Book.

———. 1978. "Terrorism and the Political Process." *Terrorism: An International Journal* 1(3/4): 255-263.

Leedy, Paul D. 1993. *Practical Research Planning and Design Fifth Edition*. New York: MacMillan Publishing Co.

Legrain, Jean-Francois. 1994. "Palestinian Islamisms: Patriotism as a Condition of Their Expansion." In *Accounting for Fundamentalisms: The Dynamic Character of Movements*, eds. Martin E. Marty and R. Scott Appleby, 413-427. Chicago: The University of Chicago Press.

Lehn, Walter. 1988. *The Jewish National Fund*. New York: Kegan Paul International.

Lenczowski, George. 1980. *The Middle East in World Affairs*. Ithaca, NY: Cornell University Press.

Lewis, Bernard. 1960. *The Arabs in History*. London: Hutchinson & Co.

———. 1979. *The Emergence of Modern Turkey*. London: Oxford University Press.

———. 1993. *The Arabs in History*. London: Oxford University Press.

Lifton, Robert Jay. 1986. *The Nazi Doctors: Medical Killing and the Psychology of Genocide*. New York: Basic Books.

Livingstone, Neil C. and Terrell E. Arnold. 1986. "Democracy under Attack." In *Fighting Back: Winning the War against Terrorism*, eds. Neil C. Livingstone and Terrell E. Arnold. Lexington, MA: D.C. Heath and Company.

Livingstone, Neil C. and David Halevy. 1990. *Inside the PLO: Covert Units, Secret Funds and the War Against Israel and the United States*. New York: William Morrow.

Long, David E. 1990. *The Anatomy of Terrorism*. New York: The Free Press.

Lopez, George A. 1986. "National Security Ideology as an Impetus to State Violence and State Terror." In *Government, Violence and Repression: An Agenda for Research*, eds. Michael Stohl and George Lopez. Westport, CT: Greenwood Press.

Luckabaugh, Robert, H. Edward Fuqua, Joseph P. Cangemi, and Casimir J. Kowalski. 1997. "Terrorist Behavior and United States Foreign Policy: Who is the Enemy?: Some Psychological and Political Perspectives." *Psychology: A Journal of Human Behavior* 34(2): 1-16.

Lustick, Ian S. 1980. *Arabs in the Jewish State: Israel's Control of a National Minority*. Austin: University of Texas Press.

———. 1988. *For the Land and the Lord: Jewish Fundamentalism in Israel*. New York: Council on Foreign Relations.

————. 1993. *Unsettled States Disputed Lands: Britain and Ireland, France and Algeria, Israel and the West Bank.* Ithaca, NY: Cornell University Press.

Makovsky, David. 1992. "Bomb destroys Israel's embassy in Buenos Aires: 5 dead 81 hurt." *Jerusalem Post*, 18 March.

Makovsky, David and Dan Izenberg. 1992. "Hope fading for victims buried in embassy rubble." *Jerusalem Post*, 19 March.

Maoz, Moshe. 1968. *Ottoman Reform in Syria and Palestine 1840-1861: The Impact of the Tanzimat on Politics and Society.* London: Oxford University Press.

————. 1982. "Communal Conflict in Ottoman Syria during the Reform Era: The Role of Political and Economic Factors." In *The Arabic-Speaking Lands. Vol. 2 of Christians and Jews in the Ottoman Empire: The Functioning of a Plural Society*, eds. Benjamin Braude and Bernard Lewis. New York: Holmes & Meier.

Marcus, Raine. 1993. "Gaza Sealed after terror attack in Tel-Aviv." *Jerusalem Post*, 2 March.

Martin, R. C. 1987. "Religious Violence in Islam: Towards an Understanding of the Discourse on Jihad in Modern Egypt." In *Contemporary Research on Terrorism*, eds. Paul Wilkinson and Alasdair M. Stewart. Great Britain: Aberdeen University Press.

McEwen, Michael T. and Stephen Sloan. 1980. "Terrorism Preparedness on the State and Local Level: An Oklahoma Perspective." *Clandestine Tactics and Technology: A Technical and Background Information Service*, 1-15. Gaithersburg, MD: International Association of Police Chiefs.

McKinley, James C. Jr. 1990. "Suspect in Kahane Slaying Kept List of Prominent Jews." *New York Times*, 1 December.

————. 1998. "Bombs Rip Apart 2 U.S. Embassies in Africa: Scores Killed; No Firm Motives or Suspects." *New York Times*, 8 August.

————. 1998. "Toll Rises as Rescue Effort Goes on in Kenya." *New York Times*, 9 August.

McKnight, Gerald. 1974. *The Terrorist Mind.* Indianapolis: Bobbs-Merrill.

Medd, Roger and Frank Goldstein. 1997. "International Terrorism on the Eve of a New Millennium." *Studies in Conflict & Terrorism* 20: 281-316.

Melman, Yossi. 1986. *The Master Terrorist: The True Story Behind Abu Nidal.* New York: Adama Books.

Merari, Ariel and Yosefa (Daiksel) Braunstein. 1984. "Shi'ite Terrorism: Operational Capabilities and the Suicide Factor." *Terrorism Violence Insurgency Journal* 5(2): 7-10.

Merari, Ariel, Tamar Prat, Sophia Kotzer, Anat Kurz, and Yoram Schweitzer. 1986. *Inter 85: A Review of International Terrorism in 1985*, Tel-Aviv: Jaffee Center, for Strategic Studies.

Merari, Ariel. 1978. "A Classification of Terrorist Groups." *Terrorism: An International Journal* 1 (3/4): 331-346.

Meri-Lichter, S. 1984. "There is More Than One T.N.T. Group (*al Ha'mishmar*)." *Israeli Mirror,* No. 680/8.3.1984.

Mergui, Raphael, and Phillippe Simonnot. 1987. *Israel's Ayatollahs: Meir Kahane and the Far Right in Israel.* London: Saqi Books.

Merkel, Peter H. 1986. "Approaches to the Study of Political Violence." In *Political Violence and Terror: Motifs and Motivations,* ed. Peter H. Merkel, 19-59. Berkeley: University of California Press.

Mickolus, Edward, F. 1976. "Negotiating for Hostages: A Policy Dilemma." *Orbis: A Journal of World Affairs* 19(4): 1309-1325.

———. 1980. *Transnational Terrorism: A Chronology of Events, 1968-1979.* Westport, CT: Greenwood.

———. 1993. *Terrorism: 1988-1991: A Chronology of Events and a Selectively Annotated Bibliography.* Westport, CT: Greenwood Press.

Mickolus, Edward F., Todd Sandler, and Jean M. Murdock. 1989. *International Terrorism in the 1980's: A Chronology of Events: Volume I 1980-1983.* Ames, IA: Iowa State University Press.

———. 1989. *International Terrorism in the 1980's: A Chronology of Events: Volume II 1984-1987.* Ames, IA: Iowa State University Press.

Miller, Reuben. 1986. "Acts of International Terrorism: Governments' Responses and Policies." *Comparative Political Studies* 19(3): 385-413.

Moore, John V. and Robert G. Smith, Jr. 1953. "Some Aspects of Noncommissioned Officer Leadership." *Personal Psychology* 6: 427-443.

Moxon-Browne, Edward. 1981. "Terrorism in Northern Ireland: the Case of the Provisional IRA." In *Terrorism: A Challenge to the State,* ed. Juliet Lodge. New York: St. Martins Press.

Murphy, John F. 1978. "Protected Persons and Diplomatic Facilities." In *Legal Aspects of International Terrorism,* eds. Alona E. Evans and John F. Murphy, 277-339. Lexington, MA: Lexington Books.

Myers, Steven Lee, Barbara Crossette, Judith Miller, and Tim Weiner. 1998. "U.S. Says Iraq Aided Production of Chemical Weapons in Sudan." *New York Times,* 25 August, A-1, A-6.

Nasr, Kameel B. 1997. *Arab and Israeli Terrorism: The Causes and Effects of Political Violence 1936-1993.* Jefferson, NC: McFarland & Company, Inc.

Nassar, Jamal R. 1991. *The Palestine Liberation Organization: From Armed Struggle to the Declaration of Independence.* New York: Praeger

Publishers.

National Foreign Assessment Center. 1980. *International Terrorism in 1979.* PA 80-1007 2U. Washington, DC: Central Intelligence Agency.

National Geographic Society. 1990. *National Geographic Atlas of the World Sixth Edition.* Washington, DC: National Geographic Society.

National Governor's Association Emergency Preparedness Project. 1979. *Domestic Terrorism.* Washington, DC: Center for Policy Research, National Governors Association.

Nef, Jorge. 1978. "Some Thoughts on Contemporary Terrorism: Domestic and International Perspectives." *Terrorism in Theory and Practice: Proceedings of a colloquium,* ed. John Carson. Toronto: The Atlantic Council of Canada.

Nelan, Bruce W. 1994. "Raging Against Peace: Still furious over the Hebron massacre, palestinians insist Rabin's concessions are not enough." *Time,* March.

Netanyahu, Benjamin. 1986. "Terrorism: How the West Can Win." In *Terrorism: How the West Can Win,* ed. Benjamin Netanyahu. New York: Farrar, Straus and Giroux.

New York Times. 1961. "South Africa Blasts Protest Apartheid." 18 December.

———. 1975. "US Life Insurance Office Wrecked in Lebanon Blast." 12 February.

———. 1977. "4 Killed in Second Attack in 2 Days In a Christian District of Beirut." 5 January.

———. 1977. "Palestinian Dies of Wounds in Greece." 20 November.

———. 1988. "Clemency Declined by Britain for Six Convicted Irishmen." 30 January.

Norton, Augustus R. 1987. *Amal and the Shi'a: Struggle for the Soul of Lebanon.* Austin: University of Texas Press.

———. 1988. "Terrorism in the Middle East." In *Terrorist Dynamics,* ed. Vittorfranco S. Pisano. Arlington, VA: International Association of Chiefs of Police.

Norušis, Marija J. 1990. SPSS/PC+ Advanced Statistics 4.0 for the IBM PC/XT and PS/2. Chicago: SPSS.

———. 1991. *The SPSS Guide to Data Analysis SPSS/PCt, 2nd Edition.* Chicago: SPSS.

Nutting, L. Ruth. 1923. "Some Characteristics of Leadership." *School and Society* 18(457): 387-390.

Nye, Jr., Joseph S. 1993. *Understanding International Conflicts: An Introduction to Theory and History.* New York: Harper Collins College Publishers.

O'Ballance, Edgar. 1997. *Islamic Fundamentalist Terrorism: 1979-95; The Iranian Connection.* New York: New York University Press.
———. 1998. *The Palestinian Intifada.* New York: St. Martin's Press.
O'Brien, William V. 1985. "Counterterrorism: Lessons from Israel." *Strategic Review* 13(4): 32-44.
O'Day, Alan. 1994. *Dimensions of Irish Terrorism.* New York: G. K. Hall.
Oked, Yitzhak. 1985. "El AL: Attack in Rome came some twenty minutes 'too early'." *Jerusalem Post,* 29 December.
O'Neill, Bard E. 1978. "Towards A Typology of Political Terrorism: The Palestinian Resistance Movement." *Journal of International Affairs* 32(1): 17-42.
Oots, Kent Layne. 1984. "Transnational Terrorism: A Political Organization Approach." Ph.D. dissertation. Northern Illinois University.
Organization of African Unity. 1986. African Charter on Human and Peoples' Rights, 21 October. OAU Doc. CAB/LEG/67/3 Rev. 5.
Organization of American States. 1948. American Declaration of the Rights and Duties of Man, March 30-May 2. OAS Off. Rec. OEA/Ser. L/V/I.4 Rev. (1965).
———. 1978. American Convention on Human Rights, 18 July. OAS Treaty Ser. No. 36, OAS Off. Rec. OEA/Ser. L/V/II.23 doc. 21 rev. 6 (1979).
———. 1987. Inter-American Convention to Prevent and Punish Torture, 28 February. OAS Treaty Ser. No. 67, OAS DOC OEA/Ser. P, AG/doc. 2023/85 rev. 1.
Osmond, Russell Lowell. 1979. "Transnational Terrorism 1968-1974: A Quantitative Analysis." Ph.D. dissertation. Syracuse University.
Pace, Eric. 1975. "Assad's Hand is Firm, and His Ear Attentive." *New York Times,* 29 November.
Parry, Albert. 1976. *Terrorism From Robespierre to Arafat.* New York: The Vanguard Press.
Parsons, Talcott. 1964. *Max Weber: The Theory of Social and Economic Organization.* New York: The Free Press.
Pear, Robert. 1989. "Cuts Threatened in Aid to Israel." *New York Times,* 12 February.
Pearson, Frederic S. 1974. "Geographic Proximity and Foreign Military Intervention." *The Journal of Conflict Resolution* XVIII (3): 432-460.
Pearson, Frederic S. and J. Martin Rochester. 1998. *International Relations: The Global Condition in the Twenty First Century.* Boston: McGraw Hill.
Peleg, Ilan. 1988. "Terrorism in the Middle East: The Case of the Arab-Israeli Conflict." In *The Politics of Terrorism Third Edition, Revised and Expanded,* ed. Michael S. Stohl. New York: Marcel Dekker.

Peri, Yoram. 1983. *Between battles and ballots: Israeli military in politics.* Cambridge, England: Cambridge University Press.

Perlmutter, Amos. 1969. *Military and Politics in Israel: Nation-Building and Role Expansion.* New York: Frederic A. Praeger, Publishers.

Perry, Duncan M. 1988. *The Politics of Terror: The Macedonian Liberation Movements 1893-1903.* Durham, NC: Duke University Press.

Pfaltzgraff, Robert L. 1986. "Implications for American Policy." In *Hydra of Carnage: The International Linkages of Terrorism and Other Low-Intensity Operations The Witnesses Speak,* eds. Uri Ra'anan, Robert L. Pfaltzgraff, Jr., Richard H. Shultz, Ernst Halperin and Igor Lukes. Lexington, MA: D. C. Heath and Company.

Philipp, Thomas. 1982. "Image and Self-Image of the Syrians in Egypt: From the Early Eighteenth Century to the Reign of Muhammad Ali." In *The Arabic-Speaking Lands. Vol. 1 of Christians and Jews in the Ottoman Empire: The Functioning of a Plural Society,* eds. Benjamin Braude and Bernard Lewis. New York: Holmes & Meier.

Pion-Berlin, David, and George A. Lopez. 1991. "Of Victims and Executioners: Argentine State Terror, 1975-1979." *International Studies Quarterly* 35, 87-108.

Pisano, Vittorfranco S., ed. *Terrorist Dynamics.* Arlington, VA: International Association of Police Chiefs.

Piscatori, James. 1994. "Accounting for Islamic Fundamentalisms." In *Accounting for Fundamentalisms: The Dynamic Character of Movements,* eds. Martin E. Marty and R. Scott Appleby, 361-371. Chicago: The University of Chicago Press.

Pluchinksy, Dennis. 1981. "Political Terrorism in Western Europe: Some Themes and Variations." In *Terrorism in Europe,* eds. Yonah Alexander and Kenneth A. Myers, 40-78. New York: St. Martins Press.

Post, Jerrold M. 1984. "Notes on a Psychodynamic Theory of Terrorist Behavior." *Terrorism: An International Journal* 7(3): 241-256.

Quandt, William B. 1977. *Decade of Decisions: American Policy Toward the Arab-Israeli Conflict, 1967-1976.* Berkeley: University of California Press.

Quester, George H. 1988. "Some Explanations For State-Supported Terrorism in the Middle East." In *Terrible Beyond Endurance? The Foreign Policy of State Terrorism,* eds. Michael S. Stohl and Gary A. Lopez. Westport, CT: Greenwood Press.

Rabi, Muhammad Mahmoud. 1967. *The Political Theory of Ibn Khaldun.* Leiden, Netherlands: E. J. Brill.

Rapaport, Era. 1996. *Letters from Tel Mond Prison: An Israeli Settler Defends His Act of Terror.* New York: The Free Press.

Rapoport, David C. 1984. "Fear and Trembling: Terrorism in Three Religious Traditions." *American Political Science Review* 78: 658-675.

Rapoport, D.C. 1987. "Why Does Religious Messianism Produce Terror?" In *Contemporary Research on Terrorism*, eds. Paul Wilkinson and Alasdair M. Stewart, 72-88. Great Britain: Aberdeen University Press.

Reiss, Albert J. and Jeffrey A. Roth, eds. 1993. *Understanding and Preventing Violence*. Washington, DC: National Academy Press.

Richardson, David and Robert Rosenberg. 1984. "15 arrested in sabotage attempt on 5 Arab buses." *Jerusalem Post*, 29 April.

Roncek, Dennis W. 1991. "Using Logit Coefficients to Obtain the Effects of Independent Variables on Changes in Probabilities." *Social Forces* 70(2): 509-518.

Ronchey, Alberto. 1978. "Terror in Italy, Between Red & Black." *Dissent* 25(2): 150-156.

Rosenberg, Robert. 1983. "Security Forces probing West Bank vigilantes." *Jerusalem Post*, 16 May.

———. 1984. "Major anti-Arab terror cases cracked by security services." *Jerusalem Post*, 3 May.

———. 1984. "Suspects show pride in Jewish terror action." *Jerusalem Post*, 4 May.

———. 1984. "Seven more Jewish terror arrests." *Jerusalem Post*, 8 May.

———. 1984. "Gush Emunim leader claims: Political, military chiefs 'urged settlers to act'." *Jerusalem Post*, 19 June.

———. 1984. "Bomb is disarmed in Jerusalem." *Jerusalem Post*, 29 November.

———. 1985. "2 bombs exploded in capital, 2 others found in Tel-Aviv." *Jerusalem Post*, 19 June.

Rotem, Michael. 1993. "Hamas gang arrested, plotted TA bombing." *Jerusalem Post*, 9 April.

———. 1993. "No Hostages for Hizbullah." *Jerusalem Post*, 26 July.

———. 1993. "Hizbullah reaps benefits from past." *Jerusalem Post*, 30 July.

Rotem, Michael and David Rudge. 1993. "IDF Continues to Hit Terrorist Targets." *Jerusalem Post,* 27 July, 1, 2.

Rubenstein, Richard E. 1987. *Alchemists of Revolution: Terrorism in the Modern World*. New York: Basic Books.

———. 1989. "Rebellion in America: The Fire Next Time?" In *Protest, Rebellion, Reform. Vol. 2 of Violence in America*, ed. Ted Robert Gurr, 307-328. Newbury, CA: Sage Publications.

Rubin, Barry. 1993. "Hizbullah's goal: Islamic Statehood." *Jerusalem Post*, 30 July.

Rudge, David. 1991. "New terror group appears in Lebanon." *Jerusalem Post*, 13 October.

―――. 1991. "Hizbullah vows attacks will escalate." *Jerusalem Post*, 29 October.

Rudge, David and Michael Rotem. 1993. "Katyusnas Hit Upper Galilee After Two Gunmen are Killed in Security Zone Clash." *Jerusalem Post*, 13 June, 1.

Russell, Charles A., Leon J. Banker, and Bowman H. Miller. 1979. "Out-Inventing the Terrorist." In *Terrorism: Theory and Practice*, eds. Yonah Alexander, David Carlton, and Paul Wilkinson, 3-42. Boulder: Westview.

Sacher, Howard M. 1976. *A History of Israel: From the Rise of Zionism to Our Time*. New York: Alfred A. Knopf.

Safran, Nadav. 1969. *From War To War The Arab-Israeli Confrontation, 1948-1967: A Study of the Conflict From the Perspective of Coercion in the Context of Inter-Arab and Big Power Relations*. New York: Western Publishing.

―――. 1978. *Israel The Embattled Ally*. Cambridge, MA: Harvard University Press.

Schachter, Jonathan and Michael Rotem. 1990. "Security forces on alert for Kahane's funeral." *Jerusalem Post*, 7 November.

Schiller, David Th. 1988. "A Battlegroup Divided: The Palestinian Fedayeen." In *Inside Terrorist Organizations*, ed. David C. Rapoport. New York: Columbia University Press.

Schlagheck, Donna M. 1988. *International Terrorism: An Introduction to the Concepts and Actors*. Lexington, MA: Lexington Books.

Schmemman, Serge. 1996. "Israeli Forces Seal Off Big Parts of West Bank" *New York Times*, 6 March.

Schmid, Alex P. 1983. *Political Terrorism: A Research Guide to Concepts, Theories, Data Bases and Literature*. Amsterdam: Transaction Books.

Schmid, Alex P. and Albert J. Jongman. 1988. *Political Terrorism: A New Guide to Actors, Authors, Concepts, Data Bases, Theories and Literature*. Amsterdam: North Holland Publishing Company.

Schmitt, Eric. 1993. "U.S. Says Strike Crippled Iraq's Capacity for Terror." *New York Times*, 28 June.

Schul, Ze'ev, Macabee Dean and Jack Maurice. 1968. "Algiers holds 22 Israelis: Others aboard hijacked plane freed." *Jerusalem Post*, 24 July.

Seale, Patrick. 1992. *Abu Nidal: A Gun for Hire*. London: Hutchinson.

Segaller, Stephen. 1987. *Invisible Armies; Terrorism into the 1990's*. Orlando, Harcourt-Brace Jovanovich.

Sela, Michal. 1989. "Sicarii threaten 'anyone who meets with PLO'."

Jerusalem Post, 31 March.

———. 1989. "Sicarii intimidate women." *Jerusalem Post*, 12 April.

———. 1989. "Defense Ministry outlaws Islamic Movement Hamas." *Jerusalem Post*, 29 September.

Selth, Andrew. 1988. *Against Every Human Law: The Terrorist Threat to Diplomacy*. Australia: Australian National University Press.

Senate Government Affairs Committee Hearing, July 15, 1991. "Terrorism after the Gulf War." CSPAN July 20, 1991.

Seriphis, Matthew. 1990. "Hamas Founder Freed from jail." *Jerusalem Post*, 6 September.

Shapiro, Haim. 1983. "Harassers of peace now held." *Jerusalem Post*, 25 February.

Shenon, Philip. 1996. "US to Transfer Most of Its Force in Saudi Arabia." *New York Times*. 18 July.

Shimko, Keith L. 1991. *Images and arms control: perceptions of the Soviet Union in the Reagan administration*. Ann Arbor: University of Michigan Press.

Shultz, Richard. 1978. "Conceptualizing Political Terrorism: A Typology." *Journal of International Affairs* 32(1): 7-15.

Shultz, Richard H. 1986. "Can Democratic Governments use Military Force in the War Against Terrorism?" *World Affairs* 148(4): 205-215.

Simpson, Howard R. 1982. "Organizing For Counter-Terrorism." *Strategic Review* 10(1): 28-33.

Skendi, Stavro. 1982. "The *Millet* System and its Contribution to the Blurring of Orthodox National Identity in Albania." In *The Central Lands. Vol. 1 of Christians and Jews in the Ottoman Empire: The Functioning of a Plural Society*, eds. Benjamin Braude and Bernard Lewis. New York: Holmes & Meier.

Smart, Ian. 1987. "International Terrorism." *Behind the Headlines* 44(3): 1-19.

Smith, Charles D. 1996. *Palestine and the Arab-Israeli Conflict Third Edition*. New York: St. Martin's Press.

Smooha, Sammy. 1978. *Israel: Pluralism and Conflict*. Berkeley: University of California Press.

Sobel, Lester A., ed. 1975. *Political Terrorism*. New York: Facts on File, Inc.

Sprinzak, Ehud. 1988. "From Messianic Pioneering to Vigilante Terrorism: The Case of the Gush Emunim Underground." In *Inside Terrorist Organizations*, ed. David C. Rapoport, 194-216. New York: Columbia University Press.

———. 1991. *The Ascendence of Israel's Radical Right*. New York: The

Oxford University Press.

———. 1998. "The Great Superterrorism Scare." *Foreign Policy* 12, Fall: 110-124.

Starr, Harvey and Benjamin Most. 1976. "The Substance and Study of Borders in International Relations Research." *International Studies Quarterly* 20(4): 581-620.

———. 1983. "Contagion and Border Effects on Contemporary African Conflict." *Comparative Political Studies* 16(1): 92-117.

———. 1985. "Patterns of Conflict: Quantitative Analysis and the Comparative Lessons of Third World Wars." In *Approaches and Case Studies. Vol. 1 of the Lessons of Recent Wars in the Third World*, eds. Robert E. Harkavy and Stephanie G. Neuman, 33-52. Lexington, MA: D.C. Heath and Company.

Stephenson, T. E. 1954. "The Leader-Follower-Relationship." *The Sociological Review* 7: 179-195.

Stogdill, Ralph M. 1974. *Handbook of Leadership: A Survey of Theory and Research*. New York: The Free Press.

Stohl, Michael S. 1987. "Terrorism, States and State Terrorism: The Reagan Administration in the Middle East." *Arab Studies Quarterly* 9(2): 162-172.

———. 1988. "States, Terrorism and State Terrorism: The Role of the Superpowers." In *Current Perspectives on International Terrorism*, eds. Robert O. Slater and Michael Stohl, 155-205. Basingstoke, Hampshire: MacMillan Press.

Stohl, Michael and George A. Lopez. 1984. "Introduction." In *The State as Terrorist: The Dynamics of Governmental Repression and Violence*. Westport, CT: Greenwood Press.

Struminski, Wladimir. 1987. "4 Americans also abducted in Beirut." *Jerusalem Post*, 22 January.

Taheri, Amir. 1987. *Holy Terror: Inside the World of Islamic Terrorism*. Bethesda, MD: Adler & Adler.

Terrorism Violence and Insurgency Journal. 1985. "A Chronology of Significant Attacks on Israel and Israeli Reprisal Operations." *Terrorism Violence and Insurgency Journal* 5(4): 26-31.

———. 1989. "TVI Report Profile Al Fatah." *Terrorism Violence and Insurgency Report* 8(3): 1-3.

———. 1989. "TVI Report Profile Popular Front for the Liberation of Palestine (PFLP)." *Terrorism Violence and Insurgency Report* 8(3): 9-11.

———. 1989. "TVI Report Profile Popular Front for the Liberation of Palestine: General Command (PFLP-GC)." *Terrorism Violence and Insurgency Report* 8(3): 13-14.

————. 1990. "TVI Report Profile Hizbollah (Party of God)." *Terrorism Violence and Insurgency Report* 8(3): 1-6.

Theen, Rolf, and Frank L. Wilson. 1996. *Comparative Politics: An Introduction to Seven Countries Third Edition*. Upper Saddle River, NJ: Prentice Hall.

Tibi, Bassam. 1993. *Conflict and War in the Middle East, 1967-91*. New York: St. Martins Press.

Tilbury, Neil. 1992. *Israel–A Travel Survival Kit*. Australia: Lonely Planet Publications.

Toy, Eckard V. 1989. "Right-Wing Extremism from the Ku Klux Klan to the Order, 1915-1988." In *Protest, Rebellion, Reform. Vol. 2 of Violence in America*, ed. Ted Robert Gurr. Newbury Park, CA: Sage Publications.

Trent, Darrell M. 1979. "A National Policy to Combat Terrorism." *Policy Review* 9: 41-54.

Tsur, Batsheva. 1993. "Peres: Israel almost certain of identity of terrorists behind Buenos Aires embassy bombing." *Jerusalem Post*, 18 March.

Turgay, Uner A. 1982. "Trade and Merchants in Nineteenth-Century Trabzon: Elements of Ethnic Conflict." In *The Central Lands. Vol. 1 of Christians and Jews in the Ottoman Empire: The Functioning of a Plural Society*, eds. Benjamin Braude and Bernard Lewis. New York: Holmes & Meier.

United Nations. 1945. Agreement for the Prosecution and Punishment of the Major War Criminals of the European Axis Powers and Charter of the International Military Tribunal, 8 August. UNTS no. 279. 59 Stat. 1544.

————. 1945. Charter of the United Nations, 24 October. TS no. 993, 59 Stat 1031.

————. 1945. Statute of the International Court of Justice, 24 October. TS no. 993, 59 Stat 1031.

————. 1948. Universal Declaration of Human Rights, 10 December. UNGA Res. 217 A(III), UN Doc. A/810, at 71 (1948).

————. 1950. Convention for the Amelioration of the Condition of the Wounded and Sick in Armed Forces in the Field, 21 October. TIAS no. 3362, 75 UNTS 31.

————. 1950. Convention for the Amelioration of the Condition of the Wounded and Sick and Shipwrecked Members of Armed Forces at Sea, 21 October. TIAS no. 3363, 75 UNTS 85.

————. 1950. Convention Relative to the Treatment of Prisoners of War, 21 October. TIAS no. 3364, 75 UNTS 135.

————. 1950. Convention Relative to the Protection of Civilian Persons in Time of War, 21 October. TIAS no. 3365, 75 UNTS 287.

————. 1951. Convention on the Prevention and Punishment of the Crime of Genocide, 12 January. 78 UNTS 277.

————. 1953. European Convention for the Protection of Human Rights and Fundamental Freedoms, 3 September. 213 UNTS 221.

————. 1954. Convention Relating to the Status of Refugees, 22 April. 189 UNTS 137.

————. 1954. Protocol (No. 1) To the European Convention for the Protection of Human Rights and Fundamental Freedoms, 18 May. 213 UNTS 262.

————. 1954. Convention on the Political Rights of Women, 7 July. TIAS no. 8289, 193 UNTS 135.

————. 1955. Standard Minimum Rules for the Treatment of Prisoners, 30 August. UN Doc. A/CONF/6/1, Annex I, A (1956).

————. 1959. International Labor Organization Convention (No. 107) Concerning the Protection and Integration of Indigenous and Other Tribal and Semi-Tribal Populations in Independent Countries, 2 June. 328 UNTS 247.

————. 1959. Communications Concerning Human Rights, E.S.C. Res. 728 (XXVIII), 30 July. 28 UN Doc. E/3290 (1959).

————. 1960. Convention Relating to the Status of Stateless Persons, 6 June. 360 UNTS 117.

————. 1960. Declaration of the Granting of Independence to Colonial Countries and Peoples, 14 December. UNGA Res. 1514 (xv), UN Doc. A/4684 (1961).

————. 1963. Convention on Offenses and Certain Other Acts Committed on Board Aircraft, 14 September. TIAS no. 6768, 704 UNTS 219.

————. 1965. European Social Charter, 26 February. 529 UNTS 89.

————. 1965. Declaration on the Inadmissability of Intervention in the Domestic Affairs of the States and the Protection of Their Independence and Sovereignty, 21 December. UNGA Res. 2131 (xx).

————. 1966. UN Security Council Resolution 232, 16 December. UN DOC. S/INF/21/Rev. 1 (1966).

————. 1967. Economic and Social Council Resolution 1235 (XLII), 6 June. UN Doc. E/4393 (1967).

————. 1967. Protocol Relating to the Status of Refugees, 4 October. TIAS no. 6577, 606 UNTS 267.

————. 1967. Declaration on Territorial Asylum, 14 December. UNGA Res. 2312 (XXII), UN Doc. A/6716 (1968).

————. 1968. United Nations Security Council Resolution 253, 29 May. UN Doc. S/INF/23/Rev. 1 (1969).

————. 1969. International Convention on the Elimination of All Forms of

Racial Discrimination, 4 January. 660 UNTS 195.

———. 1970. Procedure for Dealing with Communications Relating to Violations of Human Rights and Fundamental Freedoms, 27 May. UN Doc. E/4832/Add. 1 (1970).

———. 1971. Convention for the Suppression of Unlawful Seizure of Aircraft, 14 October. TIAS 7192, 860 UNTS 105.

———. 1973. Convention for the Suppression of Unlawful Acts Against the Safety of Civil Aviation, 26 January. TIAS 7570, 1971, UN JURID. YB 143.

———. 1974. Universal Declaration on the Eradication of Hunger and Malnutrition, 16 November. UN Doc. E/Conf. 65/20, Ch. IV (1974).

———. 1974. Resolution on the Definition of Aggression, 14 December. UNGA Res. 3314 (XXIX), UN Doc. A/9631 (1975).

———. 1976. International Covenant on Economic, Social and Cultural Rights, 3 January. UNGA Res. 2200 (XXI), UN DOC A/6316 (1967).

———. 1976. International Covenant on Civil and Political Rights, 23 March. UNGA Res. 2200 (XXI), UN Doc. A/6316 (1967).

———. 1976. Optional Protocol to the International Covenant on Civil and Political Rights, 23 March. UNGA Res. 2200 (XXI), UN Doc. A/6316 (1967).

———. 1976. International Convention on the Suppression and Punishment of the Crime of "Apartheid," 18 July. UNGA Res. 3068 (XXVIII), UN Doc. A/9030 (1974).

———. 1977. Convention on the Prevention and Punishment of Crimes Against Internationally Protected Persons, Including Diplomatic Agents, 20 February. TIAS no. 8532.

———. 1978. Protocol Additional to the Geneva Conventions of August 12, 1949, and Relating to the Protection of Victims of International Armed Conflicts, 7 December. 1977 UN JURID YB 95.

———. 1978. Protocol Additional to the Geneva Conventions of August 12, 1949, and Relating to the Protection of Victims of Non-International Armed Conflicts, 7 December. 1977 UN Jurid YB 135.

———. 1978. Resolution on Disappeared Persons, 20 December. UNGA Res. 33/173, UN Doc. A/33/509 (1978).

———. 1980. Vienna Convention on the Law of Treaties, 27 January. UN Doc. A/CONF.39/27 at 289 (1969), 1155 UNTS 331.

———. 1981. Convention on the Elimination of All Forms of Discrimination Against Women, 3 September. UNGA Res. 34/180 (XXXIV), UN Doc. A/34/830 (1979).

———. 1981. Declaration on the Elimination of All Forms of Intolerance and of Discrimination Based on Religion or Belief, 25 November.

UNGA Res. 36/55, UN Doc. A/36/684 (1981).

———. 1983. International Convention Against the Taking of Hostages, 4 June. UNGA Res. 34/146 (XXXIV), UN Doc. A/34/786 (1979).

———. 1984. Declaration of the Right of Peoples to Peace, 12 November. UNGA Res. 39/11/Annex, UN Doc. A/39/L.14 (1984).

———. 1985. Resolution on Measures to Prevent International Terrorism, 9 December. UNGA Res. 40/61, UN Doc. A/40/1003 (1985).

———. 1985. Security Council Resolution Condemning Hostage Taking, 18 December. UNSC, Res. 579, UN Doc. S/Res/579 (1985).

———. 1986. Food Aid Convention, 1 July. S. Treaty (Security Council) DOC. No. 1.

———. 1986. Declaration on the Right to Development, 4 December. UNGA Res. 41/128, UN DOC A/41/925 (1986).

———. 1987. Convention Against Torture and Other Cruel Inhuman or Degrading Treatment or Punishment, 26 June. UNGA Res. 39/46 Annex, UN Doc. E/CN.4/1984/72.

———. 1990. Convention on the Rights of the Child, 26 January. UNGA Res. 25 (XLIV), UN Doc. A/Res/44/25 (1989).

United States Congress, Senate Governmental Affairs Committee. 1991. *Terrorism After the Gulf War*. 102 Cong., 15 July. C-SPAN video #91-07-16-02-2.

United States Department of Defense. 1988. *Terrorist Group Profiles*. Washington, DC: US Government Printing Office.

United States Department of State. 1910. Convention (No. IV) Respecting the Laws and Customs of War on Land, with Annex of Regulations, 26 January. TS no. 539, 36 Stat. 2277.

———. 1974. Antihijacking Act of 1974. 49 USCA §§1301, 1472, 1514 (Supp. 1989).

von der Mehden, Fred R. 1973. *Comparative Political Violence*. Englewood Cliffs, NJ: Prentice-Hall.

von Pufendorf, Samuel. 1964. *De Officio Hominis Et Civis Juxta Legem Naturalem Libri Duo,* ed. James Brown Scott. New York: Oceana Publications.

Wallerstein, Immanuel M. 1974. *The Modern World-System: Capitalist Agriculture and the Origin of the European World Economy in the Sixteenth Century*. New York: Academic Press.

Walsh, Anthony. 1987. "Teaching Understanding and Interpretation of Logit Regression." *Teaching Sociology* 15(2): 178-183.

Wardlaw, Grant. 1982. *Political Terrorism: Theory, Tactics, and Countermeasures*. Cambridge, England: Cambridge University Press.

———. 1986. "Policy Dilemmas in Responding to International Terrorism."

The Australian Quarterly 58(3): 278-285.

————. 1988. "State Response to International Terrorism: Some Cautionary Comments." In *Current Perspectives on International Terrorism*, eds. Robert O. Slater and Michael Stohl, 206-265. Basingstoke, Hampshire: MacMillan Press.

Waugh, William L. 1982. *International Terrorism: How Nations Respond to Terrorists*, Salisbury, NC: Documentary Publications.

Webster's New Collegiate Dictionary. 1977. Springfield, MA: G.R.C. Merriam Company.

Weimann, Gabriel and Conrad Winn. 1994. *The Theater of Terror: Mass Media and International Terrorism*. White Plains, NY: Longman Publishing Group.

Weinberg, Leonard and William Lee Eubank. 1988. "Neo-Fasicist and Far Left Terrorists in Italy: Some Biographical Observations." *British Journal of Political Science* 18(4): 531-553.

Weisburd, David. 1989. *Jewish Settler Violence: Deviance as Social Reaction*. University Park: The Pennsylvania State University Press.

Weston, Burns H., Richard A. Falk, and Anthony D'Amato, eds. 1990. *Basic Documents in International Law and World Order*. St. Paul: West Publishing.

White, Louis G. 1990. *Political Analysis: Technique and Practice Second Edition*. Pacific Grove, CA: Brooks/Cole Publishing.

Wilkinson, Paul. 1974. *Political Terrorism*, New York: John Wiley & Sons.

————. 1979. "Terrorist Movements." In *Terrorism: Theory and Practice*, eds. Yonah Alexander, David Carlton, and Paul Wilkinson. Boulder: Westview.

————. 1984. "State-sponsored international terrorism: the problems of response." *The World Today* 40(7): 292-298.

————. 1986. *Terrorism and the Liberal State Second Edition Revised, extended and updated*. London: MacMillan.

Wonnacott, Thomas H. and Ronald J. Wonnacott. 1990. *Introductory Statistics for Business and Economics Fourth Edition*. New York: John Wiley & Sons.

Yaari, Ehud. 1970. *Strike Terror: The Story of Fatah*. New York: Sabra Books.

————. 1993. "Middle East Peace Talks." Speech presented at Washington Institute for Near East Studies, Washington, DC, C-SPAN Video #93-02-10-18-2.

Yanai, Nathan. 1994. "Israel." In *Political Parties of the Middle East and North Africa,* ed. Frank Tachau. Westport, CT: Greenwood Press.

Yudelman, Michal. 1984. "Lifta suspect nabbed at cafe in Netanya."

Jerusalem Post, 25 June.

Zariski, Raphael. 1989. "Ethnic Extremism among Ethnoterritorial Minorities in Western Europe: Dimensions, Causes and Institutional Responses." *Comparative Politics* 21(3): 253-272.

Zeleney, Leslie Day. 1939. "Characteristics of Group Leaders." *Sociology and Social Research* 24: 140-149.

Zinnes, Dina A. 1976. "The Problem of Cumulation." In *Search of Global Patterns*, ed. James Rosenau. New York: Free Press.

———. 1976. *Contemporary Research in International Relations: A Perspective and A Critical Appraisal.* New York: Free Press.

Subject Index

Author Index

About the Author

Dr. Richard J. Chasdi is an adjunct faculty member at Wayne State University at the Center for Peace and Conflict Studies and Department of Political Science, where he teaches courses in international politics, peace and conflict studies, and comparative politics. He has been a news consultant on Middle Eastern affairs and Middle East terrorism for several television networks in the greater Detroit metropolitan area. He was born in Boston, Massachusetts, where he received a B.A. in Politics at Brandeis University in 1981, and his M.A. in Political Science from Boston College in 1985. Dr. Chasdi received his Ph.D. in Political Science from Purdue University in 1995. In addition to his articles, "Terrorism: Stratagems for Remediation from an International Law Perspective," in *Shofar: An Interdisciplinary Journal of Jewish Studies,* and, "Middle East Terrorism 1968-1993: An Empirical Analysis of Terrorist Group-Type Behavior," in *The Journal of Conflict Studies,* Dr. Chasdi is a co-author of an international relations textbook teaching manual.